Police Officer's Guide

Police Officer's Guide

Bill Clede

STACKPOLE BOOKS

Published by
STACKPOLE BOOKS
Cameron and Kelker Streets
P.O. Box 1831
Harrisburg, PA 17105

Printed in the United States of America

10 9 8 7 6 5 4 3 2 1

First Edition

Photos by author unless otherwise credited.

Cover photo by Ichiro Nagata.

Cover design by Tracy Patterson.

Interior design by Marcia Lee Dobbs.

Library of Congress Cataloging-in-Publication Data

Clede, Bill.
    Police officer's guide / Bill Clede.
        p.   cm.
    Bibliography: p.
    Includes index.
    ISBN 0-8117-2298-8
    1. Police—United States. 2. Criminal justice, Administration of—
United States. I. Title.
HV8138.C564   1989
363.2'3'028—dc19

88-24987
CIP

Contents

Part III—Skills

Part IV—On the Street

Part V—Weapons

Part VI—Appendices

Publisher's Note

Police officers follow a profession in which they are "at risk." Their job is to serve society, protect the citizenry, and enforce the law with judicious discretion. To accomplish this, society grants them authority to use whatever force the situation requires and to take offenders into custody.

This book is intended to present an understanding of the profession, the skills needed to succeed, and options that might be used to fulfill the responsibilities of the job. It is NOT training.

Officers must be personally trained in the laws, practices, policies, and procedures that apply in their jurisdiction. Learning psychomotor skills requires hands-on training by a qualified instructor. The proper application of law or of forceful techniques or tools must be justified under the law as it applies in that jurisdiction. Alleged misapplication or misuse of any law, technique, or tool, whether or not discussed here, may make an officer vulnerable to a lawsuit.

The publisher, consultants, and author accept no liability of any sort for any personal injury or property damage that might result from the use or misuse of any of the information, techniques, or applications presented or implied in this book.

Foreword

The name of Bill Clede has become almost a household word in law enforcement. Besides a long and distinguished career in the firearms industry, Bill has served four different agencies, either as a full-time sworn officer or as one of the thousands of part-time police officers who annually volunteer millions of hours in the interest of making their communities safer. Bill is one of the most prolific writers in the United States on subjects such as law enforcement and shooting sports.

When Bill told me that he wanted to write a police officer's guide, I was thrilled. Like Bill, I have long seen a need for such a publication. This book should be required reading for anyone considering a police career, since it gives an inside look into what law enforcement is all about.

Those officers already hired and awaiting attendance at a police academy will find that a few hours spent with *Police Officer's Guide* will better prepare them for academy training, and provide valuable tips on how to survive the first few months on the force. Even experienced officers will benefit from the up-to-date information on the latest techniques.

This book is all the more valuable because it is presented in Bill Clede's inimitable writing style—practical, down to earth, and interesting.

Earl M. Sweeney, Director
New Hampshire Police Standards and Training Council
Concord, New Hampshire

Acknowledgments

Many minds contributed to this book. I purposely sought counsel from those who are actively engaged in training police officers. I am particularly grateful to those who contributed directly to the store of knowledge in this book, critiqued my explanations, and reviewed the mammoth manuscript for technical accuracy and completeness:

Earl M. Sweeney
Director
New Hampshire Police Standards and Training Council
Concord, New Hampshire

Lt. Walter J. MacDonald
Commander, Tactical Operations and Narcotics
Plymouth County Sheriff's Department
Stoughton, Massachusetts

Lt. Doris M. Hughes
Retired, Connecticut State Police
H&S Associates, Investigations and Security
Wethersfield, Connecticut

A larger group of experts reviewed drafts of certain chapters, provided guidance, and offered constructive criticism along the way:

Capt. Mel L. Risch
Arizona Department of Public Safety
ALEOAC Business Manager
Phoenix, Arizona

Ben Yarrington
Director
Iowa Law Enforcement Academy
Johnston, Iowa

Larry D. Welch
Associate Director
Kansas Law Enforcement Training Center
Hutchinson, Kansas

M. Michael McHargue
Assistant Director, FDLE Academy
Florida Department of Law Enforcement
Tallahassee, Florida

Officer Ronald Hackney
Detroit Metropolitan Police Department
Firearms Training Unit
Detroit, Michigan

Thomas B. Miller
Director
Nebraska Law Enforcement Training Center
Grand Island, Nebraska

Peter M. Tarley
Police Training Division, Inc.
Monsey, New York

Lt. Richard Rosenthal
New York City Police Department
New York, New York

Capt. J. T. Flannery
Former Training Officer
Virginia State Police Academy
Richmond, Virginia

Lex T. Eckenrode
Division Director
Virginia Department of Criminal Justice
Richmond, Virginia

I am also grateful to Scott Kingwell, publisher, and Bruce Cameron, editorial director, of *Law & Order* magazine, for their help in providing leads, information, and photographs; and to a number of other magazine editors who granted permission to use material from their publications, credited throughout the book.

Thanks are due to Gerald Seagrave, librarian at the Law Enforcement Resources Center, Municipal Police Training Council, Meriden, Connecticut. He found references and resources I could never have found on my own.

Many working police officers provided information, ideas, and tips that are used in this book, and they are credited where their information appears. The patience and tolerance of my wife Lois enabled this project to be completed. And now my lieutenant, Joel Kent, will understand why I was not able to work as many PJs as usual as the deadline drew near.

Introduction

There is something unique about a law enforcement career. Few understand why some people would want to be called out in the worst weather, expose themselves to dangers others would avoid, or deliberately place themselves between a threat and an honest member of society.

Policing is one of the most stressful professions, and officers aren't known for living many golden years. It's one of the few professions where you are literally looking for trouble, with citizens' reports and a two-way radio to help you find it. Only in recent years has the pay scale of police officers reached the level of a living wage. Yet there have been police officers as long as there have been laws to enforce.

Why do they do it? All officers have their own personal reasons for wanting to be a cop, but none of them would be lasting reasons if it weren't for something else, something I consider a fundamental motivation for choosing a career in law enforcement. Flashing red lights and screaming siren, being at the scene of a disaster, solving a mystery, wearing a gun—these are only fleeting moments of excitement compared with the lasting satisfaction of *making your community a better place in which to live.*

Sgt. Michael Maudlin of the Lakewood, Colorado, police department said it best in his article "The Right Stuff" that appeared in the September 1987 issue of *POLICE* magazine:

> "The Right Stuff" is a great title for a movie. Maybe it takes the "right stuff" to be a police officer.
>
> The right stuff not to give up on someone's life when he has given up. To be tough enough to fight and arrest someone one minute and be a marriage counselor the next. To show compassion for the bereaved one minute and to point a gun at a suspect the next. To give your coat to a naked woman running for her life, or to a child who is cold and tired because the paramedics are trying to save her mommy.
>
> Perhaps it takes the right stuff to see so much you cannot change because the damage is done before you arrived, to be a lawyer, doctor, nurse, counselor, roadside mechanic, taxi driver, traffic controller, compassionate lis-

tener, an enforcer of society's laws, perhaps all during the same shift . . . and still keep a sense of purpose.

Sometimes you do save a life, help an accident victim. Every once in a while you meet someone who respects what you do and isn't shy about saying so. We do make a difference and that is what matters. We can't solve all the world's problems, but we can have a positive impact, however small.

It was all these things that attracted me to police work. The demands of a young family finally pushed me into higher-paying employment with manufacturers who produced the products used by police. But I remained a police consultant or a part-time sworn officer even when not employed full time by a police agency.

This gave me the opportunity to observe many different kinds of law enforcement activities: in a small town with six part-time cops and one cruiser, as a military police shift commander, with a medium-size department with fifty cops and nine cruisers (where I last served), to large metropolitan agencies. They're all different, yet they're all the same when it comes to the concerns and careers of the people who make it all work—police officers.

When the concept of a police officer's guide first came up, my reaction was, "Impossible!" Each jurisdiction is unique, with its own employment manual, union contract, demography, geography, and several levels of laws. But they are all the same in fundamental philosophies, principles of law, operational procedures, personal skills, and personalities needed to do a good job.

There is one thing I want to emphasize: this book, by itself, will not qualify you to be a police officer. You must be trained in your own state and by your own department to meet certification requirements. I aim to give you an overview of what's involved, an understanding to help you get more out of training, or provide a reminder for those of you who went through the academy long ago.

Some new technologies and techniques are only now filtering down to the patrol officer's level. I raise questions where questions should be raised, and present both sides of controversies so you can make up your own mind. However, this is a fluid field. What's right and proper today may be only partly right tomorrow—maybe even wrong. Techniques improve. Methods change. And law is influenced daily by court decisions.

For these reasons, I encourage readers to send critical comment to me in care of the publisher. Perhaps you have a better way than something presented here, a unique solution that other officers should know about. Later editions of this book will incorporate this input and credit sources as others are credited throughout this text.

You might think of this book like the veteran who takes you under his wing and gives you the benefit of what he's learned on the street. If this material makes you think, makes you want to improve your skills and enhance your career, then you will benefit and this book will have served its purpose.

Bill Clede
Wethersfield, Connecticut

Part I   Background

1

Police Work—Then and Now

1.1. Origin of Police

Back before recorded time, it probably fell to one person to decide quarrels among the cavemen, but organized law enforcement began in Great Britain, when Sir Robert Peel (1788–1850) reorganized several different "patrols" into a real crime-preventing police agency. That's why English police are called "bobbies"; at one time they were also called "peelers."

Sir Robert Peel   Peel was born in Lancashire and first entered the House of Commons in 1809. He became undersecretary for the colonies in 1811, and from 1812 to 1818 he was secretary for Ireland. In 1822 he became Home Secretary, where he distinguished himself in the police fraternity for all time.

In the 1820s, London's population was approaching 1,500,000. Suburban towns were already growing together into a metropolis. This conglomeration of people and jurisdictions was policed under a chaotic and inefficient system inherited from the eighteenth century. At the time of Peel's service, England had a criminal code, a court system, and a penitentiary for "penitents." But the idea of preventive police, apart from the court, was only a vague concept.

Peel was an astute politician, and he quickly learned how to get things done. He chaired a committee in 1822 that began making overtures toward an organized police force, then turned his attention to improving the prison system. He took the lead in reforming the criminal code, pushing through five laws during the closing months of the 1823 session. One abolished the death penalty for petty larceny; another abolished capital punishment for such minor infractions as breaking river-banks or cutting down hop vines. One empowered judges to withhold formal sentence of death in all capital convictions except murder, and another abolished the custom of burying suicides on the high road with a stake driven through the body. Altogether, Peel's efforts at consolidating the criminal code resulted in the repeal of 278 acts from 1825 to 1828, with some of their provisions retained and summarized in eight new laws.

1

In 1828, Peel rose in the House of Commons to propose another committee inquiry into the state of police and the causes of increased crime in the metropolis. That committee produced a two-part report: first, it quantified increased crime; second, for the first time in history, it declared in favor of a radical reform of police organization. No more could be done during the 1828 session, but Peel's intentions were clear.

All the night police of London, the existing magisterial forces, and the horse, day, and night patrols already under the supervision of the Home Department were to be amalgamated. The difficulty lay in the details: assuming authority over the outlying parishes, determining proportions of expenses to be raised from different parochial areas. By spring of 1829 the bill was ready and, with the strong support of the Duke of Wellington, the Metropolitan Police Act passed on June 19, 1829.

A New Concept of Police   The act made the metropolitan police possible. It remained to Peel, as Home Secretary, to establish its character. Since the police force itself was an innovation, there were no readymade candidates to fill the three posts at the head of the organization. Yet those men would essentially define the character of police for all time to come.

Almost from the beginning, the heads of the metropolitan police were known as commissioners, executives who administered and directed a force of several thousand men. For one of the three, Peel hoped to find a practical and efficient lawyer; for the other primary post, a soldier accustomed to discipline and capable of enforcing it. For the third and lesser post, he wanted a man with legal training and business experience.

The headquarters of the new police force was established at 4 Whitehall Place, with a rear entry on Scotland Yard. The general use of this back door soon provided the popular name for the whole headquarters building.

Londoners saw the first blue uniforms and iron-framed top hats of the new metropolitan police on the evening of September 29, 1829.

Peel wasn't able to carry out his wider plan of national police reform, but the metropolitan police remained both the model and recruiting ground for the various borough and county police forces that gradually built up over the next quarter-century.

1.2 Police in the United States

The concept of a single nationwide police force to prevent crime and apprehend offenders has existed throughout the world for centuries. There are still national police agencies in some countries today, with absolute central authority. But those who left Europe for the New World in the eighteenth century had different ideas.

The authors of the Constitution were well aware of the potential abuse of power, and they set down guiding principles that would forever protect certain rights. In fact, the U.S. Constitution was not adopted until the first ten amendments, the Bill of Rights, were discussed and an agreement reached that they would be adopted at the next session of Congress. The Tenth Amendment states: "The powers not delegated to the United States by the Constitution, nor prohibited by it to the States, are reserved to the States respectively, or to the people."

Thus, the power to police is retained by the states. There are federal investigative agencies and security forces, some armed and with powers of arrest, but police power belongs to local jurisdictions.

The result is a mix of state police, county police, municipal police, even a water company police department, all exercising jurisdiction over slices of the same pie.

There are capitol police, campus police, conservation officers, marine police, military police, park police and park rangers, railroad police, and transit police. Each agency is given police power to enforce the law in its jurisdiction: all over the state, in a particular county or municipality, around state offices, university, military base, park, or lands and facilities of a water company, railroad, or transit company.

Some police are charged with paying particular attention to a specific group of statutes. Conservation officers emphasize fish and game laws. Marine police enforce boating laws. In some states, a state highway patrol enforces motor vehicle laws and a separate state police enforces criminal laws. Texas is one example with a highway patrol and the famous Texas Rangers.

Filling Manpower Needs   It is as important for a law enforcement agency to have a reserve component as it is for the Army, Navy, Air Force, or Coast Guard. Taxpayers cannot afford to maintain a standing force capable of handling all situations that might arise.

Many agencies make provisions for extra manpower, and these part-time officers are known by many names: supernumeraries, specials, auxiliaries, sheriff's posse, or reserve officers are some of the terms used. There is no way to generalize such officers because the situations are so different. Some may be required to complete the same training requirements and have the same powers as a regular officer. Some may not be armed or have power of arrest but may exercise all the other duties of a police officer. They may work without supervision in one jurisdiction but only in the company of a regular officer in another. Some are volunteers and are used only for traffic control during disasters or special events.

Iowa, for example, has a reserve officer's bill that spells out the powers and training requirements of such officers: "While in the actual performance of official duties, reserve police officers shall be vested with the same rights, privileges, obligations, and duties as any other police officers."

Part-time police officers may be paid at the regular's rates under certain circumstances, or at a reduced rate in other situations. In many areas, they work only for the satisfaction of doing community service. An area may have both paid part-timers and unpaid volunteers working together with regular full-time officers.

Overlapping Jurisdictions   Crime is too big for any one agency. It doesn't respect political boundaries that define a police officer's jurisdiction. Different agencies may be conducting investigations of different crimes yet come down to the same perpetrators.

There are times when officers of different agencies work together, even with federal agencies involved. Drug task forces, for example, might be composed of federal agents from the Federal Bureau of Investigation and the Drug Enforcement Administration and local officers—state, county, and municipal—from several cities and towns. (Federal agencies are discussed in Appendix A.) Even individual departments may employ different kinds of officers, including everything from sworn part-time officers to Explorer Scouts who perform helpful functions. Different agencies—federal, state, or local—may see themselves as the principal players. In this cauldron of diverse interests, there is potential for turf wars.

Getting Along   Where jurisdictions overlap, guidelines evolve between police agencies. The state police pay primary attention to the major highways, but in some states they have jurisdiction in any town that has an organized police department. Town police pay primary attention to local streets, but they may have jurisdiction over that part of the interstate highway that runs through their town.

and work together very well to accomplish more than any one agency working alone.

It was gratifying to hear David Margolis, chief of the Justice Department's Organized Crime and Racketeering Section, while addressing a meeting of the Connecticut Police Chiefs Association, say "Federal law enforcement would fall apart if it weren't for local police involvement. You are the ones who know the nuances within your local jurisdictions. You know who the players are, and you are the first to see signs of suspicious situations."

Federal agents investigate violations of federal laws. But RICO (the Racketeer Influenced and Corrupt Organizations Act) blurs the technical lines of jurisdictional differences. RICO attacks criminal organizations (the very existence of which is a federal offense) that may be committing violations of state statutes (a local offense).

Where there is a state highway patrol, the town officers spend their time on local streets. But if they run the expressway to reach another area of town, they won't close their eyes to a violation. Besides, highway patrolmen are sometimes few and far between and need the local police for backup in serious situations. By the same token, the highway patrolmen spend their time on the expressway, but they wouldn't pass by an accident on a city street.

Fresh Pursuit   There is another aspect to this question of contiguous jurisdictions. You could be in a different jurisdiction legally in the performance of your duties. Say a suspect commits a crime in your state and you chase him across the state line. The principle of fresh pursuit lets you apprehend the offender and take him into custody. However, barring some compact between the states, you have to get local help. If you make an arrest where you have no arrest powers, or in a circumstance where no offense has occurred in the second state, then the second state will hold the offender for extradition back to your state. You may not drag the suspect back across the state line without the consent of the governor of the second state.

Within the state, it depends on your state law. Some states empower a police officer of any jurisdiction to make a felony arrest anywhere in the state, or even a misdemeanor arrest when acting on a warrant. Whenever you take a police action outside your jurisdiction, it is simple courtesy, if not a legal requirement, to notify local authorities.

2

Understanding the Differences

Police officers are proud individuals—sometimes a bit too proud. I've heard derisive comments about "park rangers" and "game wardens," usually indicating a lack of enthusiasm in working with someone who isn't "really" a cop.

Don't you believe it.

Law enforcement is a broad term that includes many sorts of agencies engaging in many activities. A specific agency may emphasize a particular area of law or geographical jurisdiction, but its officers are "cops" in their individual way just as much as those in state, county, or municipal police departments. And they are just as professional as any other police officer wearing a badge.

It may help you to understand and appreciate the other person's point of view if I tell you about a few specialized law enforcement responsibilities.

2.1 Conservation Law Enforcement

What do game law violations have to do with police work? Let me tell you about an incident I was involved in.

The conservation officer stood in the darkness beside the dirt road, waiting. Coming slowly toward him was an automobile, its headlights stabbing the night. A powerful spotlight was playing from the car window into the open fields beside the road. It was too cold for just curious tourists. Besides, it was the eve of deer season.

But the men in that car didn't care about seasons or bag limits. They were jacklighters.

Darkness makes deer less wary. They come out into open fields at night to graze. A bright light suddenly shining into their eyes stuns them for a moment. The animal just stands there, motionless, staring into the light, a fine target for the jacklighter's bullet. Hunting on the eve of opening day gives jacklighters a chance to make their ill-gotten gains legal the next day, so it's an active night for conservation officers.

District conservation officer Clay Messenger waited in the bushes until the jackers drew near. Then, so their car's headlights would fall full on his green uniform and shiny badge, he stepped out onto the road. The driver reacted violently. He slammed his car into second gear and careened directly toward the officer. Clay jumped to one side just as the fender brushed his pants leg. Gravel from under the spinning wheels spewed around him.

Two hundred yards farther down the road, Bill Brown waited in Clay's radio car. Seeing the attack, he pulled the cruiser across the road to block the escape route. The jackers saw they didn't have a chance of making it around the blockade, so the driver put the car into a quick skidding turn on the loose gravel and headed back the way he had come. As they passed Clay for the second time, someone inside the car threw a piece of lead pipe at the officer's head. It missed, but the chase was on.

I was two miles away in another cruiser with Arthur Bachman, then chief conservation officer. Coordinating with Brown by radio, we tried to head off the fleeing violators, but failed. A description of the car was broadcast within minutes of the escape. It took a while but they were eventually caught, miles away.

Jacklighters too often get nothing more than a slap on the wrist when brought into court. But such vicious attacks launched against solitary officers show that conservation officers face threats much like any other police officer. In fact, a recent study by the U.S. Fish and Wildlife Service (USFWS) shows that assaults on wildlife officers are nine times more likely to be fatal than those on other law enforcement personnel. Four out of five persons who assault wildlife officers are carrying firearms, compared to one in five of their urban counterparts.

During the study year of 1987, there were 128 assaults on the 8,997 conservation officers employed by state and territorial agencies plus 186 special agents working for the USFWS. Injuries resulted in 28 of those incidents, and two state officers, in Kentucky and Florida, were killed. "Too many state and federal wildlife officers are put in harm's way," said USFWS Director Frank Dunkle. "With some 16 million hunters roaming the woods, it's fortunate there were only 128 assaults."

Virginia recorded the highest assault rate, with 4.9 percent. Utah was second with 3.8 percent, followed by Washington and Alaska each with 3.7 percent. The assailant's most frequent weapon was the body—hands, fists, and feet—used in 35 percent of the incidents. Firearms were second with 31 percent.

The problem isn't the poor person taking an out-of-season deer for food. It's more serious than that.

After World War II, jacklighting flourished. Many amateurs got into the act but they were easily caught. As the new generation of sportsmen learned more about conservation, they helped to police their sport and amateur jacklighting declined.

"Today, jacklighting is still as bad as it ever was, in some areas worse, but a different kind of person is doing it," Bachman explained. "The modern poacher is a professional. He uses a small-caliber, high-velocity rifle that won't be heard over long distances. He has a sealed-beam handheld light that can point out the shining eyes of a deer (or cow) a quarter mile away. His car is fast but usually a cheap one he wouldn't mind losing if it's confiscated. He may be out several nights a week all during the year, and he switches his areas of operation to throw the officers off his trail. And the conservation officer usually has a big area to patrol all by himself. He stands little chance of catching these poachers without sportsmen's help."

Conservation officers never know what they might encounter in the field. Officer Don Deane once suspected a certain individual of jacking deer but hadn't been able to catch him in the act. One night, Deane spotted his suspect in the field where Deane believed he was jacklighting. Always before, the suspect had reached home in time to dispose of the evidence. This time, Deane positioned himself between the suspect and his house.

In full uniform, Deane stood in plain sight on the path. When the suspect's light shone full on him, a thundering roar came from the man's rifle. He turned and ran but Deane switched on his own light and called, "Halt!" Deane captured his culprit and got the evidence for a conviction in court, but it cost him a bullet hole in his thigh. Fortunately, the slug missed the bone and major arteries. At the trial, the man testified he thought the uniformed officer was a predator who had been killing chickens.

Another conservation officer saw a man fishing through the ice on a restricted reservoir. He went over to check his license. The man ran back into the woods with the officer hot on his heels. The officer quickly learned that the man didn't want his license checked. Two shots were fired in his direction. Fortunately, they missed.

This officer wisely went back to his car to get his gun—and to radio for a backup. Together they searched the area, found the empty cartridge cases, checked witnesses, and with topnotch investigation found the suspect and brought him to trial. He was sentenced to a year in jail.

A criminal is a criminal, even when he masquerades as a sportsman.

2.2 Marine Law Enforcement

What is marine policing really like in the United States today? To find out, I spent some time with the Connecticut Marine Patrol, part of the law enforcement division of the State Department of Environmental Protection.

Conservation officers Myron Van Ness and Jim Williams eased out of Westbrook harbor in the V-20 Boston Whaler and made for the lee of Duck Island, a popular overnight anchorage for cruisers on Long Island Sound. They were checking lobstermen in the early-morning calm; instead, they found a sailor with a problem. A man and his young son were in an inflatable dinghy, wrestling with an anchor line. As we watched, the little boat nearly tipped over.

Connecticut Conservation Officers Myron Van Ness (left) and Jim Williams are among the 14 officers you're likely to see along the north side of Long Island Sound. This 20-foot Boston Whaler is a typical marine patrol boat.

"I can't free this anchor without swamping the dinghy," the sailor called over. "Could you help?"

"Guess we could," Van Ness responded. He took the anchor line as Williams eased the bow up to the tiny craft, and made it fast to the bow cleat. Williams backed the boat down and the anchor came free.

"Here's your anchor," Van Ness said, handing it to the sailor. "But you've got another problem." The boat showed no registration numbers, even though it had an outboard attached, and there were no personal flotation devices (PFDs) on board.

Operating an unregistered vessel carries a fine of $35 plus a $5 fee; insufficient PFDs adds another $40. But because the man had just bought the dinghy and promised to get it registered immediately on his return to home port, Van Ness wrote the ticket only for the lack of PFDs.

Did you ever wonder why marine police officers always know where the fish are biting? As we pulled up to a Grady-White, Van Ness called over, "How're you doing?" The fishermen held up two nice-sized fish and explained where they'd caught them. Meanwhile, Van Ness calculated that the five people on board were within the capacity of the boat. He could see a fire extinguisher mounted near the helm. But he couldn't see any PFDs.

"You got life jackets on board, Captain? Show me five of them."

The man opened the bow compartment and counted out five Coast Guard–approved PFDs.

"That's fine," Van Ness said. "Have a safe day."

As we worked our way down the Connecticut River, we spotted an outboard racing past the marinas at Saybrook, a "6 mph, No Wake" zone. Our blue strobe light came on and the loudspeaker blared, "Stand by for inspection."

The speedster slowed down and started to maneuver alongside. "You put it in neutral," Williams called. "Let me do the maneuvering."

Van Ness put the fenders over and grabbed the other boat's windshield to hold us together. "You realize you were speeding through a no-wake zone?" he asked. Of course not. "Do you have a fire extinguisher?" There was one, still in the box it came in from the store. "What about PFDs?" There were none on board. "Well, let me see your registration." The boater didn't have that with him either.

Unsafe operation, failure to carry vessel registration, insufficient personal flotation devices—the three infractions added up to a possible fine of $120. The point isn't to gouge people, but sometimes it takes a monetary reminder to make a lesson memorable. The boater was ticketed for not having the required PFDs.

As we came alongside one lobsterman to check his catch, Van Ness had some information for him. "We've got one of your traps, Charlie. Caught a poacher with it and we need it for evidence for a while."

"Good work," the lobsterman replied. "I probably wouldn't have missed it until fall anyway."

It had happened just a few days before. Van Ness recalled it was barely dawn when a "lobsterman" was seen pulling some blue-buoyed traps. Then he pulled some red and white buoys. The marine patrol officer, staked out on an island and looking through a telescope, knew that buoys of two different colors couldn't belong to one person. By radio, he alerted the patrol boat hiding on the other side of the island.

"When we checked him, he had both color buoys on board and a bunch of short lobsters," Van Ness explained. "He had one of Charlie's traps. We'll get it back to its rightful owner as soon as the case is heard in court."

This marine patrol, staffed by conservation officers, primarily enforces boating laws and fish and game laws. They spend at least three-fourths of their time on the water, but you might find them involved in everything from checking fish imported by a fish market to investigating a gang of poachers—for lobster usually, but even deer in areas within the agency's marine district.

Some marine patrols are manned by police departments. They range from a single reserve officer using his own boat, to a fleet of several small pleasure craft manned by full-time police officers.

Norwalk, Connecticut, is a good example. It's a major recreational port on Long Island Sound with some 5,400 vessels berthed in the harbor area. The Norwalk police department has a full-time, year-round marine division staffed with regular officers, four in summer and two in winter. The division has three large boats, all equipped with standard rescue gear, pumps, and firefighting equipment.

"We'll handle perhaps 500 to 600 cases a year, which are mostly assistance to disabled or stranded boaters," Lt. Tom Reidy, officer in charge, said. "We'll issue some 200 infractions, mostly for safety equipment violations, but we enforce all laws. With seventeen natural islands, some with residents on them, we are the first responders to a police, medical, or fire problem offshore.

"A lot of our work is assisting the detective bureau. Our scuba team has recovered evidence thrown off bridges, and we've recovered lots of cars. Once a man shot another man in a bar, then went bluefishing. We had to go get him. We had a kidnapping last year; recovered the car from the water but no trace yet of the victim. When the *Celtic*, a tug, sank two years ago with six lost, our scuba team recovered three bodies."

There are aspects to the life of a marine policeman you don't like to think about. It isn't all weekend recreationists.

It's just a matter of time before a marine patrol boat tries to stop some cruiser that loaded an illegal cargo from a freighter offshore. One man was already caught running drugs up the peaceful Connecticut River. Fortunately, it wasn't a marine police boat that caught him. Officers with handguns in a small patrol boat are no match for drug runners armed with submachine guns.

It's a tribute to the work these men do that a boater, caught without required safety equipment, will say, "Thank you for the ticket, officer. You may have prevented a far greater tragedy."

2.3 Military Police

When I was in the Air Force during Korea, we were called air police officers. In 1966, they changed the name to security police, and in 1971 it was split into separate security and law enforcement sections. Earlier, when I was in the Navy (during World War II) we were known as shore patrol. I was never in the Army but a number of friends were military police officers. We'll accommodate all under the generic term *military police*.

The law enforcement function of military police on a military base is much like that of police officers in the town outside the main gate: traffic enforcement, accident investigation, criminal investigation, and keeping the peace. A military base is a city in itself, with potentially the same crime problems as a civilian city. Military police responsibility travels wherever the military travels.

An armed forces police officer (let's say "MP" for brevity) is a composite of law enforcement and military. The MP is one of the troops, lives where soldiers, sailors, and airmen live, and wears the same uniform except for a white hat, brassard, and gun. The MP gets no special pay, but it costs him more to live.

The MP works crazier hours and is home less than other officers. When others are off, he's on, and no one gives him credit because it's expected. He makes more decisions in a single day than most junior commissioned officers. He must settle differences between individuals so that each will think he won, yet maintain proper respect for higher ranking officers. He must be first at an accident and infallible with a diagnosis. He must be able to start breathing, stop bleeding, tie splints, and above all be sure the victim goes home without a limp—or he's subject to a lawsuit. He must be able to whip two men twice his size and half his age without damaging his uniform and without being "brutal." If the MP hits a subject, he's unprofessional; if a subject hits the MP, that's life. The MP carries a gun, but he'd better not use it unless to save a life—then be prepared to show why. And would you believe he's sometimes ordered to shoot to wound, with a .45 caliber cannon?

Just like any other police officer, an MP must know everything and not tell; know where all the sin is and not partake; from a single hair, be able to describe the crime, the weapon, and the criminal, and tell you where the criminal is hiding; chase bum leads to a dead end; stake out night after night to find one witness who saw it happen but refuses to remember.

The MP runs files and writes reports until his eyes ache to build a case against a suspect who'll get dealt out of service on a Chapter 10. When the MP does get to court, he explains the facts in detail, while the defense lawyer tries to make him look stupid and find out if he has violated the rights of the accused.

The MP is a lawyer, a minister, a social worker, a diplomat, a tough guy, and a gentleman—and does all these things with only eight weeks of training.

2.4 Railroad Police

Yes, even railroads have police. They date back to 1855, when Allen Pinkerton became the first law enforcement officer hired to protect railroad interests. Pennsylvania was the first state to commission railroad police, in 1865. It might even be argued that a select group of railroad special agents, formed as the Rangers in 1899 to chase the infamous Hole-in-the-Wall Gang, was the first police SWAT unit. The Rangers had a specially equipped baggage car designed to carry eight men and their horses. When a train robbery occurred, the Rangers were taken to the area in their special train car, then pursued the outlaws on horseback.

Like all other kinds of law enforcement, today's railroad policing has become more complex and technical. In some states, railroad police, or special agents, must meet the same training requirements as other police officers. In others, requirements are less stringent, and a few have no requirements at all. The Association of American Railroads' National Railroad Police Academy, located at the Mississippi State Law Enforcement Officers' Training Academy in Jackson, trains some 500 railroad police each year.

What do railroad police do? In New York's South Bronx, after hours of tedious surveillance, officers arrested four men for stealing fuel from reefer cars. In Detroit, a task force captured a gang of boxcar burglars in the process of stealing tires. A K-9 officer in Chicago was called to help local police track a lost seven-year-old boy. In Harrisburg, Pennsylvania, Sgt. William Houtz and other officers responded to the sound of gunshots and found a dead body—and a man with a gun. The man, turned over to Harrisburg city police, was later convicted of murder.

These incidents happened not to municipal or state police but to railroad police. The typical activities and responsibilities of railroad police are much the same as police in the public sector. Some railroad agents are commissioned by the state or province in which they serve so they have the same powers as any other police officer. The only differences are in the processing of arrests and responsibility to private rather than public interests.

There is one other big difference. While city police officers are concerned with the geographical area of their political jurisdiction, the railroad cops's "precinct" is the miles of track owned by their employer—more than 200,000 miles of mainline track in America.

Railroad police provide vehicle and foot patrols for yards and industrial areas where freight cars are located. When high-value or high-risk loads must be left where they are vulnerable, a stakeout is often used to ensure its protection. It may be eyeball observation, remote radio sensing, closed-circuit television, or night vision surveillance.

Of course, the nation's estimated 4,500 railroad police can't do it all alone. They work closely with the FBI on thefts from interstate shipments, and with local, county, and state police where appropriate.

3

Personal Concerns

Just what is a police officer? Generically, the term means any member of an organized police force. Police officers are "commissioned" by their jurisdiction to enforce its laws. They are empowered by their state's laws with responsibilities to maintain order, to enforce the law, and to detect and prevent crime.

There are so many terms and titles it can be confusing. A town that employs a lone law enforcement officer probably calls him a constable. A deputy sheriff may be part of an organized police force. Some police officers are called patrolmen. A Western town may have a marshal. Many states have what they call "peace officers," a broad, all-inclusive term, and use "police officer" in the narrower sense of one employed by an organized police force.

But among all the court decisions defining a police officer, there is one that puts a different perspective on the profession. In *People* v. *Glennon,* 74 N.Y.S. 794 (1902), the court said that a policeman is only a citizen dressed in blue clothes and brass buttons, with no right or power to arrest without a warrant. Citizens have not made him their master, but only their honorable servant, with no power to arrest anyone *except as provided by law.* The court noted an exception: where a felony has been committed. Police officers may arrest anyone they have reasonable grounds to believe is the person who committed a felony. And that is usually what defines a police officer—the power of arrest.

3.1 P-I-G

Police officers are called by a variety of terms. "Cop" spoken by a street person may be a derogatory term, but when used by a fellow officer it could be a compliment. One common name in recent years is "pig." It was used so frequently and so contemptuously that police have given it a new definition. PIG now stands for Pride, Integrity, and Guts.

Anyone who becomes a police officer should feel pride in that accomplishment. It means they have survived a process of evaluation and selection, and then completed a grueling twelve to sixteen weeks of recruit academy before earning the right to ride along with a field training officer.

In law enforcement, integrity can never be compromised. Because police officers are trained to enforce the law, they are held to a higher standard of conduct than others. When an officer encounters stranded motorists on a lonely stretch of country road, their reaction will usually be, "Boy, am I glad to see you." An officer is a comfort, the solution to what might be, at the moment, the most important problem in the world. Such esteem has developed over history—and it continues to exist despite the pig-sayers.

Guts means going into a crisis situation with confidence in your ability to handle it; facing danger to protect a citizen; being society's first line of defense.

So, when someone calls you "pig," say "Thank you."

3.2 Qualities

It takes a special kind of person to be a police officer. Aside from the stamina to endure verbal abuse, police officers must remain alert during hours of monotonous patrol and react quickly when need be. They must be able to switch instantly from a state of near somnambulism to an adrenalin-filled struggle for survival. They must learn their patrol area so well they can recognize what's out of the ordinary. They become an integral part of their community.

Police officers need strong motivation to become a jack-of-all-trades when it comes to solving society's ills. It takes initiative, effective judgment, and imagination in coping with the complex situations that must be faced—family disturbance, potential suicide, robbery in progress, gory accident, or natural disaster.

Officers must be able to size up a situation instantly and react properly, perhaps making a life-or-death decision. They need mature judgment to determine whether an arrest is warranted or if a warning would better serve society's purpose. They need self-restraint to use only the degree of force necessary in the circumstance.

They face far greater challenges in interpersonal contacts—dealing with derelicts in a back alley one moment and the proprietor of a boutique the next. One time they may stop a senior citizen who inadvertently ran a stop sign, and the next car may be driven by a felon fleeing an armed robbery.

Officers need the initiative to perform their functions when their supervisor is miles away, yet they must be able to be part of a strike force team under the direct command of a superior when called upon. They need to take charge in chaotic situations yet avoid alienating participants or bystanders. They must be a helpful influence when crowds of citizens gather for a special event, yet single out and placate an agitator trying to precipitate a riot.

Officers must have curiosity tempered with tact, yet be skillful in questioning people, ranging from a traumatized victim to a suspected perpetrator. They must be brave enough to face an armed criminal, yet help a woman deliver a baby; cope with the stress of a high-speed chase, yet remain alert on patrol during the wee hours when everyone else is asleep. They must maintain a balanced perspective in the face of constant exposure to the worst side of human nature, yet be objective in dealing with special-interest groups, from relatives of those just arrested to members of the press.

As if all that isn't enough, officers must be adept in a variety of psychomotor skills: operating a vehicle in normal and emergency situations; firing weapons accurately in adverse conditions; maintaining their own agility, endurance, and strength in applying techniques to defend themselves while apprehending a suspect with a minimum of force.

Then, when it's all over, they must be able to explain what happened—in writing, to someone who wasn't there, in such a way there's no opportunity for misunderstanding—and to document their actions so they can relate their reasons years later.

3.3 The Look of Authority

Police officers are society's representatives of authority. As the protectors of citizens' rights and the impartial enforcer of laws, they must be immaculate in personal appearance, grooming, and conduct. Since physical appearance telegraphs what a person thinks of himself, officers need to be concerned about being physically fit, with their weight under control.

Every jurisdiction decides its own uniform. Keeping it neat and clean can be a problem, especially after you've chased a suspect through the swamp, but that's no excuse when you report for your next duty shift.

Remember that you are held to a high standard. You are the most frequent contact most citizens have with their government. The impressions they form, on the basis of these contacts, have a direct influence on how they feel about their town or state.

3.4 RHIP and RHIR

We can borrow two axioms from the military: rank has its privileges, and rank has its responsibilities. That's certainly true in law enforcement as well. But beyond the usual privileges and responsibilities of higher rank, your rank as police officer carries obligations.

In the performance of their duties, police officers are exempt from many state laws. They don't need permits to carry a gun, knife, handcuffs, or baton. They needn't obey speed limits when they must travel fast, or "no parking" signs when arriving at the scene of an accident. But some "privileges" can get you into trouble.

There is a fraternal feeling among police. Certainly there is such a thing as professional courtesy, but don't count on it. Remember that higher standard. In another jurisdiction, an officer may be tempted to overlook a minor traffic violation when he learns you're a cop—but he's under no obligation to do so. It's universal that he won't overlook a violation of drunk driving statutes.

Accepting gratuities is another gray area. The recommended Code of Ethics (see Section 3.6) includes the words "and never accepting gratuities" with good reason. If a local merchant gives you free meals or products, the implication is that you will extend special consideration, and that can be a problem when you have to arrest him for some violation. It's difficult sometimes to avoid petty gratuities. Some departments allow a free cup of coffee if the courtesy is extended to all uniformed officers and not just to you personally. You must be guided by your department policy, but if there's any question in your mind, that's reason enough to decline.

The responsibilities you incur when you put on a police officer's badge are all the things discussed in this book. Essentially, it is an officer's personal responsibility to live up to that higher standard of conduct.

3.5 "A "Police" Personality

Many people have an image of police officers as authoritarian, suspicious, racist, hostile, insecure, conservative, and cynical—among other things. Some believe that this profession attracts that kind of person; others claim it's a result of the job we must do. Is there such a thing as a "police" personality? I doubt it. I've met as many different personality types in police work as I have in any other line of work.

Nonetheless, there is one thing that binds us all—we're cops. We're all faced with the overriding necessity to cover our backsides, keep the sergeant happy, back up our partners in dangerous situations, and be as threatening as necessary when facing a hostile adversary. The demands of this profession tend to mold us alike. Police work can bring out the best in a person, and provide a continuing potential for personal and professional growth. It offers much personal satisfaction and pride in a job well done.

3.6 Code of Ethics

The International Association of Chiefs of Police developed a Law Enforcement Code of Ethics that it encourages its members to adopt.

As a Law Enforcement Officer, my fundamental duty is to serve mankind; to safeguard lives and property; to protect the innocent against deception, the weak against oppression or intimidation, and the peaceful against violence or disorder; and to respect the Constitutional rights of all men to liberty, equality and justice.

I will keep my private life unsullied as an example to all; maintain courageous calm in the face of danger, scorn, or ridicule; develop self-restraint; and be constantly mindful of the welfare of others. Honest in thought and deed in both my personal and official life, I will be exemplary in obeying the laws of the land and the regulations of my department. Whatever I see or hear of a confidential nature or that is confided to me in my official capacity will be kept ever secret unless revelation is necessary in the performance of my duty.

I will never act officiously or permit personal feelings, prejudices, animosities or friendships to influence my decisions. With no compromise for crime and with relentless prosecution of criminals, I will enforce the law courteously and appropriately without fear or favor, malice or ill will, never employing unnecessary force or violence and never accepting gratuities.

I recognize the badge of my office as a symbol of public faith, and I accept it as a public trust to be held so long as I am true to the ethics of the police service. I will constantly strive to achieve these objectives and ideals, dedicating myself before God to my chosen profession . . . law enforcement.

4

Career Concerns

The professional development of its officers is a concern of every department. As part of in-service training responsibilities, virtually all departments send officers to outside courses that help them develop into more valuable employees. You may have to argue, cajole, and stubbornly persist in submitting applications, but opportunities are there. Professional development is a key factor in anyone's success, but it won't just come to you. You need to work on it through your entire career.

4.1 It's Up to You

Few people in today's work force have active professional development agendas, according to Patricia McLagan, principal of McLagan International, a St. Paul, Minnesota, management consulting firm. Those who do usually have rigid plans that are out of step with the times.

McLagan recommends five steps an individual can take to make professional development happen:

1. Have a future vision. Anticipate what conditions and requirements will be in your field in the future. Projecting that, identify what you must do and accomplish to fit into that picture.

2. Know yourself. Recognize your own levels of knowledge and skill, career stage, professional and organizational contributions, competency strengths, and the knowledge and skills you want to develop. Ask those who have worked with you to help you assess yourself.

3. Have a scanning system. What are the top professional challenges you'll face in the next five years? Who else will be facing these issues or who will have a useful perspective on them? Seek associates who will be helpful in developing your own skills. Attending conferences of professional associations puts you in touch with others who have similar interests: you learn not only from the seminars but also through conversations beside the swimming pool.

4. Have an action plan and vision of success. Define your goals, set reasonable short-term intentions, and plan what you need to do to meet those aims. Then

Police cadets at the New Hampshire Police Standards and Training Council Academy march between classes under the command of commandant Jerry Smith-Pearson. NHPSTC.

review and revise your plan annually. You may accomplish a step earlier than planned, or a better opportunity might present itself.

5. Develop learning skills.   Continually improve the ability to listen, concentrate, read, think, explore ideas openly, and generate creative ideas. You can learn from surprising sources, but you need to think critically in order to recognize and control your own biases and blind spots.

4.2 Getting Promoted

A department's policies, and possibly a union contract, normally spell out the exact procedures for promotions. There's usually an interview, a written exam, and an oral board hearing before you can be considered for promotion. Then, once all but the top few are eliminated, how is the final decision made? Very likely a selection of subjective opinions that your superiors passed on as recommendations to the chief will be important. Everything you do from day one, your total performance on the job, influences those opinions. Do you arrive for work on time? Are you eager to learn? Do you find things to investigate when you're on patrol?

I know one officer who has a reputation of just going through the motions. One of his shift mates commented, "He'll call in a plate and if the dispatcher says it's a stolen car, he'll answer 'Roger' and that's the last you hear of it."

Another officer was on patrol when two subjects burgled a clothing store in a neighboring town and escaped in a car. The broadcast was coming over the hot line with an incomplete description when he spotted a certain car coming across the bridge. He could not have known it was the burglar's car but something struck him as suspicious. He turned on his overheads and siren. They burned rubber fleeing, and he gave chase. He finally pinned their car against a roadside berm and captured two suspects with some $4,000 worth of clothing in their car.

There's much more to a promotion decision than just one incident, but these examples show how two officers view their job. One puts in his time and does what he has to do. The other took the trouble to train himself to recognize something out of the ordinary. He is now a sergeant—and no one complained about the wrinkles in the side of his cruiser.

A positive job attitude is the willingness to slosh through a swamp after a suspect, to accept onerous assignments and do them with a professional effectiveness, to back up your partner in the face of danger, to plan a patrol so you're likely to be in the right spot at the right time, and to seek out every opportunity to improve yourself.

An officer's professional performance is the basis for the effectiveness reports that a supervisor writes periodically. In the past, evaluations were often based on data easy to define: the number of arrests, for example. Now, the quantity is not as important as the quality. More and more, case preparation and successful presentation in court are criteria for evaluation. The completeness of reports, judgment in exercising the powers of office, relationships with the community, all these can influence supervisors' opinions when they are asked to evaluate an officer.

4.3 Continuing Education

"Postgraduate" training is important for several reasons. One of them has to do with liability. Through decisions on liability suits, courts are plainly stating that basic academy training is only a foundation upon which an education is built. Here are a couple of cases that prove the point.

A police officer's training never ends. These experienced SWAT team members practice handling different situations and draw the attention of the neighborhood. **L&O.**

In *Leite* v. *City of Providence,* 463 F. Supp. 585 (1978), the court decided that the town and not just the officer could be held liable if the plaintiff's injury resulted from nonexistent or *grossly inadequate* training and supervision of a police department.

Popov v. *City of Margate,* 476 F. Supp. 1237 (1979) applied the Leite decision to the type of training provided. Margate's officers received basic training at the state police academy and in-service firearms training on the range every six months. The case concerned the fatal nighttime shooting of an innocent bystander by a police officer in the residential community. Range training provided no instruction in shooting at a moving target, night shooting, shooting in residential areas, or shooting decisions. Evidence was presented that the chief considered the rules of firing in residential streets a matter of common sense, not requiring detailed explanation. The court held that to be "grossly inadequate" training and found for the plaintiff.

The need for continuing education is well recognized in law enforcement, in fact, it's required by many

Even if your department doesn't lecture, you'll find seminars and exercises to add to your knowledge and skills. Ed Nowicki of the American Society of Law Enforcement Trainers addresses a group of instructors at a regional seminar.

states. But many state training councils also conduct elective courses, some targeted to officers with specific duty assignments. It's up to you to find them and to apply for those that will enhance needed skills and provide preparations for advancement.

Kinds of Training Available

Training services can be categorized several ways. Federal, state, and regional police academies are unquestionably legitimate. Everyone wants to go to the FBI National Academy in Virginia or the Federal Law Enforcement Training Center in Georgia. But not everyone can get in.

Many private-sector universities offer accredited training for police officers. Just to name a few: John Jay College Criminal Justice Center in New York City, Police Training Institute of the University of Illinois, Institute of Police Technology and Management of the University of North Florida, the Criminal Justice Center Police Academy at Sam Houston State University in Texas, Northwestern University Traffic Institute, University of Houston Criminal Justice Center, LSU Law Enforcement Training Program.

There are also schools conducted by manufacturers of products used in police service. Most of them began by providing training specific to their products, but many expanded into other areas. The Smith & Wesson Academy in Massachusetts, for example, teaches more than just firearms courses. Among other companies with such training services are Heckler and Koch, Detroit Armor Corporation, Monadnock Lifetime Products, and Sirchie Finger Print Labs.

Associations are deeply involved. The International Association of Chiefs of Police has been conducting training courses for years. The National Rifle Association has a Law Enforcement Activities division that conducts firearms training. Others have formed for the purpose of training, such as the American Society of Law Enforcement Trainers, International Association of Law Enforcement Firearms Instructors, Defensive Tactics Institute, and Justice System Training Association.

And there are private police training consultants—a growing group of dedicated professional trainers whose business it is to provide the best possible training, using the most timely techniques.

Training Consultants
The use of private training consultants is growing rapidly. One reason may be that they aren't influenced by the politics inside a department. They don't have to work under the ranking officer who wants to phone in the requalification scores. An outside consultant might be just what the chief needs to convince a town council to budget funds for more training. It's been proved that people are more receptive to learning innovative techniques from an outside expert than from someone they work with.

Many training consultants are former police officers, instructors, or administrators. Now they earn their living by providing the knowledge a department doesn't have the time to develop in-house. It's their business to keep up to date, evaluate new ideas, and make their programs more than a department could do for itself.

Tim Powers, chief of a small department, became so concerned over the lack of physical training that he started the Fitness Institute. John Skaggs of the Firearms Training Institute was a street cop for twelve years, ten of them as firearms instructor. Emanuel Kapelsohn was a trial lawyer who saw legal problems with what was being taught, so he formed the Peregrine Corporation to conduct training. Roland Ouellette was an instructor at the state-run recruit academy but he saw a lack of followup training for officers in medium and small departments. Now he runs the Connecticut Law Enforcement Training Institute.

A martial arts master, Jim Lindell of the National Law Enforcement Training Center in Missouri drew on different disciplines to develop his Handgun Retention System. It's not a martial art in itself but it applies principles of four different martial arts disciplines to a few simple reactions that work.

Consultants tend to become specialists. Frank Bolz earned a national reputation as a hostage negotiator when he was with the New York City police department. Now he heads Frank Bolz Associates and trains others in his specialty. Focus on the police flashlight and I think of John Peters of the Defensive Tactics Institute. Verbal strategies calls to mind Daniel Vega of Catalyst, Inc. The father of practical shooting is Jeff Cooper of the American Pistol Institute. Probably no one has taught police shotgun more than John Farnum of Defense Training. Peter Tarley of Police Training Division, Inc. ran a seminar at the National Training Conference of the International Association of Law Enforcement Firearms Instructors that made it strikingly clear what happens under stress.

"A training consultant isn't a guru," Massad Ayoob of the Lethal Force Institute said. "He's really a conduit through which all the information he gathers can be developed, digested, and explained to his students in a way they can understand."

Consultants themselves caution that they aren't the final authority. They are really full-time students of their specialty. Each is a little different. Their programs are continually reviewed and revised. You may attend one course and find something you don't agree with. That's why John Peters believes instructors should attend outside trainers' courses. "The consultant gives you the ingredients to bake a cake," Peters said. "How you bake it is up to you."

5

Stress and Family Concerns

Law enforcement can be stressful. Many things induce stress: the challenges, quick changes of attitude, tragedies witnessed, odd working hours, physical demands, testifying in court.

But notice I said the profession *can be* stressful.

When you keep hearing about how stressful the job is, pretty soon you come to believe it.

Stress *is* a problem and it needs to be addressed. But it doesn't negatively affect every police officer. For example, it has been said that 37 percent of police marriages experience severe difficulties. That means 63 percent do *not*.

Stress is a complex phenomenon. Research links it with psychological and physiological problems. There are individual differences in the ways people react to stress. The stress of a domestic disturbance can send one person into a tantrum, another into melancholy. A study of concentration camp survivors twenty-five years after their release found a fourth of them with no evidence of any chronic physical disease or mental disorder. Yet institutions are filled with patients who suffered far less.

Stress factors range all the way from a demanding superior to a threat against your life. But when you perceive danger, your body responds to prepare you to cope. Hormones flow, causing what you feel as a pounding heart, sweating, trembling, or fatigue. Adrenalin is pumped into your bloodstream. Your blood pressure falls, then rises sharply. You may find yourself incredibly strong (you've probably heard a story of a mother lifting a car off her baby). Besides focusing your physique, stress may focus your mind. Suddenly you see nothing but the gun in the guy's hand. It's like looking down a tunnel. Of course, that could lead to serious consequences if the culprit is standing among a crowd of innocent bystanders.

Every officer needs to know how to recognize the symptoms of stress — and how to cope with it.

5.1 Recognizing Stress

Decisive and prolonged changes in a person's attitude may indicate a problem. Everyone has a bad day once in a while, but a distinct personality or physical change is a warning sign. Those under stress may become easily agitated, depressed, want to quit, drink increasingly, or feel emotionally exhausted. You might recognize the signs when a mild-mannered and even-tempered friend becomes irritable and unreasonable, or a normally well-groomed officer loses interest in her appearance.

If there's the slightest inkling you have a problem, do something about it.

5.2 Handling Stress

There are as many recommendations for handling stress as there are psychologists, and that is fine. What people need to overcome whatever is bothering them depends on them and on the problem. It takes a trained specialist to determine the problem and suggest appropriate remedial actions. It also takes a big man to admit he needs counseling.

Stress management is very complicated, because what's right in one case may be ineffective in another. The best purpose this discussion could serve is to convince you that it's okay to chat with a psychologist if you feel you have a problem a specialist could help with.

Some basic principles, however, should be helpful to everybody. Recognize your own limits. Off duty, do pleasant things. Learn to laugh. Accept that the struggle never ends; life is often unfair; the past is over.

One antidote to worry is to be analytical. Ask yourself: What's the worst possible consequence? How likely is it to happen? What can you do about it?

Recognize also that you are the one who helps others overcome their concerns and conflicts. You should be able to do it for yourself, if you approach it the same way.

This prayer has often helped me:

> God give me the strength to endure that which I cannot change,
> the courage to change that which I can,
> and the wisdom to know the difference.

5.3 Effects on the Family

Stress problems carry over to the family. You snap at your spouse, yell at the kids. You become more concerned with your own problems than with theirs. A spouse is the one most concerned with the effects that stress has on an officer. Because of the more intimate relationship, a spouse is frequently the brunt of anger or irritability.

The common complaint "My wife doesn't understand me" really is true in this business. How many people truly understand what a police officer experiences during a tour of duty? Ride-along programs have proved successful in helping a spouse or fiancée better understand the problems, and ultimately help the officer cope with them.

It was a little thing that used to upset my wife. With a police radio in my personal car, I feel obligated to stop and help stranded motorists. My wife was often irritated at what she considered a longer than necessary delay in my arrival home—until one day she was with me when it happened. A car was stranded on a lonely stretch of road and the motorist needed a tow. I called it in and the dispatcher acknowledged that a tow truck had been assigned. Since the car was in a safe place, I cleared and started to leave. It was my wife who asked, "Do you think we should leave him here all alone?" We stayed, and she hasn't complained since.

Since most police officers are males, and since the concerns

HOT TIPS FROM OLD HANDS

Don't mix business with pleasure. To those young and single studs with the shiny badge, tailored uniform, and big gun, the rule is, *Don't date on your beat.* It will only lead to trouble.

Sgt. Frank Thornton
Shelburne, Vermont,
police department

---

of a female spouse are not the same as those of a male spouse, it isn't chauvinistic to say police wives are special people. Dorothy Fagerstrom, a research editor for *Law & Order* magazine, got to know cops pretty well. In "Open Letter to Police Wives," May 1971, she wrote, "Police officers want an orderly society . . . want to help people. . . . They expect their wives to understand that this is something they *must* do and to approve. . . . They present a rough, tough exterior to the world; yet . . . they have hearts as big as all outdoors and they are sentimental softies."

Pat James and Martha Nelson present a revealing understanding of the challenges facing a police wife in their book *Police Wife* (Charles C. Thomas, 1975). Every police wife should read it. When a police officer is suffering stress, the family suffers. But it isn't a one-way street. The family is also one of the best sources of support. Most spouses are interested in what their officers do, and in their problems and frustrations.

5.4 Effects on the Children

Any job that imposes odd working hours means that you can't spend as much time with your kids as you'd like. A psychiatrist once told me that what's important is how much you are really *with* them when you are with them. That's true in any family relationship. Officers could actually spend more time with their family than someone who works 9:00 to 5:00, especially when the kids are young and have early bedtimes.

In my first marriage, I had three sons. They never had any social problems in school. The eldest once overheard an older boy say to another, "Don't fight with him. His father's a cop." Your career could be an asset to your children!

A cop's child also faces challenges others don't. The police parent has been exposed to the seamier side of life. When the child takes the car keys, the police parent sees the mangled bodies in the automobile accident she just investigated. When daughter's date arrives with a corsage, the police parent relives the rape case he handled the day before.

In their preteen years, your kids may find their friends fascinated by your profession. When they reach rebellious adolescence, they will find a wide variety of reactions, including some very negative. During these years the youngster is expanding horizons and confronting peer-group attitudes. What they find depends a lot on the general attitude of the community.

Officers need to help their families understand the "good samaritan" side of the profession, that they make the community safer for honest citizens, that they may be threatened but are trained to handle those situations. A youngster who appreciates the role of the police will be proud to be a "cop's kid."

6

Human Relations

The police officer's job is to prevent crime and apprehend offenders, and many still say that's all it is. However, a popular police motto is "To Protect and to Serve." As law enforcement evolves into a profession, it increasingly involves dealing with human behavior. A majority of your dispatches concern public service of some kind, rather than a crime. For many people, the police officer is the first contact in resolving all sorts of problems. Regardless of your personal opinions, you need to understand how many people are viewing the role of police.

As Harold Russell and Allan Beigel said in their book *Understanding Human Behavior for Effective Police Work*, "No one expects a psychologist to be a police officer, but a police officer is expected to be a psychologist—a practical, street-level psychologist."

Even more than the psychologist, the police officer is directly involved in dealing with the public, one on one. What you say and do directly influence how a situation develops. A bit of applied psychology on the street can serve you in many ways. You are better off defusing a situation with talk, rather than resorting to physical force. In dealing with citizens, it can help you to project a favorable image of yourself and your department.

In all stress situations, every human being will experience normal emotional reactions. That includes you. But professionals anticipate not only their own emotional reactions, but also the reactions of those they're dealing with. You've reduced the number of unknowns so you can direct your attention to other factors that make you effective. All behavior is motivated by something. When you identify why a person is doing whatever he's doing, you can deal with it.

The theory behind this sociological approach to police work is that it helps you handle confrontations better. You don't take offense at an insult. Instead, you probe for the cause of such anger and hostility. Once you understand it, you are better able to control it. It isn't always easy when you apprehend a rapist who just violated a seven-year-old or an armed robber who beat up a senior citizen. But, while personal involvement is unavoidable, emotional involvement is controllable.

People learn behavior patterns. The child abuser was likely abused as a child. Besides, if you lash out at him emotionally, you just might give his defense attorney the ammunition needed to get the client off because of violated civil rights.

6.1 Community Relations

Public relations and community relations programs attempt to enhance the police image, but such programs are not enough. The cop on the street deals with the public and the community every day. What that really means is simple: you're dealing with human beings.

Officers may encounter attitudes of mistrust and apprehensiveness not only along racial

and ethnic lines, but between ranks, sexes, age groups, perhaps even between officers working side by side. Your dealings with humans must recognize that mankind is basically the same in all societies; the basic values are the preservation of life, liberty, and equality.

Robert N. Pemberton conducted a field research project called "A Human Relations Program for Criminal Justice Agencies" when he was with the Nassau County, New York, police department. Some of his ideas are very relevant here.

Our Declaration of Independence says "all men are created equal," but you know that isn't so. Some are larger or stronger than others. All people are different—

Dealing with people is a big part of police work. You're the one who knows the area and can direct a newcomer. **L&O.**

physically, socially, and in personal preferences. Instead of looking at differences, Pemberton suggests you look for similarities. Under the skin, people are alike. In this sense, all men *are* created equal.

It's easy to become cynical in this job. You're exposed to the seamier side of life, to the worst of people, or to good people at their worst. Pemberton believes the keys to avoiding cynicism are education and training. Experience alone may not be the answer. The officer with twenty-one years on the force could have only one year of experience, repeated twenty times.

"The best advice I could give any police officer is to *read*," Pemberton adds. "Read the professional journals. Read the abstracts of studies reported by the National Institute of Justice. Be interested in developments in your profession, and in the needs of all individuals in your community. And be objective, rather than subjective."

How do you get along with kids? Liaison officers with a school system present programs to school children on topics such as traffic safety and crime prevention. **L&O.**

6.2 Troubled Youth

Everyone is mischievous sometimes. Lord knows, I played hooky from school. There really isn't a clear distinction between delinquent behavior and delinquent criminal behavior. Many offenses for which a juvenile may be arrested are not offenses if committed by an adult—running away from home and possession of alcohol, for example. We tend to categorize all juvenile behavior that comes to police attention as delinquency.

Broken homes, neglect, poverty, low intelligence, brain damage, and mental illness have all been proposed as "causes" of delinquency. It's more complex than that. The American Psychiatric Association's *Diagnostic and Statistical Manual* describes two disorders common in delinquent behavior: adjustment reactions of childhood, and adjustment reactions of adolescence. These are reactions to the stresses of two difficult ages.

There are many childhood conflicts. Children may feel rejected and run away or try to test their parents. A death of a loved one may lead to antisocial actions. Adolescents add other conflicts as they expand their horizons beyond the family or local neighborhood. As they search for an identity, they may be troubled with self-image or popularity, defining an acceptable moral code for relating with the opposite sex. Anxiety can be horrendous.

The police officer may symbolize bad experiences with authority figures. The juvenile's peer group may view the police as enemies. That means you need to project a professional, courteous, and respectful image. The kid's problems are the biggest things in life at that time. You should be firm but not overbearing. Listen when the kid wants to talk. Be concerned. In minor offenses, a firm but respectful warning may accomplish more than a citation. By the same token, be helpful when a kid asks for help.

Even if a youngster is wrong, you should respect a juvenile as you would an adult. Be patient. Show compassion. Be humorous when it helps. Always explain your actions to a juvenile and answer questions. Remember that kids soak up information and impressions like a sponge at that age and your influence could be lasting.

HOT TIPS FROM OLD HANDS

Be cool, never cold. It's trite but very true: getting involved emotionally with the victim is detrimental to good police work. Too many officers seem to think this means projecting a cold, impersonal attitude and not caring at all. Not true! A cop without empathy is worthless. The main concern is to remember the objective of bringing the criminal to justice. Arrest and conviction are the correct route, not wanting to roast the perp over a slow fire. Empathy is fine, just don't wallow in it.

Sgt. Frank Thornton
Shelburne, Vermont,
police department

6.3 Abnormal Behavior

The prefix *ab* means "away from," so abnormal behavior is behavior that deviates from whatever the community considers normal. "Normal" is a statistical average with society writing the rules. One definition of abnormal is any behavior that is ineffective, self-defeating, self-destructive, or that alienates the individual from those who are important to that individual.

When you are dealing with a person who is emotionally disturbed, don't try to handle the situation alone. Call for backup. But stay with the person, move slowly, reassure, get help from the person's family or friends, never try to deceive or threaten with weapons. However, a show of force can work. Try to convince the person to do what you want; then tell him or her that the choice is to do it with dignity or be carried out in a strait jacket. Experts tell me that, faced with this show of force, most patients will elect to proceed under their own power.

Don't be fooled by a person's size. Emotional stress can make people impervious to pain and give them unusual physical strength. Meet hostility and anger with calm, objective compassion. Try to find out why the person is upset. That distracts attention and helps to calm a subject. Most disturbed individuals are afraid because they don't understand their own feelings and are uncertain how others will treat them. And don't be fooled by a sudden return to reality; delusions can return just as quickly. Remain alert even after things have calmed down.

Dealing with personality disorders is a unique problem for police officers. Behavior is probably out of control and violence threatening by the time you arrive. Remember that the person adopted a maladaptive pattern to protect himself from life's stresses. Threaten the pattern and the person could become potentially dangerous, acting impulsively in desperation.

Such persons usually react positively when something or someone acts to remove that stress. It may mean taking a spouse into another room to separate the combatants. It may mean forcefully and tactfully leaving the person no choice to fret over. Confronting reality in clear terms can have a calming influence; it can help the person reestablish a contact with reality that was temporarily lost.

6.4 Mentally Disabled

Problems that police face when dealing with mentally disabled persons became a growing concern when the preferred treatment changed from hiding them away in asylums to putting them into community programs. A network of public and private agencies to provide health care and assistance was slow to develop and even then was often inadequate or ineffective. People who are unable to manage for themselves often have no choice but to do it anyway. Police are asked to "do something" about people whose offenses are minor, if any offense at all, but who are major aggravation to others.

The general public is uneasy and intolerant, perhaps fearful, of bizarre or deviant behavior. Whether a crime has been committed or not, their first reaction is to call the police. Then officers are faced with determining if the person is mentally ill and evaluating whether the person is a danger. They need to determine the person's mental health history, without the help of experts, and then decide what they're going to do. It's the sociologist's view that officers need to deal with such situations from three perspectives: law enforcement, civil, and social service.

Most often, disposition is providing referral information or simply separating the individuals involved, but that's not always the best resolution. Arrest is also often inappropriate. A voluntary mental health examination is usually the most desirable disposition but is also the hardest to achieve. An involuntary mental examination is often chosen simply because the problem is of a mental health nature rather than criminal.

Managing an encounter with a mentally disturbed person is unfamiliar to most police officers. It can be frustrating, even frightening. But an inadequate response leads to future encounters and perhaps bigger problems for police.

You can't ignore the call from a person who is threatened by laser rays from outer space or being followed by an assassin with a gun. But these are often repeat calls, and knowing what has transpired before will help you decide on an appropriate action. You need to project a calm, take-charge image to placate distraught or panicky persons. Bystanders who aren't witnesses should be dispersed, even disruptive family members. But identify those who may be helpful and keep them close. Do what you need to do to calm the person. Then you can start to manage the situation.

Obviously, your first concern is stopping or preventing a crime, but you're going to need all the information you can get. Check the scene for signs of results of bizarre behavior. Interview family members and witnesses. Was the mentally disturbed person threatening or using violence, or threatening suicide? Was the person acting dangerously, neglecting personal care or bodily functions? Has the person suffered a recent traumatic experience?

Other questions will help develop information needed for an involuntary commitment. Does the person have a history of mental illness? Feel controlled by outside forces? Receive messages from strangers, radio, or television? Hear voices others do not? See things others do not? Feel the victim of a plot? Claim others can read his or her thoughts? Claim to be able to read other's thoughts? Note if the person is oriented to the environment, changes moods during the conversation, presents a mood appropriate to the nature of the call, or appears to be under the influence of alcohol or illegal drugs.

These answers and observations also help you to recognize mental disorders. The person may be quite lucid by the time you get reach an appropriate facility and your concern may appear unfounded. Then you need to provide "probable cause" for bringing in a mentally disturbed person. These general characteristics are symptomatic of mental disorder: behavior and mood are inappropriate to the setting, and behavior tends to be inflexible or impulsive.

Before interacting with a mentally disturbed person on the scene, follow these six guidelines suggested by psychologists:

1.   Gather as much information as you can.

2.   Be discreet and avoid attracting attention.

3.   Be calm, avoid excitement, and portray a take-charge attitude.

4.   Remove distractions or upsetting influences.

5.   Gather information from helpful witnesses, family, and friends.

6.   Then be firmly gentle.

7

The Judicial System

Police agencies are just one part of the criminal justice system in America—the first part. The actions of the police feed the next part of the system—the courts. What you do, how you prepare your case, the evidence you gather, and how you present all this in court play a large role in determining the outcome. Obviously, you are an important part of the judicial system. Of course you have help.

The tripartite system of criminal justice—police, courts, corrections—is really a three-part extension ladder with many rungs, and the parts overlap.

Within the first (police) phase of the system, you have to detect the crime. Whether you find it accidentally or by design, respond to a dispatch or a complaint by a citizen, you become aware that a crime has been committed. Then you investigate. You determine the facts, gather the evidence, and develop a case report that, you hope, leads to the identification of the perpetrator. Once you know there really was a crime committed and who probably committed it, then you can make an arrest, an apprehension. The administrative process of taking a person into custody, booking, is now a familiar term, thanks to movies and television shows.

Now comes the first overlap between police and courts. You don't just arrest someone and let it go at that. Within a time specified by law, you must present the accused to a judicial officer for formal charges and consideration of release on recognizance or bond. From the information you have developed, the formal complaint is prepared by the prosecutor, the attorney who represents the state in a criminal trial. He or she decides, on the basis of the evidence you present, the specific charges to be brought against the accused.

You may arrest because of a citizen's complaint, and you usually determine the charges when you arrest someone, but you now see that the real complaint and charges the accused must answer in court are those prepared by the prosecutor.

In the case of a felony, the next step is a preliminary hearing, followed by a grand jury indictment. Once the prosecutor decides to charge the suspect, he or she must demonstrate there is probable cause that the suspect committed the crime. The prosecutor prepares an information, a document that presents to the court all relevant information regarding the charge. This is simply to determine whether the prosecutor's evidence is sufficient for trial. Once it's established that there is probable cause and that the cause is sufficient, an arraignment is held in the court where the accused will be tried. This is where the defendant is officially informed of the charges.

Then there's the process of plea bargaining. To expedite a case through the court system, the prosecutor and defendant's attorney may agree to a plea of guilty to a lesser offense, just to avoid a long and costly trial. It could be that the accused has information that's worth bargaining for. If no bargain is reached, the next step is adjudication. Here various pretrial motions to dismiss or suppress evidence are heard by a judge and decided.

Then the trial can begin, before a judge or judge and jury. If there is a jury trial, the petit jury decides on the facts, and the judge rules on disputed points of law. If the defendant is found guilty the trial is over, but another process, *sentencing*, begins. There may be a presentence investigation to help a judge (or jury in some jurisdictions) determine the most appropriate disposition before bringing the offender back into court for sentencing. The offender may be required to pay a fine, put on accelerated rehabilitation, be put on probation under supervision, or be incarcerated behind bars.

And that leads to the third part of this ladder, *corrections*. But that's the next chapter. Police overlap with the court at the front end of the process; probation and corrections overlap at the other end.

This seems like an orderly and logical progression of criminal justice, but it doesn't work that way. Police are part of the executive branch of government, courts a part of the judicial branch. Corrections may be part of the executive branch, but often there are separate agencies involved—one responsible for supervising probation, another handling parole, and a totally separate structure operating jails and prisons. Despite the efforts of politicians, bureaucrats, and academics, a rampant lack of coordination among these components once led the American Bar Association to call the criminal justice system a "nonsystem."

While the components of the criminal justice system are distinct, separate, and independent of each other, each is very much affected by the actions of the others.

7.1 Court Officers

The three principals of any judicial proceeding are the judge, the prosecutor, and the defense attorney. The offices of each may be staffed with assistants, paralegals, investigators, and clericals, but the person in charge is the responsible party.

The Prosecutor   The prosecutor—who may be called state's attorney, district attorney, county attorney, county solicitor, local prosecutor, or U.S. attorney—has a complex function. His or her purpose is to see that justice is done, although the goal of many prosecutors may appear to be to convict as many defendants as possible. The sentiment expressed in the American Bar Association's Code of Professional Responsibility (1977) suggests that prosecutors be concerned more with justice than simply with convictions.

In larger offices, many prosecutors have sophisticated investigation teams, career criminal units, diversion programs, and such nonprosecutorial functions as crime prevention, community education, and victim and witness services.

Joan Jacoby, author of *The American Prosecutor* (Lexington Books, 1980), developed four categories for the decisions facing the prosecutor: legal sufficiency, systems efficiency, defendant rehabilitation, and trial sufficiency. Legal sufficiency refers to the legality of the case, including the elements of the crime and other legal and constitutional issues. Systems efficiency is the priority the case should receive. Facing overloaded dockets, budget constraints, and overcrowded jails and prisons, they cannot prosecute minor offenses as vigorously as major crimes. The defendant is part of this consideration. A first offender is treated differently than a career criminal. One with an alcohol problem may be better treated in "accelerated rehabilitation," going through an alcohol program rather than going to jail. Finally, trial sufficiency: is the evidence sufficient to convict the defendant in court?

It is the stuff of jokes that attorneys go at each other's throats in court, then make a date for their golf game. The prosecutor and defense attorney may have been classmates in law school. They may be neighbors. Such relationships aren't lost on perplexed police officers or disgruntled defendants. It might serve the system quite well if such informal liaisons led to wholesale resolutions of stacks of similar cases, but people are wont to take things personally. When a victim or a defendant sees the "adversaries" laughing together over some unrelated subject, it's human nature to feel that one was somehow dealt less than an advantageous hand by the dealer of justice.

The defendant's hope is the defense attorney.

The Defense Attorney   It seems strange in today's society of *Miranda* warnings and free legal counsel to the indigent, but until 1963 defense counsel was available only to those who could pay for it. An elderly white inmate in Florida claimed that the Sixth Amendment guaranteed him the right to be represented by counsel. A young lawyer named Abe Fortas, later to become a U.S. Supreme Court justice, argued the case for Clarence Earl Gideon. The Supreme Court agreed with Gideon and ruled that anyone charged with a felony is entitled to court-appointed representation (*Gideon* v. *Wainwright,* 372 U.S. 335, 1963.)

Later cases extended the Gideon ruling to include the right to counsel at all critical stages of prosecution, and in 1972 the court ruled that no person may be imprisoned for any offense without legal counsel (*Argersinger* v. *Hamlin,* 407 U.S. 25, 1972). It boils down to a simple fact: if the person you are arresting *may* face incarceration, he's entitled to a lawyer, even if he can't afford one.

Many of the problems associated with appointing volunteer counsel were resolved when the concept of the public defender emerged. These offices may be similar to the office of the prosecutor, with investigators, paralegals, and funds to hire expert witnesses. But critics claim that public defenders, being paid by the court, must maintain a harmonious relationship with the court and perhaps are not as adversarial as they might be. The opinions of experts differ, but some say that a person's ability to choose his own legal counsel is important because defendants often perceive private counsel as better than public defenders.

Despite the popular view that the defense counsel's job is to get the client off, his or her purpose really is to make sure the client gets a fair shake. If there is any error or omission in the prosecutor's case, you can be sure the defense will make the most of it. The defense attorney's job is to grill you on the witness stand and try to blow holes in your story, to do everything possible to cast doubt on the client's guilt.

With two lawyers arguing from different viewpoints, there must be a final arbiter, and there is—the judge.

The Judge   The broad term *judge* includes magistrates, trial judges, appellate judges, and justices. In large jurisdictions, some judges may be responsible for pretrial matters only, while others hear only traffic cases, or misdemeanors, or felonies, or appeals.

The major roles for a judge are to issue arrest and search warrants, rule on pretrial motions, plea bargain, "referee" the trial, and rule on appeals. They ensure a fair trial by enforcing the rules of evidence and law, deciding on objections raised by either side. In jury trials, the judge explains the law to the jury and instructs them on the presumption of innocence and the state's burden of proving guilt beyond a reasonable doubt.

In their court, judges are all-powerful. When you appear, your police powers are virtually left at the door.

7.2　Layers of Legal Jurisdiction

The court system is a complex structure with related but independent components, as we have seen. To understand it, you need to understand the principle of separation of powers written into the U.S. Constitution. The legislative branch of government writes the laws, the executive branch (police) enforces the laws, and the judicial branch (courts) interprets the laws and decides differences of opinions. As we'll see, those decisions themselves become law.

Jurisdiction　　Police officers function within the boundaries defined by their employer: a town, county, state, or perhaps a particular area of law. Courts also have their own jurisdictions. There are tax courts, traffic courts, civil courts, criminal courts, county courts, state courts, superior courts, federal courts broken down into districts and circuits. Whichever one is the appropriate place to bring a particular case before is called the court of *original jurisdiction*.

State Courts　　While the organization of criminal courts may differ from state to state, the basic structure and processes are similar. Some trial courts may hear all criminal cases; in other jurisdictions, they may be divided, with one level hearing only misdemeanor cases and another hearing felony cases. All states have some form of appellate procedure, either intermediate appeal courts or one court of appeals.

Generally, appellate courts hear only issues of law, rather than the facts and witnesses of a case. There may be a succession of courts through which a case may be appealed until, ultimately, the most serious reach the state Supreme Court. Whenever a court rules, its decision has the force of law and all lower courts within its jurisdiction must abide. The state Supreme Court's decisions are binding on all state courts.

Federal Courts　　Federal courts are similarly structured, but organized on a regional basis. There may be several federal court districts within a state. Appeals go up to one of thirteen federal circuit courts, and then to the U.S. Supreme Court.

When the U.S. Supreme Court renders a decision, its majority opinion becomes binding on all lower courts, including state courts where federal constitutional questions are involved. When a circuit court rules, it is binding on all lower courts *within that circuit*. Should two federal circuit courts disagree, the Supreme Court decides the issue.

7.3　Historical Precedent

The American system is modeled after the British system, and the British system goes back to the Magna Carta of 1215. It is an adversarial process, in which all parties cooperate in a search for the truth. The process assumes that there are two sides to every question. Each side has its champion in the prosecutor and defense attorney, with the judge sitting as referee.

In reality, you soon realize that lower courts, especially, seem to be a bureaucratic system of disposing of as many cases as possible in the shortest possible time. The system is stretched to its limit, and sometimes perfunctory disposition becomes a matter of necessity.

8

The Penal System

Police officers have little to do with the penal system, and corrections officers are going to study more comprehensive texts than this. This chapter is included to broaden your understanding of the overall criminal justice system.

Punishment for wrongdoing dates back to before recorded history. While it could hardly be considered "law," the earliest remedy for wrongs was simply retaliation. Atonement for murder by payment to appease the victim's family became common, and it is still practiced in some parts of the world. In our modern society, the practice continues in the form of fines for lesser offenses.

The most common forms of state punishment over the centuries have been death, torture, mutilation, branding, public humiliation, fines, forfeiture of property, banishment, and imprisonment. There was very little knowledge of behavior modification and other modern techniques to control violent persons. Feared offenders were put to death, by ever more sophisticated techniques in modern times, to serve as an object lesson, a deterrent to others.

The idea that capital punishment is a deterrent is not held in high regard nowadays. But former Los Angeles police chief Ed Davis was once asked by a reporter if he felt the death penalty was a deterrent. He replied that he had done a study and found that not one of the criminals put to death had ever committed another crime. Of course, that exchange was during his political campaign for state senator. The theory that capital punishment is more economical than life imprisonment is argued down by some who say the cost of imposing the death penalty, with all its inherent appeals, is more than the cost of keeping the prisoner alive.

I mention this to illustrate the wide range of opinions about punishment today. The concept of penalty—the penal system—is influenced by personal philosophy, so you can understand why it has changed over the years.

8.1 Corrections

There are three theories of corrections, and they can be categorized as punishment, treatment, and prevention.

Punishment   Punishment has been officially sanctioned since the beginning of law. It can be traced back to the victim's need for retaliation and vengeance. It is intended to have a deterrent effect, convincing others of the futility of committing similar crimes. The weakness of this theory is that most criminals don't think they'll be caught and so are not deterred by fear of punishment.

Incapacitation has been used as punishment. The theory is that there is no hope for rehabilitation, and the offender must be prevented from committing another crime. In some countries, for example, castration has been used to punish sex offenders.

Obviously, some punishments can be effective when applied in the proper amounts at the right time. Every parent applies this principle. But, institutionally, the effects of punishment can be negative. Minority-group members may blame their incarceration on repression by the rich, political persecution, or attempted genocide. Harsh punishments may motivate offenders to become more sophisticated criminals.

If those punished see their punishment as unjust and this view is supported by their peers, results are negative. If they feel it is deserved and their peers agree, punishment can be more positive. Prisons generally become places where inmates look to one another for support and the agents of the law become the enemy.

General and uniform punishment is still the rule rather than the exception. The move toward a treatment or preventive model is slow.

Treatment   A major trend today is to approach the offender as you would the mentally ill, neglected, or underprivileged. This ideology sees criminal behavior as a pathological manifestation that can respond to some form of therapy.

Procedures vary. Classic psychiatric treatment is rare. Group therapy, including staff and inmates, is more commonly used. Such programs try to shift the offender's allegiance from the values of the criminal group to those of the noncriminal group. The main purpose of the treatment approach is to help people identify their defect or problem and overcome it.

Prevention   Of the prisoners who served their time nearly 63 percent are arrested for a serious crime within three years of release, according to a 1989 Justice Department study. *Recidivism* is the term. You hear it used to justify a variety of concepts. "Problem children" in school become delinquents who become criminals. Prevention programs in schools today treat the problem child by providing special classes, vocational education, and counseling.

Another aspect of prevention is removing what we've come to call "career criminals" from the opportunity to commit crime. Chronic repeat offenders are a small part of the criminal population, but they commit a majority of the crimes. In Marvin Wolfgang's 1972 study of criminal careers in Philadelphia, chronic offenders comprised just 23 percent of all male offenders but they committed 61 percent of all the crimes: 61 percent of homicides, 76 percent of rapes, 73 percent of robberies, and 65 percent of aggravated assaults. If we selectively incapacitate these career criminals, the number of crimes committed should be reduced.

8.2 Incarceration

After 1976, when crime took a temporary downturn, ever-increasing crime rates have pushed society toward the punishment ideology. But prison populations have grown to unmanageable proportions. The trend toward determinate sentences and "get tough" policies make the situation worse. Treatment is becoming rare. The pendulum has swung far right, in the view of some administrators, and decisions are being made now that will influence the future of corrections.

Whatever concept of "correcting" criminals is popular, incarceration is a punishment. Concerned citizens want crooks put behind bars.

When a judge passes sentence, it means what it says, right? Not necessarily. "Most offenders released from prison in 1984 had served a little less than one-half of their court-ordered maximum sentences," said Steven R. Schlesinger, director of the Bureau of Justice Statistics. "The median time served was 45 percent."

According to statistics released by the National Corrections Reporting Program in 1988, the average offender released from prison in thirty-three states had served one year and five months behind bars. The median term for those released after serving sentences for murder or nonnegligent manslaughter was six and a half years, including pretrial jail time. For rape the median was three years and eight months; for robbery two years, six months; for burglary one year, five months; and for drug trafficking one year, four months. The National Corrections Reporting Program surveys both the anticipated and actual time prisoners serve in state prisons.

Repeat offenders—those who had previously served time for felonies—spent more time behind bars than those who had no previous conviction. For violent offenses this difference was six months; for property offenses three months; and for drug offenses, one month.

8.3 Probation

Probation is not the same as a suspended sentence. A sentence can be imposed, with its execution suspended, or *both* imposition and execution can be suspended. However, this practice has generally been replaced with supervised probation. The American Bar Association defines probation as "a sentence not involving confinement, which imposes conditions and retains authority in the sentencing court to modify the conditions of sentence or to resentence the offender if he violates the conditions. Such a sentence should not involve or require suspension of the imposition or execution of any other sentence."

"The problems associated with a lack of organization in the criminal justice system are exemplified in probation services," says Harry E. Allen and Clifford E. Simonsen in their book *Corrections in America* (Macmillan, 1986). Under the original concept, judges themselves were to administer probation. In small jurisdictions, this may still be the case, but most states offer probation services at the state level. In some, the system is set up at the county or even municipal level.

Most probation officers have the problem of serving two masters. They are usually required to meet with probationers, doing casework like a social worker analyzing problems. Then they must report back to the court and recommend subsequent action. An inherent drawback in this casework model is that probation officers are likely to go beyond probationary functions by placing probationers in foster homes, operating shelters, or trying to deal with such extreme problems as alcoholism, drug addiction, and mental illness. Yet they are expected to account for their probationers if they get into trouble again. The court is bound to ask, "When did you last see your client?"

Large caseloads have been the bane of probation officers everywhere. The San Francisco Project, a 1969 study of the relationship between recidivism and probation caseloads, set 50 cases as the ideal, 25 if they require intensive supervision, but found 100 the norm and some as high as 250. The study also found little relationship between the number of contacts and the success of probation.

Restrictions and conditions of probation are set by law and the opinion of the sentencing court, so the decision is only as good as the presence information available to the judge. But the conditions cannot be standard operating procedure. Conditions for continued probation must be tailored to the needs of the individual offender, rather than the offense. Unfortunately, courts frequently delegate this rule-making power to the probation officer. That puts the officer in the impossible position of being lawmaker, enforcer, and confidant.

A number of courts require the probation officer, who does the presentence investigation, to recommend conditions for probation on the basis of expectations of where the offender will be living, how he'll earn a living, and so on. The judge discusses terms of probation with the candidate, his counsel, and the probation officer. In this way, restrictions are usually few but important, and they give the probationer a clear understanding of what constitutes acceptable behavior.

Victim compensation is sometimes a condition of probation. Reimbursement of medical costs or financial losses has followed recent studies of victimization. Sometimes, a judge may impose an order to do voluntary community service as a form of symbolic restitution.

Probation is similar to parole, but it occurs at a point in the judicial process that tends to minimize the damage that incarceration inflicts on first-time offenders. Most states administer probation and parole by separate agencies, although some combine them into one. The number of people on probation continues to grow. According to the *Sourcebook of Criminal Justice Statistics* (Government Printing Office, 1987), there were 986,000 people on probation in 1984. By 1985, the total had risen to 1,064,000.

Probation may be imposed without adjudication. The judge can put the offender on probation without the stigma of being a convicted felon. Or she can find him guilty and sentence him to probation. Actually, probation without adjudication was John Augustus' original idea. A philanthropic Boston shoemaker, Augustus is said to have bailed out nearly 2,000 offenders between 1841 and 1858. When a defendant came back to court for sentencing, Augustus would report on his progress. The judge would usually impose a fine of one cent and costs in lieu of a term in an institution.

Probation gives offenders a chance to prove themselves so they can remain in the community, under supervision, and without a criminal conviction. Massachusetts passed the first probation law in 1878. Since then, probation was developed into the main component of corrections. With continued emphasis as a preferred disposition, it will remain in the forefront of penal reform.

8.4 Parole

Parole and probation have similar histories and operate in much the same way, even though they occur at opposite ends of the correctional process. Early in American history, a sentence to prison for a fixed term meant just what it said. It left little hope for early release or little incentive for prisoners to change their ways.

"Good time" laws began in 1817 in New York state and were enacted in every state and the District of Columbia by 1916. They gave administrators a means to reward good behavior.

Since World War II, parole boards have taken three forms: those made up of correctional staff, those made up of people independent of the penal system, and a consolidation of correctional and parole services with the best aspects of the first two.

A national study in 1979 determined that parole boards consider specific factors in determining a prisoner's readiness: his participation in prison programs, good behavior, change in attitude, increased maturity, and development of insight.

Most parole boards operate by assigning cases to individual board members, who investigate and recommend actions to the board as a whole. A member may visit the prison to interview the inmate and prison staff, or the board may convene inside on a regular schedule. Penal administrators consider it a problem that boards keep secret the standards a candidate is expected to meet and the reasons for his failure to win parole. There is virtually no appeal process, because criteria for parole are not specified. Some states have begun to define criteria and establish appeal procedures. The U.S. Parole Commission has been in the forefront of this trend.

Parole has gained an important place in the penal system, but it is not without its problems and detractors. Criteria for the selection of parole authority personnel needs to be defined by statute, and training should be provided on a national scale. Despite the trend toward determinate sentencing that releases prisoners unconditionally, about 75 percent are still released to parole supervision. Some states have changed the title of parole officer to community corrections officer.

In the United States, Bureau of Justice Statistics data show that 158,000 people were on parole in 1985. But the process is far from perfect. What's needed most is a way to determine the moment when an inmate is most likely to benefit from parole.

8.5 Pardon

Another way to escape punishment is by some form of pardon. A governor may extend executive clemency to one who has achieved significant social accomplishment while behind bars. Later evidence might develop that shows the convicted person was really innocent, and a full pardon wipes the slate clean. A class of criminals might be offered amnesty. The murderer on Death Row might win a reprieve, with his death sentence reduced to life imprisonment. Punishment may also be lessened by commutation, which is a shortening of the sentence, usually to time already served.

You learned about the U.S. Constitution in school, but you need to learn about it again. English common law was the foundation on which American law was built. Now it's more complicated. The constitutions of the United States and your state, along with federal and state statutes, published court decisions, town ordinances, and regulations promulgated by regulatory agencies are the basis for everything you do.

It really isn't all that complex, once you are reminded of the fundamentals of the U.S. Constitution. No state law may contravene this basic law of the land.

9.1 U.S. Constitution

The U.S. Constitution went into effect in 1789 and established our form of government. It divides the federal government into three parts: legislative (Article I), executive (Article II), and judicial (Article III), and one branch may not encroach upon the province of another. The legislature writes laws. The executive branch enforces laws. The judiciary interprets laws. The Constitution defines the functions that are appropriately done by the federal government—for example, maintaining a defense force, handling mail, making treaties, coining money, declaring war—and it limits the powers of states in these areas.

The Bill of Rights   The first ten amendments were ratified in 1791 as the Bill of Rights. They address concerns not specifically covered in the basic document. Since this original document was written, other amendments have been added over the years.

Amendment	Purpose
First	Guarantees freedom of speech, religion, press, peaceable assembly, and redress of grievances.
Second	Prohibits infringement of the right of the people to keep and bear arms.

Third	Prohibits quartering soldiers in a home without the consent of the owner.
Fourth	Prohibits unreasonable search and seizure. Requires "probable cause" supported by oath, and particular description of places to be searched and persons or things to be seized.
Fifth	Requires indictment by a grand jury in major crimes. Prohibits putting a person in double jeopardy, confiscation of property without just compensation, deprivation of life, liberty, or property without due process of law, or compelling persons to incriminate themselves.
Sixth	Guarantees right to a speedy trial and counsel. (The 1963 case of *Gideon* v. *Wainwright* defined the right to counsel: if there is a likelihood of imposing a jail sentence, a defendant must have counsel, even if he or she is indigent.)
Seventh	Guarantees trial by jury.
Eighth	Prohibits excessive bail and cruel or unusual punishment.
Ninth	States that listing rights in the Constitution shall not be construed to deny or disparage others retained by the people.
Tenth	Provides that powers not delegated to the federal government, or prohibited to the states, are reserved to the states or to the people.

Other Amendments

Another amendment, important to you, was added in 1868. The Fourteenth Amendment guarantees due process of law. It says, "Nor shall any State deprive any person of life, liberty, or property, without due process of law; nor deny to any person within its jurisdiction equal protection of the laws."

Let's look again at the Fourth Amendment:

The right of the people to be secure in their persons, houses, papers, and effects, against unreasonable searches and seizure, shall not be violated, and no warrants shall issue, but on probable cause, supported by oath or affirmation, and particularly describing the place to be searched, and the person or things to be seized.

A key word here is *unreasonable*. When you apply for a warrant, you must include as much information as possible to show that your conclusion is reasonable.

The phrase *probable cause,* which I'll discuss in greater detail later, is another key concept in the Fourth Amendment. This principle applies only to the police officer, and it can protect you in many ways—if you can explain your reasoning.

The Fourth Amendment permits police to augment their own senses with tools provided by science and technology. For example, *United States* v. *Knotts,* 460 U.S. 276 (1983) concluded that no search existed when a beeper was used to track a purchased container to the defendant's cabin. *California* v. *Ciraolo,* 10 LOB 127 (1986) upheld warrantless surveillance flights by aircraft over a drug dealer's property.

Other Supreme Court decisions have established precedents where plain view or exigent circumstances are involved.

Plain view. If you inadvertently see incriminating evidence in plain view, when you are in a place you have a right to be for a proper reason, you can seize it (*Coolidge* v. *New Hampshire,* 403 U.S. 443, 1971).

Exigent circumstances. Because you are a police officer, sworn to protect the public, you are expected to act in shady situations. You might define *exigent* here as "emergency." Drugs are being flushed down the toilet, screams inside indicate someone is in grave danger. You don't have time to get a warrant or ask permission to enter a dwelling (*Mincey* v. *Arizona,* 437 U.S. 385, 1978).

Neither do you have time to think up all those justifications you put into a warrant affidavit. But as soon as you can, you'd better write a report that clearly explains all the reasons that led you to believe immediate action was necessary. Whenever you act without a supervisor's overview, an attorney for the plaintiff in a civil suit will look for a way to discredit your action. The U.S. Supreme Court has held that a warrantless search of a home is unconstitutional in the absence of exigent circumstances (*Payton* v. *New York,* 445 U.S. 573, 1980). To arrest a subject in the home of a third party requires both an arrest and a search warrant (*Steagold* v. *United States,* 451 U.S. 204, 1981).

Interpretation   You should understand that all laws are interpreted by the courts. While you may read a law one way, what's important is how a court of your jurisdiction has read it.

Article IV, Section 2, the U.S. Constitution says, "The Citizens of each State shall be entitled to all Privileges and Immunities of Citizens in the several States." Amendment XIV, Section 1, says, "No State shall make or enforce any law which shall abridge the privileges or immunities of the citizens of the United States."

This means that you don't need to get an operator's license for every state you drive through. And you and your bride were not living in sin when you visited a honeymoon resort in a neighboring state. However, my state granted me a permit to carry a concealed pistol or revolver. Other states do not recognize this permit, and courts have upheld this as "reasonable" restriction. I told you I'm not a lawyer.

The police officer is not expected to be an attorney. Even attorneys specialize because they can't know everything either. But you have to understand the law as it applies to you. For example, under the principle of "fruit of the poisoned tree," if you violate a suspect's rights, any evidence gathered as a consequence is inadmissible. And that can blow the whole case.

9.2 Fruit of the Poisoned Tree

A grocery store was robbed. A person already in custody on unrelated charges told a policeman he heard that Omar Taylor was involved. The officer arrested Taylor without a warrant, acting solely on that information. The defendant was advised of his rights and taken to the stationhouse, where he was fingerprinted and again advised of his rights. In a lineup, victims failed to identify him but police found his fingerprints on items taken from the grocery. After a brief visit with his girlfriend and a neighbor, and some six hours after his arrest, the defendant signed a waiver of his rights and gave a written confession.

At trial, Taylor's defense counsel objected that the evidence of his waiver and confession were the fruits of his illegal arrest. The judge overruled and Taylor was convicted. On appeal, the U.S. Supreme Court voted five to four to overturn his conviction. They found a lack of probable cause for the original arrest. No matter how many times his rights were read later, anything that followed the illegal arrest is fruit of the poisoned tree. It's all reported in *Taylor* v. *Alabama,* U.S., 73 L. Ed. 2d 314 (1982).

Nuances such as this affect your daily life. But they can change day by day. The information here is as accurate as I can make it at the time this is written, but it's not gospel. Even your training is gospel only at the time you receive it. The final authority is your department's legal counsel. And his or her advice is valid only at the time you ask the question. The law can change.

Even when you have executed a warrant, you can bet the defendant's attorney will look at it carefully. If he or she can show that the warrant was improper, any evidence obtained under that warrant is "fruit of the poisoned tree" and may not be introduced in court. Defendant's attorneys will look even harder at any action you took without a warrant.

This exclusionary rule has been eased somewhat in recent years. Once, the slightest technical discrepancy was enough to invalidate a warrant. Now, if an officer acts on information he believes to be true, but it turns out it's not, he acted in good faith and the U.S. Supreme Court says that's okay (*United States* v. *Leon*, 468 U.S. 897, 1984).

9.3 Exigent Circumstances

Exigent circumstances is a term you'll hear often. It simply means that the situation requires immediate action on your part. It could be to provide safety for yourself or others, prevent the destruction of evidence, or prevent the escape of the suspect. Most often it involves a search incident to a lawful arrest. Necessity demands that you protect yourself. You can make sure the person has no weapons, access to things that would aid his escape, or evidence that he might destroy.

The arrest must be lawful. The search must be for the purposes stated above and it must be contemporaneous with the arrest. The arrest cannot be a sham just to justify a search. You may make a reasonable search of areas within the suspect's reach or distance he might leap to gain a weapon or destroy evidence. Any search beyond these limits of time and area requires a warrant.

9.4 Probable Cause

Virtually everything you do must be based on a reason for your doing it. The legal principle for an officer's actions is *probable cause*. Briefly, probable cause is defined as facts and circumstances sufficient to lead a reasonable person to believe that a crime has been or is being committed, and that the suspect has committed or is committing it (*Beck* v. *Ohio*, 379 U.S. 89, 1964).

In deciding whether probable cause exists, you may consider information known to you at the time and facts leading up to your action. To help establish probable cause, you can rely on hearsay, admissions, statements of fellow officers, witnesses, and observations. For example, you observe a person acting in such a way that you become suspicious. The officer you relieved had told you that a person matching this suspect's description had been hanging around. Then you see him running down the street. Those actions in themselves aren't enough to convince you that a crime is involved. But then you receive speedy information from a victim that a crime has been committed. Adding this together, you may then have probable cause.

A police officer is on the street, ready to protect the citizenry at a moment's notice. Thus, you are expected to act, at times, on your own initiative. You can act, providing you have sufficient probable cause. Your probable cause must be "fresh"—that is, it must relate to an event that is occurring now or occurred only a short while ago. A "short while ago" usually is measured in minutes rather than hours.

9.5 Statutory Law

Statutory law is simply the body of law comprising statutes enacted by the legislature. (The common term *statutory rape* refers to sexual intercourse with an underage person, even if the person consents.)

9.6 Common Law

Common law, case law, judicial precedent (they mean essentially the same) is the collected body of published court decisions that have the effect of law. However, since courts cover geographical areas, their decisions affect only their geographical areas. Attorneys may use case decisions of other courts to bolster their arguments, but it's only an argument and not the "law" in your jurisdiction. Therefore, while *common law* is used as an all-inclusive term, its meaning can vary from one jurisdiction to another.

Cases cited in this book are those decided by the U.S. Supreme Court. Their decisions apply all over the country. Your state courts have published decisions that apply in your state. Those that affect your function as a police officer are surely cited in your training.

10

Detention and Arrest

The Fourth Amendment of the U.S. Constitution concerns your right to detain or arrest a suspect.

An "arrest" is a restraint, a denial of freedom of movement. It happens when a person believes he is in your *custody*. When a person is not free to leave, that constitutes an arrest. You don't have to formally hold the suspect and say, "You're under arrest." If he believes that he is not free to go, regardless of what you say or do, once you deny his freedom of movement, he's arrested (*California* v. *Beheler,* 463 U.S. 1121, 1983).

But this doesn't mean that you can't detain a person while you investigate a situation. You have the right to maintain the status quo while you're checking things out. A witness may be held to determine his or her identity, for example. But it must be temporary and last only as long as it takes to confirm or refute your suspicions. Noncriminal detention is permitted under the Fourth Amendment. The U.S. Supreme Court even held that you may order an operator out of a vehicle you have legally stopped for a traffic violation (*Pennsylvania* v. *Mimms,* 434 U.S. 106, 1977). You can even use reasonable physical force to detain a person for investigation.

10.1 First Encounter

When you first come face to face with a suspect, a mistake on your part could make any evidence you develop unusable. Your conduct is governed by rules that depend on your knowledge of the suspect and the crime at the time you confront him.

Let's say you have reason to believe a person has knowledge of a crime but no reason to think he's involved. You can question him without concern over self-incrimination or right to counsel. Even if you suspect he's involved, you may still question him as long as you make it clear he is not obligated to answer and that he is free to stop answering and leave any time he wishes. But if you make him think he is not free to go, then the rules of conduct based on the Fifth Amendment apply.

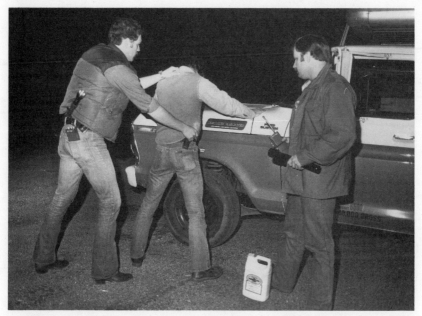

The detectives who stopped this suspect are entitled to "pat him down" for weapons to insure their own safety.

Once you restrain a person, search and seizure rules take effect. If you actually arrest him, further rules apply. Ordinarily, a person is not "detained" if you just ask for his identification. But if you take additional steps indicating he is not free to go, it's at least a detention.

If you have knowledge of facts that lead you to believe a person is involved in criminal activity, you may stop and briefly detain him for questioning, even if you do not have probable cause to arrest. You must be able to point out specific facts to support your suspicion, not just a hunch. Your decision to act may be based on your evaluation of the broad picture you see, including facts and reasonable conclusions that your experience enables you to draw from those facts. If you cannot explain all this to a judge's satisfaction, any evidence you discover cannot be used in prosecuting the person.

During a "stop" you may question the suspect, have him viewed by a witness, and detain him while you pursue other avenues of investigation. The Supreme Court has held that this may even include fingerprinting.

But time is critical. A detention without probable cause must be brief, minutes not hours. You may not detain a person any longer than reasonably necessary to accomplish the legitimate purpose of the stop.

Your right to move a suspect from where he was stopped is uncertain. Some courts have held you may take him a short distance to be viewed by a witness, but others have disagreed. Taking the suspect to the police station would likely make your detention an arrest, for which probable cause is required. If you discover nothing during the stop to give you probable cause to arrest, you must allow the suspect to leave.

This extends to stopping vehicles on the highway. Even though a safety check is not the same as a criminal investigation, motorists are protected against any form of arbitrary police intrusion. Before you stop a vehicle, you must observe speific facts that give you reasonable suspicion that some law is being violated. This doesn't mean that you can't conduct systematic safety checks. However, roadblocks and spot checks for drunk drivers, for example, are viewed differently in different states.

Once you have made a proper vehicle stop, you automatically have the right to order the offender to get out of his car and, in my state, to produce his driver's license. Getting him out of the car is recognized as a reasonable safety precaution. If you then observe his appearance or actions that lead you to reasonably fear he may be armed or involved in criminal activity, stop and frisk rules come into play.

> ## HOT TIPS FROM OLD HANDS
>
> **Think cover.** The first, and most important, thing I learned was on my first drug raid. As we drove up to the target, it reminded me of Vietnam. I thought, "They have position, strength, height, and my sergeant always said the best way was to blow them out." But that's against civilians' civil rights, so I did the next best thing. I found the biggest cottonwood tree in the front yard and stayed behind it until they all came out of the house. It worked like a charm.
>
> There's nothing cowardly about taking advantage of any cover you can find. It's smart—and beneficial to your health.
>
> *Deputy Dennis Niblack*
> *Garfield County,*
> *Colorado, sheriff's*
> *department*

10.2 Stop and Frisk

Even though you lack sufficient information to establish probable cause, you don't have to ignore suspicious activity. In the case of *Terry* v. *Ohio,* 392 U.S. 1 (1968), the Supreme Court recognized that an officer may have to briefly detain a person to establish identity, maintain the status quo, or for further investigation. If you reasonably believe the suspect may be armed, you can do a protective stop and frisk—a pat down, if you will—to ensure your own safety but not to discover evidence.

If you should happen to find evidence during this limited search, it would be admissible later because your actions to that point were proper. However, it's up to you to explain your reasons for doing a stop and frisk. If you can't satisfy a judge that it was proper, any evidence you found would be thrown out.

The moment of arrest determines what happens next. If you have good reason prior to the arrest, you can search incident to the arrest, seize evidence, use an admission, and you are protected from civil liability.

10.3 Elements of a Legal Arrest

The key element of an arrest is probable cause—facts and circumstances that reasonably lead a person of ordinary caution to believe that a crime has been committed and that the suspect did it. If you have probable cause to make an arrest, your actions are valid even if the actual crime turns out to be a different one than you suspected.

If you obtain a warrant (an order from the court), probable cause is decided for you by the judge. When you have time, get the paper. That means you have presented your information to a judge and she agrees that a crime has been committed and circumstances lead her to believe that the person named did it.

Once an arrest is made, the case belongs to the prosecutor. Statements to the press should be made by the prosecutor rather than the police.

10.4 Arrest Without Warrant

In the case of a felony, it is true in most states that, if you have probable cause, you can arrest at any time, anywhere. But to arrest a person in his own home when no exigent circumstances exist requires a warrant (*Peyton* v. *United States*, 445 U.S. 513, 1980). And to arrest a person in the home of a third party requires both an arrest warrant and a search warrant (*Steagold* v. *United States*, 451 U.S. 204, 1981). Even exigent circumstances don't justify the warrantless arrest of a person in his or her own home for a nonjailable offense (*Welsh* v. *Wisconsin*, 466 U.S. 470, 1984).

As I said earlier, the cases cited and laws quoted here reflect decisions of the U.S. Supreme Court to date and the law in most states. However, you should check your own state laws and the decisions of your state courts, because they may differ. State appellate courts are free to interpret state constitutions to give people more rights—but not fewer—than they would enjoy under the federal Constitution.

In the case of a misdemeanor, you still need probable cause to arrest. But if you witness the crime or have *speedy information* on a crime within your jurisdiction, you can arrest without warrant within your jurisdiction. Speedy information means "a short period of time." Again, check the law in your own state to be sure. You can also make a warrantless arrest during an uninterrupted fresh pursuit.

An armed robber held up a cab company. Two drivers followed and saw him run into a house. With this speedy information, officers crossed the threshold under hot pursuit. They were admitted by the defendant's wife and found the suspect. Incident to his arrest, the weapon and other evidence was found. This case established that, in "hot pursuit" of a fleeing felon, you can make a warrantless entry into a premises to search for the suspect (*Warden* v. *Hayden*, 387 U.S. 294, 1967). Warrantless misdemeanor arrests during hot pursuit are also legal in many states.

10.5 *Miranda* Warning

Miranda v. *Arizona*, 384 U.S. 436, 44 (1968) has had a profound impact on police procedures. It boils down to the suspect knowing and understanding his right to not answer questions, to have an attorney present, and to have one provided if he can't afford his own. Two circumstances are necessary to invoke the need for a *Miranda* warning: custody and interrogation. So you need to understand the term *custodial interrogation*.

Custodial Interrogation   Custodial interrogation is questioning initiated by law enforcement officers after a person has been taken into custody or otherwise deprived of his freedom of action in any significant way. This means that a suspect need not necessarily be under arrest to be in custody. If the suspect has any reason to believe he is not free to leave, *Miranda* warnings must be administered before any questions are asked. *United States* v. *Mendenhall,* 446 U.S. 544, 554 (1980) defines *seized* within the context of the Fourth Amendment.

Interrogation means some form of pressure or compulsion beyond the pressure the suspect feels simply because he is in custody. It may refer not only to specific questioning but to any actions or words by the police that the police should know are likely to elicit an incriminating response from the suspect (*Rhode Island* v. *Innis,* 446 U.S. 291, 1980).

But suppose there is no interrogation?

Five days after a shotgun murder, a suspect surrenders to police. He is arrested and taken into custody. He is given repeated *Miranda* warnings by different officers and tells a captain at the scene that he wants to talk with a lawyer. Three officers accompany him to the police station after being told by the captain not to question the suspect or intimidate or coerce him. On the way, the officers discuss among themselves what a tragedy it would be if the shotgun were found by some young-ster from the nearby school for handicapped children. They express their deter-mination to continue the search. The suspect interrupts them and leads them to the gun.

The shotgun was admissible because no interrogation had occurred.

It may be wise *not* to give a suspect *Miranda* warnings if you have no intention of interrogating him expressly or indirectly. Once he invokes his right to counsel, it is more difficult to interrogate him later.

There are situations in which you may question a suspect without a *Miranda* warning. Generally, *Miranda* need not be administered if the suspect is not in custody and is free to go at any time. It must be administered at the point that you decide to place the suspect under arrest. However, it is always prudent to advise a suspect of his rights before you interrogate him.

Voluntary Statements

If a suspect is not under arrest and voluntarily comes to the police station for questioning, *Miranda* is not required (*Oregon* v. *Mathiason,* 429 U.S. 492, 1972). However, remember that a suspect may be considered "in custody" even if not placed under arrest formally, if he did not voluntarily come to the police station (*Florida* v. *Hayes,* 470 U.S. 1643, 1985).

A "threshold" statement occurs when someone comes in, puts the smoking gun on the desk sergeant's counter, and says, "I did it." In such cases of voluntary statement, it's better not to end with an arrest. When a suspect is positively identified, not likely to leave, and you're confident you can grab him later, it isn't unusual for the officer to take his statement, thank him politely, and tell him goodbye—then use his statement to get a warrant. The suspect obviously wasn't under arrest. He was free to leave. What he said was obviously voluntary and there was no reason to read him his rights.

Whenever you take an accused into custody, you have to advise him of his rights, if you intend to question him.

Exemptions

If there is a genuine need to protect yourself or the public and the questions are limited to that protective purpose, you needn't administer *Miranda*. An instance would be asking an armed robber, while handcuffing him, what he did with the weapon (*New York* v. *Quarles,* 467 U.S. 649, 1984).

A woman told two police officers she had just been raped by a man who had then entered a supermarket and that he had a gun. They went to the market and one officer entered. He spotted the suspect, who immediately bolted. With gun drawn, the officer gave chase and soon captured him. A frisk found the empty shoulder holster but no gun. In response to the officer's question, the suspect indicated a pile of cartons and said, "The gun is over there."

After retrieving the gun, the officer read the suspect his rights. New York courts suppressed the defendant's statement, "The gun is over there," and the gun because *Miranda* had not been administered. The Supreme Court agreed that the subject was in custody and interrogated but held the evidence admissible under a public-safety exception to *Miranda*.

The public-safety exemption to *Miranda* requirements is relatively new, and no one is sure just how far it extends. But, generally, you can ask, "Where's the gun?" when a victim tells you the suspect is armed but you don't find it on him. That question is motivated by your concern for public safety. It's obvious that you need to find the gun before it is found by an accomplice or an innocent person.

This exemption may not apply if that suspect is in a remote area and you knew there was no accomplice. The failure to give warning, however, doesn't incur liability on your part. It just could make it more difficult to get a conviction because such evidence is tainted.

If a defendant leads you to the body before being advised of his rights, the evidence may be admissible. A suspect had been seen in Des Moines carrying a bundle from which two legs protruded shortly after a ten-year-old girl disappeared. He was arrested the next day in Davenport. Two Des Moines officers were sent to drive the defendant back. On the way, one talked with the defendant, lamenting how the poor girl was denied a "Christian burial." The defendant made some incriminating statements and led the officers to the body. Police and volunteers were still searching. After his second trial and string of appeals, the Supreme Court held that evidence pertaining to the discovery and condition of the body was properly admitted because it ultimately or inevitably would have been discovered regardless of the violation of defendant's right to counsel (*Nix* v. *Williams,* 467 U.S. 431, 35 CrL 3119, 1984).

If you've stopped a motorist, you needn't administer *Miranda*. But if the stop leads to a custodial arrest, even if only for a motor vehicle charge, *Miranda* is required (*Berkemer* v. *McCarty,* 468 U.S. 82, 1984). General on-scene questioning or questioning during a brief investigative detention does not normally require *Miranda*. But if you pay serious attention to a particular person and he gets the idea that he is not free to leave, that could constitute custody, filling the requirements for *Miranda*.

Statements may be held inadmissible, even though *Miranda* warnings are given, if the arrest was made without probable cause, if the interrogation was coerced, if the waiver is held invalid, or if the statement was taken after a suspect invoked his rights.

If you forget to give an in-custody suspect *Miranda* and he gives you a voluntary statement, then you correct the error by giving him the warning and he confesses *again,* the second confession will be admissible (*Oregon* v. *Elstad,* 470 U.S. 298, 1985). I realize this seems to contradict the Taylor case cited in Section 9.2, but, remember that in that case the original arrest was found to lack probable cause.

The *Miranda* warning does not have to be given verbatim, as long as you cover all the bases (*California* v. *Poysock,* 29 CrL 4110, 1981). Some states require a special, simplified form of the *Miranda* warning when interrogating juveniles.

You don't have to inquire into the mental state of a suspect before questioning him, as long as you're sure he understands the warning you're giving him (*Colorado* v. *Connelly,* 11 LOB 55, 1986).

If a suspect refuses to give you a written statement but agrees to give an oral confession, the oral confession is admissible (*Connecticut* v. *Barrett,* 11 LOB 79, 1987).

Waiving Right to Counsel

For all practical purposes, once a suspect has a lawyer, that ends your questions. In *Edwards* v. *Arizona*, 451 U.S. 477 (1981) it was made clear what the prosecution must prove to make admissible a confession of one who initially invoked his right to remain silent or have counsel present, then later waived those rights and confessed.

The scenario went like this: Edwards was arrested on a warrant and charged with murder, robbery, and burglary. He was taken to the police station and advised of his rights; he said he understood them and was willing to answer questions. When he was told that another suspect implicated him, he denied any involvement and gave a taped statement in which he claimed to have an alibi. Edwards then said he wanted to make a deal but police said they had no such authority. He phoned the prosecutor but hung up after a few moments, then said, "I want an attorney before making a statement." Police stopped their questioning and put him in jail.

The next day, two detectives went to the jail to interrogate Edwards. The jailer took him to the detectives against his will. He was again advised of his rights. He said he was willing to talk but he wanted to hear the taped statement of the suspect who had implicated him. After hearing part of it, Edwards gave an oral statement implicating himself. He was later convicted but appealed on the grounds that police had violated his rights by questioning him after he had requested the presence of an attorney before answering questions. The U.S. Supreme Court held that Edwards had invoked his right to counsel when he was first arrested, and that he had not legally waived that right.

But the decision also stated that the person may change his mind when "he initiates further communication, exchanges or conversations with the police." The concurring opinion said that the important question is not who spoke first but that there was a "free and knowing" waiver. This means that when you interrogate someone after he invoked his rights, you'd better have a good record (written, taped, or videotaped) of when rights were read, when the arrestee invoked those rights, when and why he changed his mind, who spoke first, and exactly what was said thereafter.

You cannot use evidence obtained as a result of a conversation about the crime between an in-custody suspect who has appeared before a judge and asserted his right to counsel and an officer who has been told by the lawyer not to discuss the case.

With all this discussion of admissibility, you should keep in mind that you do not act illegally if you don't give a suspect his *Miranda* warning when you should. It means only that you cannot use the information you gained from that interrogation against the suspect. But there's no law against developing that same information from other sources in a proper way and using it in court.

11

Search and Seizure

It is fundamental in all jurisdictions that a search or seizure of evidence should always be accomplished with a warrant, if at all possible. The founding fathers found it important to include in the Bill of Rights the Fourth Amendment, with its guarantee against unreasonable searches and seizures.

This protection extends to persons, houses, papers, property, or anything in which the person has manifested a reasonable expectation of privacy. (*United States* v. *Katz,* 389 U.S. 347, 1967). It does not protect under certain circumstances or where the person cannot reasonably expect privacy, such as open fields or public places. Protection extends not only to the building but also its "curtilage," the open areas immediately adjacent to a dwelling—the lawn, or more specifically, "area around the home to which the activity of home life extends."

Then there's the "open fields" doctrine. Two narcotics officers went to a farm to check reports of marijuana being grown. They stopped their car at the locked gate but followed a foot path around the gate and down a road, passing a barn and parked camper. They found a field of marijuana more than a mile from the defendant's house. He was arrested. The defendant moved to suppress the evidence, claiming violation of the Fourth Amendment. The Supreme Court held the entry and search to be lawful because protection extends to "persons, houses, papers, and effects" but not open fields. This term may include any unoccupied or undeveloped area outside the curtilage. A thickly wooded area could be an open field under this definition (*Oliver* v. *United States,* 466 U.S. 170, 1984).

11.1 Search Warrants

A search warrant is an order from the court, signed by an impartial magistrate, directing police to search a specified place for specific evidence, contraband, stolen property, or other "fruits" of a crime, and to bring the listed articles before the court. Here are some aspects of the warrant process you should remember.

Facts and Circumstances   This is the key to your warrant application. You must lay out all facts and circumstances that lead you to believe that a crime was committed and that the accused did it (probable cause).

The facts known to you must be sufficient to lead a reasonable and prudent person to believe that a crime has been committed and that the articles described can be found at the place specified. You can rely on information from a witness or even a confidential informant, but you must show why that information is probably valid. Even if a witness lies and you, in good faith, believe him, the arrest will be upheld. But courts will look to see what efforts you made to corroborate statements of witnesses.

The circumstances that lead you to this belief must be spelled out in the warrant application. Your professional opinion is only as good as the facts you used to reach that conclusion.

Oath or Affirmation   The affidavit you write to request a warrant must be sworn. No one, especially the defendant's attorney, will presume that the magistrate swore the applicant. If the oath was not administered, the warrant is faulty and any evidence gathered as a result of it is excluded.

Description   You've probably heard stories of a raid on the "house next door," or innocent citizens startled by scruffy detectives breaking down the front door to the wrong apartment. The place to be searched must be identified and sufficiently described so that officers won't make that mistake.

Property Subject to Seizure   If you don't identify and describe what you're looking for, your warrant won't justify seizing anything. You're looking for fruits of the crime, contraband, instruments of the crime, or evidence of the crime. Contraband, such as machine guns, sawed-off shotguns, explosive devices, or gambling equipment, ordinarily need not be described as stolen goods. You can seize any contraband that you inadvertently discover or that is in plain view while you're searching for something else.

Issuing Official   It's so basic that it's sometimes slighted: a warrant is only as good as the signature of the official who issued it.

Execution   Your state law describes specific procedures for executing a warrant, filing an inventory, and notifying the owner of seized property. A time limit is part of those procedures and, if you can't meet the deadline, you'd better have a good explanation.

Prior Notice, Demand, Forcible Entry   The "knock and announce" rule, in most states, requires you to knock, wait a reasonable time, and announce your authority and purpose. "Police. We have a warrant to search these premises." If not admitted, you may force entry.

Of course, if there are exigent circumstances—you have reason to believe someone inside may be harmed, the suspect will escape, or evidence will be destroyed if you delay—you may need to force your way in immediately. If you are in uniform approaching a drug outlet, you see the occupants watching you approach, and you know them to be armed or quick to destroy evidence, you need not knock and announce. This requirement varies from state to state.

11.2 Warrantless Searches

There are situations in which an officer may enter, search for, and seize evidence without a warrant. An easy way to remember is by the acronym "ICE"—incident, consent, exigent.

Incident to Arrest   When you make a proper custodial arrest, you have the right to fully search the arrestee without having to show that a weapon or evidence might be found (*United States* v. *Robinson,* 414 U.S. 218, 1973). And you may search the area within his immediate control, any area where he may reach a weapon or destructible evidence (*Chimel* v. *California,* 395 U.S. 752, 1969). At the police station, all containers and articles in the arrestee's possession may be searched, as a stationhouse inventory, as part of routine procedure (*Illinois* v. *Lafayette,* 462 U.S. 640, 1983).

Consent   The person consenting to a search must have authority to do so. He must have a right to possess the premises, be an adult, and be the owner of the house or occupant of the hotel room. An adult may consent to the search of a child's room but not the other way around. A parent may not consent to the search of an adult child's room if it is used exclusively by the adult child. A minor child's consent isn't likely to stand up, but an adult child can consent to the search of jointly used areas. A person responsible for caring for the property may consent to a search.

If you have no good reason to be where you got the evidence, it could be inadmissible. A tenant is the responsible consenter for a warrantless search. Police entry into a rented house at the request of the landlord was held unreasonable, even though the tenant was scheduled to vacate the house that same day.

Anyone may waive a right or privilege to which he or she is entitled. But courts look at such waivers carefully. After all, these protections evolved because of historical abuses. You have to show that the person made some positive action to waive his right of privacy. You'll probably have a printed form to be signed, but a verbal consent is permitted when you can corroborate it (*Schneckloth* v. *Busta-monte,* 412 U.S. 218, 1973).

As with a warrant, the search cannot extend beyond the terms of the consent in either time or area. If the resident agrees to your search of a room, you may not search the rest of the house. The resident can stop the search at any time by simply revoking his consent.

Exigent Circumstances   We already discussed screams inside the house, drugs being flushed down the toilet, and hot pursuit—reasons why you are required to act immediately. There are other circumstances in which you may properly search without a warrant.

Inventory of Impounded Vehicle   When you've impounded a vehicle, department policy may require you to inventory its contents to protect the owner, as well as the police. Most states require it as standard operating procedure, not left to the discretion of the officer. If, in the process, you discover evidence accidentally, while you are doing what you have a right to do and where you have legitimate reason to be, the evidence can be used in court (*Illinois* v. *Lafayette,* 460 U.S. 640, 1983).

Plain View   If you are in a place where you have a right to be and you see something in plain view, you can seize it. But if you are trespassing, whatever evidence you seize will be excluded (*Coolidge* v. *New Hampshire,* 403 U.S. 443, 1971).

Third Party   Curiously, the Fourth Amendment protects private persons against acts of government, but not acts of other private citizens. The police officer is a government officer and is bound. But if a private person gathers incriminating evidence and passes it on to the police officer, it is admissible even if the private person entered the premises illegally. However, if the officer instigated the private person's action or participated in it, the evidence would be excluded.

Movable Vehicles   If you stop a motorist and then develop probable cause to believe that contraband is in the vehicle, you'd lose it if you took time to get a warrant. Thus, you are permitted to search even the locked compartments (*Carroll* v. *United States,* 267 U.S. 132, 1925; *United States* v. *Ross,* 456 U.S. 798, 1982; *New York* v. *Belton,* 453 U.S. 454, 1981). However, your right to search depends on probable cause. If you have reason to believe the vehicle contains a stolen stereo, for example, you can't look for it in the glovebox.

Such warrantless searches require the same essential elements of probable cause that you'd need for a warrant. And you must be able to show those elements were known prior to the search.

Luggage   Luggage is a common repository of personal effects and thus people have a greater expectation of privacy in their luggage. If you suspect a drug courier of transporting contraband in his luggage, for example, it may be best to detain the luggage and get a warrant before you open it (*Arkansas* v. *Sanders,* 442 U.S. 753, 1979).

Remember the rule: to conduct a lawful search, you must have a search warrant. If you search without a warrant, you must demonstrate to the court that the situation falls within one of the specific exceptions.

Informants   If you rely on information from a citizen for your probable cause, you should establish that person's reliability and how he knows what he told you to be true (*Illinois* v. *Gates,* 462 U.S. 213, 1983).

11.3 Attacks on Warrants

You can prepare better warrant applications if you understand how warrants are attacked by defense counsel. Defendant's counsel will look carefully at the descriptions, the oath and signatures, how it was executed or delayed, how the search was conducted, whether items not named were seized, and will try to show a lack of probable cause in the affidavit or question its timeliness, or prove that an informant is unreliable.

12

Police Surveillance

You know you need a warrant to trespass on private property, tap telephone lines, or use electronic devices to intercept conversations that the person involved would reasonably expect to be free of government intrusion. But that doesn't mean you can't look.

You may conduct a surveillance using your unaided eyes and ears, unless it invades a suspect's reasonable expectation of privacy. This is often how you develop probable cause to arrest. If you invade privacy, you could lose your whole case.

12.1 Expectation of Privacy

It is important that you understand this concept. Even certain public places may give the person using them an expectation of privacy. For example, observation into a bathroom stall from an overhead vantage point, or looking through an overhead vent into a motel room, has been held as unreasonable invasion of privacy. Remember the difference between "curtilage" and "open fields." If you go onto the lawn and look into the window, that's an unreasonable invasion of privacy. But observation from an adjacent open field or from the street is not.

If people conduct themselves in a way that seems to disregard privacy, they may be observed even in a private home. A domestic dispute in an apartment was easily overheard by the officer standing out in the hallway; the couple had no reasonable expectation of privacy. A suspect running a numbers game in his garage had no reasonable expectation of privacy from police, who were able to look into the garage window from a nearby railroad track. A principle involved here is that you have a right to be where you are.

On the other hand, people may lose their expectation of privacy in a public place if there is reason to believe they are not using it for the purpose for which it was intended. Two men went into the restroom at a gas station and remained there for more than a half hour. The attendant called police, who entered with a passkey. That entry was held to be reasonable, and the drug paraphernalia they seized was admitted into evidence at their trial.

Modern surveillance equipment includes cameras with long lenses, discrete recording devices, biocular night glasses, and telephone taps. **CCS COMMUNICATIONS CONTROL, INC.**

12.2 Electronic Surveillance

The use of electronic devices for surveillance is strictly regulated. Without a court order (except in limited emergency situations), it is a serious federal offense. It's difficult to write black-and-white rules about the correct use of electronic surveillance (decisions may even seem contradictory), but here are comments on past court decisions.

Using an extension phone is not a tap if the subscriber on the other extension permits it. However, some states have more stringent rules requiring two-party consent in the absence of a court order. If you get a warrant to use an electronic listening device, you don't need a separate warrant to install it, even if it means forcible, covert entry of private premises. Electronic surveillance conducted on the order of a state or local judge is illegal under federal law unless there is specific state law authorizing the judge to issue such an order.

In most but not all states, however, federal and state officers may electronically overhear or intercept conversations if they have the consent of one of the parties. You "wire" an informer. He enters a suspect's home. You may overhear and record conversations between the suspect and the informer. By the same token, you can listen in on a telephone conversation if you have the consent of one of the parties. In both cases, the suspect has "misplaced his confidence" in the informer and has no reasonable expectation of privacy.

There are fewer restrictions on the use of devices that do not intercept communications. Using a pen register on phone-company property to record the number the subscriber dials is not protected in some states, although others require a court order. The subscriber has no expectation of privacy in the numbers he dials. This also applies to devices that identify the number calling a particular phone.

Using beepers is a gray area. You don't need a warrant to attach a beeper to the outside of a vehicle, but you may need one to install it inside. If you have consent to put a beeper in an object, you don't need a warrant before delivering the bugged package to an unsuspecting person. However, you will need one to continue monitoring if the beeper is taken into a private place.

The Fourth Amendment does not apply to monitoring a beeper as the target travels over public roads or open fields. But you should have one to monitor the beeper as the target moves inside his residence, where he has a reasonable expectation of privacy. As this is written, the Supreme Court had addressed beeper monitoring in only two contexts: on the open road and in a home. As a rule of thumb, if locating a beeper by ordinary methods would require a warrant, you'd better get one before locating it electronically.

13

Crimes

Police officers are not attorneys, but everything you do is influenced, governed, and regulated by law. It is crucial to your career that you understand what is expected of you when you apply the law in your enforcement activities. What constitutes a crime, felony, misdemeanor, or infraction is determined by the laws of your particular state or jurisdiction. Your state probably has a field manual or guide that lists the more frequently used statutes and identifies various offenses.

Most crimes are classed as either felonies, punishable by more than a year in prison, or misdemeanors, punishable by less than a year in jail. And that also defines the difference between a jail and a prison. A jail houses prisoners for up to one year; a prison has inmates sentenced for more than a year.

Then there are infractions, sometimes called violations or petty offenses, punishable by a fine but no time behind bars. Infractions include parking improperly, faulty vehicle equipment, running a stop sign, and such. No criminal intent is required for a person to be guilty of an infraction. To be convicted of a misdemeanor or felony, it must be proved that the person acted with wrongful intent—generally that he acted negligently, recklessly, knowingly, or purposely.

Certain offenses are criminal everywhere.

13.1 Mala per Se

Acts that are bad in and of themselves—*mala per se*—include such crimes as murder, arson, robbery, larceny, burglary, assault, rape, and kidnapping. These are crimes everywhere. But there are degrees and localized definitions of each.

Have you ever known someone to call the police and shout, "I've been robbed!" Police respond with a drawn-guns attitude because robbery implies physical force. What the victim really meant was that someone had stolen his property by stealth the night before.

Larceny means wrongfully and intentionally depriving someone of property. This could include embezzlement, false pretense or promise, extortion, receiving stolen property, theft of services, shoplifting, fraud, or failing to return rented

Radar checks speed even while you're moving, reading both the target's speed and the patrol car's speed. **L&O.**

property. Degrees in larceny are generally determined by the value of the property taken.

If in the course of committing a larceny, the perpetrator uses or threatens physical force to compel the owner to give up his property, then it's robbery. It can be robbery in different degrees, depending on whether the actor causes injury, is armed, threatens or represents that he has a deadly weapon or instrument, or is aided by another person.

13.2 Mala Prohibita

There are crimes that are bad only because society decided by act of legislation that they are crimes: *mala prohibita*. Such laws are generally founded in common sense. A liquor dealer is in the business of selling booze; that's no crime. But if he sells it to a minor, he can lose his license to do business. The person who drives his car seventy miles an hour in a

sixty-five mile zone probably has no malicious intent and certainly hasn't broken any moral law or universal cultural taboo. But he has committed a *mala prohibita* offense, one that has been prohibited in a particular jurisdiction by the legislature.

13.3 Administrative Regulation

Society elects officials who establish boards and commissions to administer a particular activity, and legislatures sometimes delegate to these persons or agencies the power to publish regulations that have the force of law. You are empowered to enforce "the law." If a particular administrative regulation allows for its enforcement by "any peace officer," you can enforce it.

An example might be the illegal dumping of hazardous wastes. While on patrol, you see a truck rolling drums into a gully at night in an uninhabited area. Your suspicions are aroused, so you investigate. You find the drums contain a substance included in hazardous waste regulations, and make an arrest for violating the regulations.

13.4 Elements and Degree of an Offense

The police officer must understand what constitutes an offense. Your field manual outlines the elements that define a particular offense. For example, to commit murder in most jurisdictions, a person must *intend* to cause the death of a person and actually *cause* it either directly or by suicide through force, duress, or deception. Presenting crimes in terms of elements gives you a checklist of points you must prove.

An offense may be further classified according to degree. The seriousness of the offense is graded according to specific elements of the offense. To continue the wrongful death example, murder in the first degree requires both willful and premeditated intent to kill and also causing the death. But what if the actor only intended to seriously injure but caused the death? That may be manslaughter in the first degree. If the actor's recklessness causes death, it could be manslaughter in the second degree.

Assault is a broad term that includes crimes ranging from a felony to a misdemeanor. If the actor intends to cause serious injury, actually causes serious injury, and uses a deadly weapon or dangerous instrument, in most states it's first-degree assault. Take away the weapon and it's assault two. If his intent was only to injure, rather than seriously injure, and he causes injury, it's assault three. If he recklessly risks serious injury with indifference to human life, it may be reckless endangerment one. Take away the indifference and it's reckless endangerment two.

In my state, we use a couple of acronyms to differentiate between breach of peace and disorderly conduct. Both offenses are predicated on a person's intent to cause alarm or recklessly creating the risk of alarm. Add any of the elements in FATCOP and it's a breach: Fights in a public place, Assaults another, Threatens to commit a crime, Creates a hazardous public condition, Obscene language or gesture, Posts offensive material. But if the additional elements are INFACT, it's disorderly conduct: Interferes with another, Noise, Fights with threatening behavior, Annoys or disturbs a lawful assembly, Congregates with others in public and refuses to disperse, Traffic is obstructed.

You may find you can use similar acronyms to help you master the law in your state. There's no point in duplicating your field manual here because the language will vary. Just be aware that your field manual is your bible. Carry it wherever you go and refer to it frequently. Read sections whenever you have a chance. This will make you familiar with it and help you to find answers when questions come up.

14

Personal Skills

A police officer must be concerned with the physical and mental preparedness required to meet the challenges of the street. When you are attacked, your body must be able to respond and your mind must be made up so your body can do what it has to do. It takes physical fitness and mental fitness.

14.1 Physical Fitness

A former police chief in a small upstate Wisconsin town, Tim Powers, made a study of police fitness. He became so concerned that the unique demands of police fitness weren't being met that he quit his job and went into fitness training full time. He is a police performance specialist. I asked him, "Tim, just how much time would a police officer have to invest to maintain a high-performance conditioning level?"

"Once we've identified just what it is a particular situation needs, a fitness program could require as little as one hour, three days a week," he answered.

That isn't much to ask of a person whose job performance depends on good physical conditioning.

Your exercise program should address four targets, according to Powers.

1. Cardiovascular and respiration.   Sudden cardiac arrest is a major threat to police officers. A properly designed program improves the heart function, improves blood circulation, and increases lung capacity. By training through aerobic conditioning, you'll find yourself better able to exert the explosive power sometimes needed to handle a situation.

2. Muscle strength and stamina.   Your punch power isn't increased by doing bicep curls. It's exercised by punching, by doing the function you want to improve. A qualified law enforcement physical training instructor can devise many simple routines that address the strengths a police officer needs.

3. Joint flexibility.   If you have freedom of movement, you can better perform the defensive tactics techniques that can save your skin. If your muscles are stiff, your performance will suffer, and lower-back problems can ensue. Lower-back pain and back injuries are major problems for police officers.

4. Low body fat.   It's a fact that excess body fat impairs coordinated body movement. The fat literally gets in the way.

14.2 Mental Well-being

Mental preparedness is too often ignored in police training, yet its importance is obvious in the concise definition given to me by *Law & Order* magazine editorial director Bruce Cameron. "This is simply having made up your mind that you will do whatever a police officer needs to do when called upon—whether shooting someone who is threatening a life, wrestling a giant drunk to the floor, or jumping into an icy river to save someone. Not many cops are properly conditioned in training on how to think positively about their duties. They get good instruction on how to perform their duties but little in regard to mental preparation."

Mental attitudes are critical to survival. They must become instinctive. All the physical skills in the world are fruitless if you aren't mentally prepared. There are a host of elements that ensure your success in a confrontation, beyond the simple attributes of ability, power, speed, strength, balance, and reaction time; and they're *in your mind.*

Andrew Casavant of the Midwest Tactical Training Institute has researched this question of mental conditioning and has organized these mental attitudes in terms of what you face on the street, starting with alertness.

Many departments provide a gymnasium with exercise equipment to help you keep in shape. **L&O.**

HOT TIPS FROM OLD HANDS

Perfect practice makes perfect. Police employment is a highly skilled occupation. Learn as much about proper tactical procedure and officer-survival techniques as possible. Practice it religiously. *Never* let your guard down. Skill and intelligence are the distinguishing characteristics of a contemporary police officer. Luck eventually runs out and cannot be relied upon. Skill is developed; it doesn't just happen.

Charles Bruni
Former patrolmen, Augusta, Georgia,
police department; deputy,
Richmond County, Georgia, sheriff's
department; and supervisor,
Augusta College police

Alertness   Alertness, awareness of where you are in relation to all things in your environment, is the overriding theme. If you're not ready when it's time to act, your skills won't help.

Jeff Cooper, a well-known combat shooting instructor in Arizona, came up with a color-code scheme to measure awareness levels that police trainers have adopted with fervor.

1. White.   You are home watching television, totally unaware of your surroundings.

2. Yellow.   Now you are aware of your surroundings, relaxed but alert. You are mentally prepared.

3. Orange.   You are aware of something specific in your surroundings that has caught your attention. Perhaps it will become a threat. You analyze the risks to yourself and others, and consider potential reactions.

4. Red.   You are ready to do what needs to be done. You may decide to move in or back off, depending on the circumstances. Your plan is decided, so your reaction will be quick and sure.

5. Black.   You've got no choice. An assault is started. If you aren't mentally prepared, you panic. You must go from white (totally unaware) to black (he shoots) in a fraction of a second. If you haven't followed the crucial self-training of always anticipating an attack, you add to the sad statistics.

With anticipation comes preparedness. Under normal circumstances, a police officer should always be in condition yellow.

Decisiveness   Once you commit yourself to reacting to a threat, be decisive about it. A mind cluttered with liability issues, department policies, and other such diversions will cause hesitation when you need to act, and that hesitation can be fatal. Make up your mind about those "what-ifs" beforehand, so that when you need to act, you can.

Aggressiveness   Before you can legally use force on another person, the force must be justified under the circumstances, and it must be no more than is reasonable and necessary.

Once you've decided you have the right and obligation to use force, do it like you mean it. Be aggressive. If you decide to apply a pain compliance technique, use enough force to make it work. If you draw your baton, *use it*—hard and properly. Don't pussyfoot around. End the confrontation with whatever force is necessary, as quickly as you can. This minimizes the risks to all involved.

But aggressiveness must be learned. It's not human nature. And certainly not the nature of smaller-statured male or petite female officers. You must learn to be assertive. That's part of defensive tactics training.

Speed   To execute any defensive technique, to gain the advantage of surprise, you must act quickly. Speed is essential. And that includes speed of thought. Don't stop to ask yourself if he really meant to swing that lead pipe at you. Quick thinking is as important as quick hands or feet.

Calmness   Remaining cool and calm in any confrontation is prerequisite to successfully ending it. Learn to control your emotions, and you can control the situation.

Ruthlessness   While it seems harsh, ruthlessness has a place in conflict. It means winning, doing whatever it reasonably takes to win and survive. It means continuing to fight, even if hurt, never giving up. However, it must be short-lived. If you can't let go after the need for force is past, you're being brutal.

Surprise   Physical aggression can't be used except to defend yourself or a third person against what you reasonably believe to be an imminent threat. You can choose the means of attack and the technique you will use, and you need not telegraph this in advance.

Gaining the element of surprise makes your technique even more effective.

14.3 Mental Defense Training

Training is a small price to pay to develop the skills and habits that enable you to win and survive. The old adage that you will do under stress what you're trained to do is really not quite correct. You will probably perform much worse in a serious confrontation than you ever did in training. So, to survive a street confrontation, you need to continually exercise the skills you learned in class. And you can do it in your head.

Suppose that little old lady were to swing her umbrella at your head. What would you do? Imagine yourself doing what you need to do to parry her blow. Suppose someone leaped out from the dark corner with a gun in his hand. What would you do? Draw and shoot? Or dive for cover? And where's cover?

If you can actually see yourself going through the motions of your newly learned techniques, it will improve your ability to respond quickly. While there's no substitute for good, hard, comprehensive physical practice, you still need the mental conditioning to enhance your response and keep you alert in more mundane circumstances.

The one emotion you can't contrive is the one that makes the greatest difference in a real threat: fear. Unlike fights on television, real confrontations aren't logical, patterned, give-and-take brawls. They are a flurry of hitting and screaming, kicking and shoving. You must mentally train for the attack that is certain to be sudden, vicious, and perhaps overwhelming.

14.4 Body Language

An officer and his partner had separated the combatants in the domestic dispute. The husband and wife were beginning to settle down when a third officer arrived on the scene. He strode into the room, baton in one hand striking the open palm of his other hand, and demanded, "What's the problem here?"

And the fight started all over again.

"When you communicate with a subject, 85 to 90 percent of the message you deliver is nonverbal. Only 10 to 15 percent of your message is transmitted verbally," says Roland Ouellette of the Connecticut Law Enforcement Training Institute. You can learn to use this phenomenon to your advantage.

Personal Space   Did you ever notice when a second person joins someone in an elevator, the two will divide the space equally? If a third person enters, they will share the space in thirds. If someone enters a nearly full car and faces rear, toward the other people, they all feel uncomfortable. "That's because your personal space extends farther to the front than it does to the rear," Ouellette says.

Every individual is circled by three rings of a size specific to that individual. For the police officer, the outermost is the alert zone. Next is the defense zone, an area in which an invader puts you on the defensive. The innermost ring, with a diameter about an arm's length plus one hand, is the attack zone, in which an invader is likely to incite a reaction. Most instructors teach four to six feet for this zone. A civilian might call these zones social, personal, and intimate.

When you are dealing with a citizen in a verbal situation, stay out of his attack zone. Don't invade his body space because you may well precipitate aggression against you. If you're that close, you are vulnerable.

You've seen pictures of the Marine drill sergeant. He intimidates the recruit by moving in close. Notice also his stance.

Stance   The Marine drill sergeant tries to tower over the poor trainee. His hands are on his hips. His shoulders are back. His chin is raised. His voice is loud and commanding. All these gestures send signals of aggression. This may be just how you want to appear when dealing with a juvenile who just snatched an old lady's purse.

If you are trying to calm a combative citizen, would you act like a Marine drill sergeant? Of course not. Such body language would likely prompt him to commit a crime against you. How much better it would be to calm him by appearing supportive, interested in finding out what his problem is, and wanting to help solve it. Assume a supportive stance and you win the citizen's support.

You can see the difference in the message you send if your head is back or bowed, chin up or down, shoulders back or forward, arms folded or open. In each case, the first is authoritative and the second is supportive.

Eye Contact   When you stare the subject right in the eyes, you are telling him that you are the powerful authority. If you are trying to elicit his cooperation, a direct stare is not likely to motivate him to be your friend. But if you drop your gaze down to about his sternum, you reduce the power role and become more of a helpful ally.

It works just the opposite if you are listening to his story. Looking him straight in the eye makes you appear interested in what he's saying; you are paying attention. If you look off in the distance, or avoid his eyes, you appear uninterested.

Defensibility   Now think back over all these gestures and postures. Expanding the body into a rigid, erect stance elicits a hostile response. Contracting the body, relaxing, bowing the head, stooping the shoulders, standing obliquely usually is effective in forestalling violence. But there is another important consideration. In general, the supportive postures put you in a much better defensive position than the authoritative stances.

14.5 Verbalization

One of your most used but least trained tools is your voice. It's the one tool you always have with you, and you use it more than any other piece of police equipment. With it you establish authority and take command of a situation. Verbalization is a force by which you exercise control.

Sometimes that control is simply a matter of letting the suspect know he can influence what is to happen. In an arrest, you may say, "You're under arrest. You can go one of two ways: you can make a fool of yourself right here in front of everybody, or you can walk out with dignity."

Writer Richard Garrison tells two stories to prove the point. A rookie, during his first shift on his own, was dispatched to "unknown trouble" at a local market. He found people milling around when he arrived and, in his best command voice, he asked what was happening. A bystander pointed to a person slipping into the crowd and said something about the subject causing trouble. The rookie called to the subject, "Excuse me, uh, hey you, uh, I want to . . . We got a complaint of . . ." He got rattled when he couldn't define the complaint. The subject paid no attention, of course. The rookie caught up with him and grabbed him by the shoulder. The subject, drunk and angry, turned with a knife in his hand and slashed at the officer. The blade sliced his jacket, glanced off his body armor, and cut his forearm.

> ### HOT TIPS FROM OLD HANDS
>
> **Take control.** It seems hard for a rookie to learn to take control of a situation, and remain in control. Old-timers do it automatically, and it seems almost magical to the new kid on the block. Yet there is no big secret. Most people will assume that police arrival on the scene indicates authority, and if the aspect of authority is assumed by the officer and projected via voice, mannerism, and body language, then that authority (and control of the situation) will be manifested in the officer.
>
> Watch how your FTO does it: cool, calm, and collected. Nervous body movements and a quavering voice have no place in police work. Step in, take control, and *be* in control. If you're nervous (and old-timers still get nervous), don't let it show. It's okay to get the sweats and the shakes afterward as long as the people you're dealing with don't see it while you are on the scene.
>
> *Sgt. Frank Thornton*
> *Shelburne, Vermont,*
> *police department*

In another case, officers responded to a domestic disturbance at an apartment house, where a number of family members stood arguing in the front yard. Neighbors were leaning out of their windows. The officers separated the most agitated combatants. Suddenly one officer and a subject began to scuffle. The subject broke free and ran with the officer in pursuit. Cornered by a fence, the subject turned and a shot rang out. The subject dropped, wounded in the leg. The officer said he struggled with the subject over a handgun the man carried in his belt. When the subject ran, then turned to point the weapon, the officer fired.

A weapon was found where the man fell, but no one had seen it before the shooting. The family said the man never owned a gun. A BATF (Bureau of Alcohol, Tobacco, and Firearms) trace proved negative. Witnesses said they saw the struggle, but didn't hear the officer say anything. They simply saw the officer chase the subject, draw his weapon, and fire. They said they saw no weapon other than the officer's. How much better if the officer had used his voice.

There are two very different lessons in these examples.

A Command Voice   Short, loud commands elicit quick obedience (remember the Marine drill instructor). A person under stress will focus on the few action words. Lengthy verbiage is superfluous and counterproductive.

Words that begin with a hard consonant, an explosive rush of air, are more effective than those with a soft sound. "Stop" is better than "Halt." "Don't move" is better than "Stand still." At the NYCPD Firearms and Tactics Training facility there are signs on every wall: "POLICE. DON'T MOVE." Three little words that accomplish two purposes.

First is identification. The word *police* establishes your identity and authority. Say it even if you're in uniform; the suspect and witnesses may be looking somewhere else. Put the accent on the first part "*po*-lice" and emphasize the explosive breath of the "P." That helps to get their attention. I'd say "*po*-lice" even if I were a special agent of the U.S. Drug Enforcement Administration.

Second, you issue a terse, loud, lawful command that people are predisposed to obey. If you're walking among the rocks on a sunny summer day and your buddy hollers, "Don't move!" you freeze in your tracks, even if you didn't hear the rattle of that snake just two steps ahead. Try a simple test. Ask your wife to slap you on the cheek. Then, as her hand starts to swing, holler, "Stop!" I'll bet her hand hesitates.

When we were toddlers, we learned to obey those short, loud, one-word commands from our mothers.

Project your voice the way an actor does on stage. When you holler, "Police!" abdominal muscles should contract to push air from the bottom of your lungs. Talking from the diaphragm, the stage actor calls it. It adds volume and distance with surprisingly little extra effort. In the first example, if the officer had hollered "Stop!" perhaps the man would have stopped. And the officer would not have been slashed.

When interviewing offenders, Garrison found that they did not try to resist or evade an officer with a good bearing,

---

HOT TIPS FROM OLD HANDS

Avoiding a showdown. Sometimes when you stop a bunch of kids, a smartaleck in the group may wise-off. If you recognize his insult, you could be forced to "save face" by doing something you don't want to do. I just spin my head and say, "*What!?,*" as if I didn't hear what was said.

The smartaleck will usually change the comment so it's not insulting and you avoid having to take him to task.

Officer Pat Springer
Windsor, Connecticut,
police department

one who seemed to know what he was doing. The officer who was hesitant or uncertain, like the officer in the first example, is the one they ignore, escape from, or even attack.

Extending Commands
Once you've identified yourself and have the subject stopped, tell him what you want him to do next. In the second example, the officer said nothing, witnesses heard nothing. Suppose the officer had hollered, "Stop!" Perhaps the suspect would have, perhaps not. But if the officer had added three more little words—"Drop that weapon!"—it would have helped to establish the fact that the subject was armed, even if the witnesses didn't see the gun.

In any case, the U.S. Supreme Court specifically states in the *Tennessee* v. *Garner,* 471 U.S. 1 (1985) decision that verbal commands must be given, wherever practical. This same decision also negates the threat "Stop or I'll shoot." The suspect knows very well that you can't shoot if he isn't threatening anybody. An empty threat makes you look foolish if he calls your bluff. If the situation is such that you have your gun in your hand, it's better to explain to the suspect, "Don't do anything that would force me to shoot you."

Giving Commands
Traveling on up the continuum of force, your response is determined by what the suspect does. But how can he comply if he doesn't know what you want him to do? Tell him—in a few, hard-consonant words. "Put your hands up!" "Drop to the ground! Face down." "Show me your hands! Slowly." "Turn around!" "Face the wall."

If he complies, these commands get the suspect into a controlled and safe position. They establish that you are in control. If he doesn't comply, reinforce the commands with "Do it now!" in a loud voice.

If he still doesn't comply, you step up to the next rung on the ladder of force. As you escalate your use of force, however, don't forget to keep talking. It may ease his resistance when you apply a pain compliance technique, for example, if you say, "Cooperate with me and there'll be no pain."

Part of verbalization is letting your partner know what you are doing, what you want him to do. If you mess up and lose control of an aggressive subject's arm, he needs to *know* that.

Debriefing
Verbalization doesn't end with the arrest. Debrief the suspect. "Are you all right? I notice you hit your head. Do you need a doctor?"

This gives you time to get your own head together, catch your breath, and regain physical control. By that time, you probably have an audience. These questions demonstrate to witnesses your concern for the subject's well-being—and they can testify to that fact.

Consider the four D's: dialogue, direction, debriefing, and documentation. Once you've accomplished your goal and made the arrest, document your actions throughout the event. Cite the subject's actions that required you to employ whatever reactions you used.

15

Professional Skills

Police officers are many things. They're not medics, but they're the first responders on the scene when people are injured. (And to get there, they need better driving skills than a New York cab driver!) They need the decorum of a British barrister, yet they must be able to quickly gain control of an uncooperative person on the street. They are the embodiment of government.

You need many skills to be a police officer. In this chapter there is information on a number of topics, but it's important to note that you need specific training in each of these subjects beyond what's presented here.

15.1 Police Communications

You get involved in a wide range of diverse activities, sometimes in emotional situations. What you say and how you say it could be critical.

Communication means conveying information from one person to another. If the receiver understands something different from what you transmitted, that's not communication. Suppose the phone rings and an excited caller hollers, "There's an accident, Main and Pearl, [cough] injuries!" and hangs up. Did he say there were no injuries? Multiple injuries? Either way, something did not get communicated. Police response could be correct, or very wrong.

Telephone Techniques   Reading and writing are taught in school. Aren't you amazed how few people ever learn how to talk properly on the telephone? A caller's impression of your agency begins when you answer the phone at the station.

There are three elements to placing or receiving a call. Identify yourself. Identify your agency. Identify the person you wish to speak to or ask how you may help.

Proper identification saves time. "Windsor Police, Officer Clede. How may I help you?" If it's a misdial, the caller knows immediately. If it's not, you sound efficient and courteous. If it's a question you have to ponder, ask if the caller would like to wait, or would prefer someone call back.

A computer aided dispatch center in Indianapolis, Indiana. **GENERAL ELECTRIC.**

Tact wins friends. If another line rings and the call you're on isn't an emergency, excuse yourself and ask if you may put the caller on hold. But return to the original call promptly, and thank the caller for waiting.

If you are calling someone and you know it will be a long call, ask if another time would be more convenient. If time is of the essence, say so. "I'm sorry to inconvenience you but we need this information right away."

Special training is given to those answering the emergency lines. Sometimes callers are distraught and you need to calm them tactfully before you can get the information you need. Your agency may have a form to prompt you with the questions to ask: exact location, any injuries, nature of the problem, other information to help a responding officer.

Radio Techniques

Your two-way radio is your link to headquarters, the means by which you can holler for help, if you have a chance. But what if you're jumped unexpectedly? Keep your dispatcher informed of where you are and what you're doing. When you stop a motorist for a moving violation, call in your location and plate number of the car you're stopping. A good dispatcher will check back, if you don't clear the stop within a reasonable time. On your way to a call, your radio is the means by which another officer, who's had experience with that particular person or location before, can give you vital information. It's a good bet that the radio has saved more grief than the gun.

No doubt you'll develop a sort of verbal shorthand to save time and be less intelligible to the thousands of citizens with scanners. On my radio you might hear one car call another and say, "Lower level?" That means the officer wants to meet the other for a chat in the remote level of the big shopping center parking lot. But be wary of picking up sloppy habits and imprecise pet phrases. When the chips are down, don't take chances on being understood. Use the procedural words dictated by your department. Speak distinctly. Be precise.

Many police radio procedure uses codes. There are many variations of the familiar 10 signals, numbers assigned their own meanings, or plain language using a specific choice of words. The purpose of such codes is not secrecy. One can soon identify a variety of codes simply by listening over time. Their real purpose is to convey a precise meaning in a minimum of time.

Almost every radio service in the world has adopted the same calling procedure: giving first the call sign of the station being called, then "this is," followed by the call sign of the station calling—except police. It's common practice among police to call just the other way around. And many's the time I've heard a car respond to such a call by saying, "Car calling 46." When the network consists of one dispatcher working a group of patrol cars, it's common for the dispatcher to call simply with a unit number; you can tell who's calling.

Good Operating Practice   With the crowded airwaves today, your radio probably uses a squelch circuit that is opened by a subaudible tone or tone burst. You don't have to listen to other stations that may get into your system. When you pick up the mike, a switch unmutes the receiver so you can listen to the frequency for a few seconds before you begin transmitting. If another officer in a distant location is in the middle of hollering for help, you don't want to activate your nearby transmitter to get a time check. FCC rules and regulations require you to monitor the frequency to be sure it is clear before you transmit.

You are responsible for what's said over your radio. Don't leave it unattended. Most radios are installed so that turning off the ignition key also turns off the radio.

Intelligibility   It's imperative that someone on the other end of your transmission understands what you are saying. So speak d-i-s-t-i-n-c-t-l-y. Practice pronouncing the words you use the most. There are a couple of guys on my department who are mumblers. Their radio transmissions are often twice or three times as long as they need to be because they have to repeat themselves.

And learn to use terms correctly. "Roger" means "I received and understand your message." It does *not* mean "yes." That's "affirmative." You wouldn't ask for a reiteration. Use "say again." "Stand by" means wait for further information, or wait a minute while the dispatcher handles an emergency phone call.

Another bad habit is reaching over to the dashboard, pushing the push-to-talk button, and talking without bringing the mike to your mouth. That may be okay for a quick acknowledgment but not for conveying information. Technicians usually set the mike audio level so that a normal voice is barely heard with the mike at arm's length. This helps to subdue the back-

The two-way radio is an important tool for the police officer. **MOTOROLA.**

ground noise inside your mobile environment so your voice comes through loud and clear when the mike is close to your mouth.

Don't get into the habit of clicking the mike key a couple of times to acknowledge a transmission, instead of saying "Roger" or "10-4." Do those clicks mean "Okay" or "Someone's got me by the neck and I can't talk"?

Spelling Phonetically   Unusual words, usually names, must be spelled out to convey them accurately. Is it Steven or Stephen? That could make a difference when you're asking for a license check.

Spelling phonetically can be done efficiently. Don't say, "G as in George, U as in Unit, S as in Sam." It takes less time to simply say, "Golf Uniform Sierra." And that brings up the international phonetic alphabet.

There used to be many different phonetic alphabets, and some used words difficult to pronounce. The old police phonetic alphabet was one. Finally, the nations of the world got together and developed a standard list of phonetics most suitable to persons of all ethnic backgrounds and languages. Sometimes you even hear it used on police frequencies by officers recently out of training.

International Phonetic Alphabet

A	Alpha	J	Juliet	S	Sierra
B	Bravo	K	Kilo	T	Tango
C	Charlie	L	Lima	U	Uniform
D	Delta	M	Mike	V	Victor
E	Echo	N	November	W	Whiskey
F	Foxtrot	O	Oscar	X	X-ray
G	Golf	P	Papa	Y	Yankee
H	Hotel	Q	Quebec	Z	Zulu
I	India	R	Romeo		

15.2 Emergency Medical

You are the first responder. It doesn't matter what kind of service your citizen needs, you're the one sent to find out what's wrong. It could be a fall down the stairs, a heart attack, a bloody accident, or a knife-slashed victim.

Most police officers today must be trained in at least basic first aid. The department in my town prides itself in that every officer is trained to the Emergency Medical Technician (EMT) level. My state requires training to Medical Response Technician (MRT), which is roughly equivalent to American Red Cross advanced first aid.

There are many excellent texts on first aid, and specific training is required, so we won't go into detail here. But understanding some of the principles will help you get more out of that training.

Emergency Medical Service (EMS) Call   Remember the ABCs of any medical emergency: check the Airway, check Breathing, and check Circulation. Until these three functions are assured, there's no point in doing anything else because the victim won't survive to benefit from your first aid.

If you're called to aid a choking victim, the Heimlich maneuver may clear the airway. Essentially, the Heimlich maneuver involves grasping the victim from behind, putting the thumb side of your fist just under the rib cage, and quickly exerting pressure inward and upward against the diaphragm. This causes an explosive expulsion of air that just may clear the obstruction.

Cardiopulmonary resuscitation (CPR) is required training for police officers because it can mean survival for a victim suffering cardiac or pulmonary arrest. Basically, CPR provides victims with air and blood circulation until either they revive or the paramedics arrive. It buys time. After the ABCs mentioned above, CPR involves chest compressions to pump blood and forced breathing to provide oxygen. Required training and practice teach you how to establish the rhythm necessary to mimic the body function. Anyone can learn it, and should. CPR has saved lives.

Trauma Call   When you respond to an accident, there is a sequence of things you must do quickly, right after you've advised the dispatcher you've arrived. First, evaluate the dangers—downed power lines, for example. Second, determine how many victims there are. A youngster could be thrown well clear of a car crash. Then survey the situation and protect against hazards that might aggravate it.

It may take several reports back to the dispatcher as you develop information on additional services needed. Do you need an ambulance? More than one? If there are no injuries, response from other agencies can be more measured. Downed power lines require the electric company. A spill of hazardous material requires notification of environmental officials.

Then you can take the time to quickly check *all* the victims. Your first survey of victims is to be sure each is breathing and to identify the more seriously injured. Then you can go back to those who need it most to inventory the injuries and take remedial action.

You need to control serious bleeding to buy time for the victim. Direct pressure with a gauze pad is best. If you add a dressing later, put it on over the old one. You might need to use a pressure point to control bleeding from a specific wound. Perhaps elevating the wound will slow bleeding. A tourniquet is a last resort. Then treat for shock. Loosen restrictive clothing and warm the victim.

Finally, you can check for signs to give you an indication of the problem. Skin tone that's gray, clammy, ashen indicates shock. Check the pupils of the eyes: if dilated, possible cardiac arrest; if constricted, possible drug use; if unequal, possible brain damage, stroke, or head injury.

This one seemed strange to me but it makes sense. You come upon the stabbing victim. The knife is still sticking out of his chest or back. *Leave it.* Bandage around it, if you must, but never remove a penetrating object.

Say it's a gunshot victim and you hear a sucking sound around his chest. The chest is a closed system. If it's penetrated, air may be inhaled through the chest wall (pneumothorax) rather than the nose. It needs to be closed with a dressing backed up by plastic to make it airtight. But it's important to cover it as the victim exhales. If breathing then becomes labored, the lung may be penetrated. If removing the dressing lets out a rush of air, a punctured lung is likely. If it's not punctured, the occlusive dressing may help respiration to improve.

If you suspect a fracture, stabilize it. That's the purpose of splinting a limb or joint in the same position as you find it.

The point of all this is simply that your purpose is to take the immediate action a situation requires, to prevent further injury, and to buy time for the victim until medical responders arrive. If your state has a Good Samaritan law, it will protect you only to the extent that you act in accordance with your training.

Good Samaritan Laws   A Good Samaritan law protects a person trained in or licensed to practice first aid, CPR, or emergency care from liability for civil damages arising from humanitarian actions. It became necessary when even physicians found themselves the target of litigation. In my state, the law specifically exempts paid or volunteer firemen or policemen from liability for forcible entry into a residence in order to render emergency first aid. You should check the laws of your state for the specific wording; it may include a lifeguard, schoolteacher, ski patrol member, or ambulance personnel.

AIDS Is Frightening   AIDS is an acronym for Acquired Immune Deficiency Syndrome. It is a virus, officially called Human Immunodeficiency Virus (HIV), that damages the body's natural defense system. AIDS is not transmitted by casual contact, but rather through transfer of body fluids, particularly blood and semen. Statistics reported by the Center for Disease Control in 1987 show 65 percent of AIDS victims are sexually active homosexual and bisexual men; 17 percent are illegal intravenous drug users; 8 percent are both drug users and homosexual or bisexual men; 4 percent are heterosexual men and women, generally sex partners of those in the other groups; 3 percent had received blood transfusions prior to routine screening; 1 percent are infants born to mothers with AIDS; 3 percent are undetermined.

Statistically speaking, police officers would not seem to be a high-risk group. But we've just seen that a police officer's contact with a victim is far from casual; he bandages a bleeding wound or gives CPR, including mouth-to-mouth resuscitation. The usual cuts and bruises on a cop's hands provide that body-fluid-to-body-fluid route. Even in the course of normal routine, he might prick his finger on the unseen hypodermic needle during a body search of an infected addict.

There is reason for fear. Recent reports show three health care workers became infected a year after their skin was splashed with the blood of AIDS patients. Six others had previously been infected on the job, all through accidentally being stuck with infected needles. Clearly police should guard against contact with blood, even though the chance of infection is still thought to be remote.

Not all the advice that's been published on AIDS can be followed by police officers in emergency situations, but you should be aware of what the medical experts are saying.

• If you're going into a situation where contact with body fluids is unavoidable, protective garments are advisable.

• Disposable latex gloves should be worn when arresting a potentially violent bleeding person, handling bodies, touching bloody items, or handling drug paraphernalia.

• Mouth-to-mouth resuscitation should be done using airways with one-way valves, hand-operated bags, or other devices.

• Any exposed part of your body should be washed quickly and thoroughly after possible exposure.

• Clothing that contacts blood or other body fluids should be removed and cleaned before being worn again.

• If you have a break in your skin, cover it with an impermeable bandage before going on duty.

• Be careful when searching an addict to avoid sharp or pointed objects.

• Exposed protective gear should be disposed of in a proper manner. Evidence items should be stored in double plastic bags and clearly labeled. Bodies of suspected AIDS victims should be identified with a distinctive toe tag.

- If you are exposed to blood or body fluids, you should document the incident. The suspected carrier should be tested for HIV antibodies. You should be tested to establish baseline data, then every six weeks for a year if the carrier tests positive.

15.3 Defensive Driving

What is the largest single source of liability suits? If you thought firearms or use of force, you're wrong. It's automobiles. Your car is a very powerful tool, and you use it constantly. Operating your patrol car calls for exemplary skills whenever you are behind the wheel. After all, your marked car is easily identified and *citizens are looking at you.*

When you go into the defensive driving course during training, you'd better believe there is something you can learn. You need to practice control, steering, fast but safe lane changes, U-turns, controlling skids, proper braking.

Your driving instructors know what has caused officer-involved accidents in the past. They've given a lot of thought to how to avoid them and they've developed techniques to teach you. They will also try to teach you judgment. Their experience will tell you what you might expect from other drivers' reacting to you. And that is the essence of defensive driving—anticipating the other drivers' actions.

Motor Vehicle Chases   Before you pull a violator over, note his license plate. If he tries to run, you'll have that critical piece of information. But just because a motorist runs doesn't mean he's a felon who can't afford to be caught.

A driver may run for any number of real or imagined reasons. Of course, you want to catch him. But if continuing hot pursuit puts others at risk, you have no choice but to break off. If you noted the plate number, you can always catch him another day. If it's a suspected felon who's running, your radio can alert other units that may be ahead of him. If the only reason to chase is that the driver was speeding, it's not worth breaking your neck. The exception is one who is likely to endanger others if he continues.

You need to consider the kind of road, weather and wind conditions, amount of traffic, and what's up ahead before deciding to chase an offender in hot pursuit.

South Whitehall Township, Pennsylvania, Police held the first gymkhana for police patrol vehicles under "hot pursuit" conditions to test driving skills.

Good judgment is the critical factor. And I haven't figured out how to explain that.

But let's say that all things (and the policies of your department) considered, you decide to chase. First, consider how you're going to startle other motorists when you switch on the lights and siren. Give them a chance to get out of your way. Then remember that high-speed operation of a motor vehicle is quite different from a Sunday drive in the country.

While draping one arm out the window and resting the right hand at the bottom of the wheel may seem comfortable, it affords little steering control. Where does the racing driver put his hands? The left at nine or ten o'clock, the right at three or two o'clock. That hand position provides optimum control.

Brake as you enter a tight turn, slowly accelerate during the turn, and exit quickly as you tromp on it. Too much braking or acceleration during a turn could cause fishtailing or a skid. Second gear was handy in city traffic back when I drove a 1949 Ford cruiser, but our 1988 Fords came through with automatic overdrive transmissions. They are placarded "Use 'Drive' under 40 mph and during high-speed chase." It helps ease the demand on the brakes.

What if the violator is traveling in the other direction? Several U-turns are possible when you need to reverse direction quickly. The simple "U" is the quickest and safest when you have room. When you don't, you can back into a drive on the right side or turn into a left-side road, then back into the street. The Y-turn is a last resort. It involves turning your nose to the right, backing in a left turn across the road so you're nearly headed in the other direction. Obviously, if traffic is heavy, it's dangerous.

Intersections are a constant problem. New York City loses some 400 cars a year in intersection crashes, according to local news media, and too many involve two cruisers with lights and sirens blaring. Other drivers are supposed to give way to your lights and siren, but don't count on it. If you enter an intersection at ninety, they'll never see you—until you hit. You are still responsible, so you must brake enough that you can avoid any crossing traffic, and let them avoid you. Then stomp on the gas *after* clearing the intersection.

The last thing you want is a parade of police cars all in a row crashing one lonely speeder. If you can position other cars ahead, fine, but let one officer handle his own chase. If two cars are in the chase, remember the safe separation distance required for avoiding an accident is multiplied as speed increases.

There's a lot of noise inside a police car with a roof-mounted siren wailing. You must keep the dispatcher informed of your location, speed, and direction of travel, but can he hear you? If your message isn't getting through, some suggest a last resort of using the microphone like a throat mike. Press it against your neck, on the soft part next to your windpipe. That should block the background but lets your voice come through your throat with perhaps a 25 percent reduction in audio. Obviously, this presumes you are in position to use the radio safely.

Highway Pursuits   Highway chases, where speeds can top 100, are not for novices. You need to know how a vehicle handles at such speed. You need to understand the dynamics of your particular vehicle. You'd better have experienced this challenge on a test track before you try it for real.

You need to know how fast you can take a particular exit ramp. If the car you're chasing enters the turn too fast, let him be the one to make the mistake. You'll save time by slowing to the maximum negotiating speed you've established for that hazard. And you might not have to chase him much farther anyway, if he doesn't make it.

Frequent braking during high-speed operation can heat up brakes and cause them to fade. Should you notice degraded performance of your brakes, call another car to take over the chase because you're likely to soon become a guided missile.

In a challenging chase, you can become so engrossed in capturing the fleeing suspect that you suffer tunnel vision. The fixation can become so strong that you continue a pursuit you normally would have broken off. You forget side-road traffic or any concern for others. At high speed, your field of vision narrows. You are looking farther ahead to detect dangers. Near objects to the side blur.

As the chase continues, more adrenalin is pumped into your bloodstream. This "kick" can impair your ability. Your time-speed sense is expanded. When you slow to 90 after traveling 120, you feel as if you're doing 40. If the car being chased spins out, you might see it in slow motion, and misjudge the safe stopping distance.

At 100 mph, you're traveling 146.6 feet per second. This means you need to predict where cars will be and what they will be doing 1.6 miles ahead, because you'll be there in one minute. If you're doing 125 and trouble develops a mile ahead, you have about 16 seconds to start stopping or else you won't be stopped by the time you reach the scene.

Rain is also a concern in high-speed operation. At high speed your tires can hydroplane, literally riding on top of a film of water. You have no traction, no control. Slow down. That's the only cure at that point.

"Finesse" is an apt description of your delicate touch in steering and braking when running at high speed. A jerk of the wheel or jam on the brakes could throw the vehicle out of control. Brake gently and increase brake pressure as the vehicle slows. Handling high-speed turns, blowouts, dips, and bumps is a skill you develop just like learning to shoot—by doing it. Experience, plus proper training, help you avoid the psychological effects of the chase.

Any time you are involved in fresh pursuit, you'd better write a report before you go off shift. Include all pertinent information and objectively describe exactly what happened and why.

15.4 Developing Informants

Part of your job is to know what's happening on your beat, but you can't know everything. You need to develop sources of information who will keep you informed. If you knew everything that all the people on your beat know, you could solve all the crimes. Informants extend your eyes and ears, let you know about events out of your purvue. Adding to your store of information through informants can make you more effective. Informants aren't just the "stoolies" who inform for pay, as depicted on television.

Who Is an Informant and Why?   Almost anyone "in the know" can be an informant. Persons with wide public contact see and hear a lot more than you do by yourself—barbers, garbagemen, delivery people, hotel personnel, money lenders, store clerks, even other investigators. And don't forget passersby. Give citizens on the street an opportunity to help you.

There are many reasons why a citizen will want to give you information, beyond the civicmindedness that most people feel. One may fear becoming a victim of someone he knows, or he may be jealous of the other guy's "successes." He may have been involved in something that he now regrets. It could be a question of vanity: knowing the police took action because of the informant's information.

Whatever the reasons, it takes time and effort to develop a rapport with people you consider to be possible sources of information.

Protecting Informants and Evaluating Information   It is ethical practice to protect the identity of your informants. It's necessary, if you expect to keep their confidence and benefit from additional information in the future. Never use their real name on the telephone and don't identify them in your reports because they are subject to subpoena by the courts. Meet your informants in a secure place and at a time they won't likely be spotted. You can't make promises or deals, but your knowledge of the informant's assistance certainly should be made known to your superiors when necessary.

Someone who is a regular informant may be protected with a fictitious name or number, with the true identity known only to the officer who "controls" him. Once you've established an informant as reliable, treat him or her fairly. If a monetary reward is the policy, make sure it is paid. You obviously won't reveal all the information you have to an informant, but if some pieces of information will help the informant develop it further, it might be smart to let him try.

No good journalist accepts a fact until she has received it from at least two separate, qualified sources. There's no reason you should be any different. *Check it out.* Check other sources and records. Then consider the motives of those providing information. You should be able to identify a good reason for someone furnishing information.

Finally, no good thing lasts forever. You might discover your informant has a record he didn't tell you about. You might determine that the informant is a security risk, or has submitted false information, or he may even ask to break off the relationship. At that point, it's important not to be antagonistic. The informant may have compelling reasons. A pleasant parting leaves him in position of perhaps becoming an informant again in the future. You must continue to protect his identity and avoid unfavorable reactions to your department.

16

Report Writing

The biggest chore a police officer has is paperwork. But your report may be the key to solving the crime later. You'd have a hard time testifying to details of an incident years later without a report to refer back to. Report writing is one of a police officer's most important functions. In fact, it could mean your career.

16.1 ABCs of Report Writing

Newspaper reporters learn that their stories must include the Who, What, Where, When, Why, and How. Your report is even more important, because it will affect people's lives, but you can borrow their format.

- *Who* must include everyone involved, whether participant or witness.

- *What* must describe the situation as you observed it and what you did because of your observations.

- *Where* needs to be specific as to location, both during the event and after apprehension.

- *When* demands specific times relative to the incident itself and later actions.

- *Why,* if known, may indicate motive for a criminal act or cause of an accident. It may also justify your actions.

- *How* may chart the development of a situation or describe your actions in relation to the challenges presented to you.

The information in your report must be sufficient to answer any questions in the mind of anyone who reads your report.

What incidents should be reported? Your department policy will govern, but, for your own good, write up any situation in which you acted in any way. As long as you have a written record, you can use it later to show cause for your actions. Your report is a permanent record and should be complete, accurate, and clear.

The ABCs of report writing are Accuracy, Brevity, and Clarity and Completeness. If laboratory analysis, doctor's examination, or other tests are pertinent, include them in your report.

I've got bad news for you: you have to be able to write your reports using correct English. Just to show you how important it is, suppose you respond to an automobile accident. When you call in the plate, the dispatcher tells you the vehicle was just used in an armed robbery. The dispatcher describes the felon and it fits the subject behind the wheel. You order driver and passenger out of the car.

Now, suppose you write in your report, "As the driver got out of the car, he tossed a gun to the passenger. He opened his door and took aim at me. I fired and he dropped. I covered the driver and ordered him to lie spread eagle on the ground. I handcuffed him. The passenger appeared to be dead and I gained control of the situation."

Writing the report is a necessary chore but you need the facts from a witness. **L&O.**

Notice the ambiguity in the first part of the statement. You don't know who took aim until later in the paragraph. A lawyer may quote you out of context to make a point of your confusion about the situation.

This is obviously a "good shoot." You had all sorts of probable cause and a definite threat to which you responded properly. But it could be a couple of years before the case comes to court, and you'll have to testify to those minute details that went into your shooting decision.

16.2 Importance of a Notebook

The basis of your report, and perhaps your testimony two years later, is your field notes. No one expects you to remember all those details; you are permitted to refer to your notes. But remember that what you bring into court is subject to subpoena. The little spiral-bound pad you carry in your shirt pocket is convenient but it doesn't constitute your field notebook. Better that you keep your "real" notebook in the car and prepare your field notes with a bit more thought and consideration.

When I went through training, the instructor recommended a looseleaf notebook. Your department may specify the type of notebook you will use. But if it's looseleaf, you can take only the pages pertaining to a particular case into court. Then, if the defense counsel grabs them, you don't lose your whole notebook.

For this reason, your field notes need to be complete, clear, and accurate. "A young scruffy-looking character in a blue outfit" tells little. How young? What made him look scruffy? What color blue, light or dark? What type of clothing? What condition was it in? Hair length, facial hair? And, while you're at it, what was the condition of the witness, excited and agitated or calm and considered? Record your impressions.

You can make your own observation of the scene and record what you see with enough detail that someone could tell from reading your notes just what the situation was at the time.

16.3 A Lawyer's Warning

A good friend of mine, Walt MacDonald, has seen the problems of improper reports from both sides of the bar. Walt is the lieutenant in charge of tactical operations and narcotics for the Plymouth County, Massachusetts, sheriff's department. He is also a practicing attorney. He told me that report writing is much more than a lesson in English grammar.

In most jurisdictions, the opposing attorney, through the discovery process, will be provided with a copy of every departmental report filed in the case. Whether you testify as a prosecution witness, a civil defendant, or a criminal defendant, you will be subjected to cross examination based on your report. It doesn't matter that the trial is two weeks, two months, or two years down the line.

When compared to your sworn testimony, what your report does not contain may be more crucial than what it does. You will surely be asked the standard question, "Now, Officer, is your memory of these events better today than it was back when you wrote your report?"

Facts and details stated from the witness stand but omitted from the report will be branded "recent contrivances." The attorney will argue that if the incident had actually happened as you now testify, your report would coincide with your present version of the facts. "If it's not in your report, it didn't happen," MacDonald says.

16.4 Use of Force

When any amount of force is used, your report should clearly and completely state the facts justifying the kind and amount of force. Note also whether any lesser means of control were attempted and proved insufficient, such as verbal direction or unarmed physical-restraint techniques.

Too many department policies state simply that "the officer shall file a full and complete report." This leaves it up to you to determine what facts should be included. Unless the positive identification of witnesses and other facts are acquired immediately at the scene and included in your report, they are often lost forever. Frequently a Catch-22 situation occurs: the more force used,

---

HOT TIPS FROM OLD HANDS

Off-the-cuff comments. Spontaneous "off the cuff/at the scene" explanations, as well as hastily prepared reports to satisfy the news media, can bring dire consequences.

Whenever you're involved in a shooting, first aid, if needed for emotional as well as physical injuries, should be the immediate concern. This is easier if you can remove yourself from the scene as soon as possible. Don't stay where you'll be the object of intense media attention and inquiry.

You hope the justified use of force will be viewed in its proper context, as it happened. If you win what could have been a life-threatening encounter and then lose because of ill-considered comments, that would really be an injustice.

Lt. Walt MacDonald
Plymouth County,
Massachusetts,
sheriff's department

the greater the stress; the greater the stress, the greater the likelihood of faulty reporting. In your own self-interest, this is one report you do not want returned at some later date marked "incomplete."

One of the Northeast's leading administrators in law enforcement and corrections, Sheriff Peter Y. Flynn of Plymouth County, Massachusetts, has met this problem head on. His department's comprehensive policy on use of force includes a specific and detailed section on reporting requirements. Unless otherwise ordered, the officer involved is required to file a written report before the end of the tour of duty.

Here are some of the required contents:

1.   An account of the events leading up to the use of force.

2.   A precise description of the incident and the reasons for employing force.

3.   A description of the type of force used (including weapons, if any) and the manner in which used.

4.   A description of the injuries suffered, if any, and the treatment given, if known, along with attached photographs, if any.

5.   A list of all participants and witnesses to the event.

Although our reports are primarily written for our own internal use, a report explaining the use of force may well go further. Neither the content of the report nor the language used should be open to misinterpretation or put the officer in a bad light if it is read by a judge and jury. The most important thing to remember is that your report must be understandable to judge and jurors who've never been in a fight or faced a hazardous situation.

16.5 Report Checklist

1. Elements of the crime.   Your state's field manual will identify the elements that constitute a violation or crime. Those elements should be included in your report.

2. Penalty-enhancing circumstances.   Some crimes carry a more severe penalty if committed while armed, against a police officer, or against an elderly or retarded person. Those circumstances must be alleged at the time the complaint is filed.

3. Probable cause for stop, detention, or arrest.   Even an obviously guilty party may go free if you don't show probable cause for initiating your action. Be specific. Don't say you stopped the car for a traffic violation. Cite the circumstances and violation. Then issue a traffic summons even if you develop a major felony arrest; otherwise a judge may think you fabricated the infraction to justify probable cause. Court decisions have held that you must be able to state "articulable facts" to show probable cause every step of the way. Of course, you can draw on your experience to show why a subject's actions made you suspicious.

4. Basis for search and seizure or entry into private dwelling.   If you acted without a warrant under exigent circumstances, your report must include all the facts that give you a legal basis for acting: consent, search incident to lawful arrest, contraband, in plain view, imminent destruction of evidence, crime in progress. If you can cite several justifications, include them all.

5. Advisement of rights or waiver.   It isn't uncommon for a report to ignore the fact that the suspect was advised of his rights. Don't just say, "I advised him of his rights." Tell when and where, who else was there, and his or her exact words in answer to your rights questions.

6. Statements by suspect.   Should the subject make a damaging statement, be more specific than simply saying "he admitted to the crime." Use his words in a direct quote. Include everything he says in explaining his actions. It might be admissible as a spontaneous utterance, even without advisement and waiver of rights. If it's a contrived alibi, it may do as much to convict him as an admission.

7. Statements of witnesses.   If a witness seems friendly to the suspect, report his exact words. Such statements may be used to impeach him in court if his testimony is inconsistent. For other witnesses, some experts say you should be careful about reporting direct quotes. You can't testify as to what a witness told you; that's hearsay. If your report shows the victim made a statement that conflicts with his testimony, you may become a *defense* witness to prove prior inconsistent statements.

8. Suspect's demeanor.   You might expect a suspect to advance a defense of diminished capacity. Carefully record your observations of his demeanor. You might say that he appeared to show no signs of intoxication, that he appeared to respond quickly and decisively to your questions, that he seemed to know where he was, the time and day, or that he asked questions showing his awareness of the situation.

9. Cliff hangers.   Say your report shows a crime committed in January and an arrest made in July. If that report doesn't show the reason for the six-month delay, a defense attorney will file a motion for dismissal for lack of a speedy trial. And the prosecutor won't have information he needs to reply.

Your report serves many purposes. It may be the basis for followup investigation by the detective division. It will be the basis for a formal complaint. It will surely be subpoenaed by the defense attorney in the discovery process when the case goes to court. It may be used by your crime analysis section to develop new crime-prevention procedures.

16.6 Forms of Reports

Not all cops can write like Joseph Wambaugh, so the narrative form of report is not used by some departments. You may need to do a narrative for a supplemental report. But for the initial report, you're likely to see a printed form with boxes to check off, or a laptop computer that prompts you with questions.

Regardless of the form prescribed for your report writing, you must be your own severest critic. It's tempting to leave the chore for later, especially at 5:00 A.M., but an incomplete report could come back to haunt you in many ways, even if the sergeant doesn't bounce it back to you.

Sgt. Maurice McGough of the St. Petersburg police department pioneered by writing a program for the Tandy 102 laptop computer. The report is typed right at the scene, then transmitted back to headquarters over the telephone. Officer Joe Salvadore of the Lakeland, Florida, police took this idea a step further by developing software for the stationhouse computer to manage this input.

The originating officer can retrieve a disapproved report to make additions and corrections. It's department policy that the officer cannot retrieve approved reports, except to read or print them. With these computer programs, it's hard to forget important information. Like the St. Petersburg program from which it grew, Lakeland's program prompts the officer with pertinent questions.

"The state's attorney's office is enthusiastic about our project," says Lakeland's chief, Ronald Nenner. "They tell us they're getting better, more accurate and complete reports than before, and the officer can finish his report at his convenience. "Where they once had to come into the station, officers can now go home and phone in their report."

Use of laptop computers in Lakeland has cut report writing time by more than half. Detectives were first to test this new idea, and even the most reluctant diehard asked for a computer when he saw others doing two and a half reports in the time it took him to do one.

17

Interviews and Interrogation

There is a difference between an interview and an interrogation, but it can sometimes be subtle.

You might define the interview as a talk with someone who is friendly and cooperative, someone who is willing to help and has no apparent reason to lie. He may be a witness or a victim, a relative or neighbor of the accused. However, a person friendly with the accused could be biased and try to protect him. The interview is an effort to develop accurate information from a reasonably cooperative person.

An interrogation is a talk with someone who is not friendly and cooperative—the accused or a coconspirator. This person normally has something to conceal. An appearance of cooperation may be a ploy to mask deception.

Sometimes the distinction is not clear. The owner of a store that just burned may have set the fire himself. The "rape" victim could be a prostitute who's angry because she wasn't paid.

17.1 Interview

Whenever you talk with anyone, you need to establish that you are in control of the conversation. How much control obviously depends on the situation. You wouldn't treat a witness like a criminal, but neither can you afford to waste time on unrelated matters.

Do your homework; learn as much as you can about the situation, so you know what kinds of information you need to discover and what questions to ask.

Communication is fundamental. If the subject can't speak English and you can't speak his language, you have a problem. Find out beforehand if you are going to need an interpreter.

There are two schools of thought on an interviewer's dress and demeanor. One holds that the officer should be well dressed and look professional, in uniform or a business suit. The other theory is that skill is more important than appearance, especially if your normal dress is more informal and you don't want to intimidate the witness with a uniform and gun.

There are also two schools of thought on the best location for the interview. At an accident scene, you don't have much choice as you interview witnesses. Getting their information while it's fresh in their minds is more important than moving to more pleasant surroundings.

But when you set up an interview, the choice of location depends on the interviewer— where you can function best—and on the interviewee— where he will be most inclined to give you information. A relaxed and friendly atmosphere seems to work best. If possible, I prefer to meet a witness somewhere other than police headquarters—at his home or office, or another place familiar to him. Most citizens don't have

---

HOT TIPS FROM OLD HANDS

What'd he say? Beware of the nonresponsive answer. You ask, "Where do you live?" and the suspect answers, "I just got into town last week." He didn't answer your question, although it sounds like he did if you aren't listening too closely. Too often, you're too busy formulating your next question or writing down information to really hear the answer. People with something to hide will be evasive and nonresponsive. People who are simply hostile to the police will usually just decline to answer.

Officer Tim Dees
Reno, Nevada,
police department

---

much contact with the police and are somewhat uncomfortable in a police station. Of course, you may decide that a particular witness will more freely discuss the subject if he is a little intimidated, or if he feels secure in the environment of police activity.

When you're trying to develop a sequence of events, it usually works best to interview first the witness who was most directly involved. This may be the victim or someone standing nearby. They probably had the longest look at the suspect, and can give you a better description of him and of the events. This gives you the broadest picture possible, and may suggest other questions.

Someone who was standing outside the bar when the suspect held it up could have information not available to those inside. The suspect ran out and jumped into an old blue Buick with license plate 123-ABC. Of course, if you find this witness first as you roll up to the scene, it could be more important to get the vehicle description first so you can put it out on the radio.

Taking Statements   It's best to let witnesses tell their story in their own way, preferably without interruption. This narration brings out the main points, as the witness sees them. Questions can fill in the details later.

When you're taking statements from more than one witness, talk with each one individually, separate and apart from others. Eyewitness testimony is questionable at best. People don't remember every detail. One person will remember different details than another. And one who is unsure of himself will be influenced by what he hears others say. Keep them apart while waiting to be interviewed so they don't have a chance to concoct a story they want you to believe.

Bias on the part of a witness is not necessarily lying. It's human nature to shade the truth or slant the facts to support one's own beliefs. Experienced interviewers call it "selective memory."

Handling inadequate responses challenges an interviewer's skill. A strained facial expression could imply that the person is not telling all he knows. The witness may be purposefully evasive, or he just may not remember. You may prod his memory or catch him off guard by posing the right questions.

Asking the Right Questions

Most field interviews are conducted to enable you to fill out a report, so you need to ask the questions that give you the information called for in the report. Filling out an accident report is usually done right in the cruiser, perhaps with the subjects in the back seat so you can ask your questions right off the report form.

While narrating his story, a subject may need encouragement. Nodding your head at appropriate times, looking him in the eye, and assuming a supportive posture gives him a feeling that you are interested in what he's saying, and encourages him to continue.

But he may need prompting—which is very different from "leading." A leading question introduces an element that hasn't been brought up before. Even if the complaint is armed robbery, you never ask, "Did you see the gun?" before the witness says a gun was involved. It could have been a knife. Instead, you ask, "Did you see the suspect holding anything in his hands?"

Some other examples of prompting questions: "What did you do then?" "Why did you do that?" "What else did you see at that moment?" "Did you hear anything else right then?" "Was someone else there at the time?" Notice that these questions carry no implications.

You'll develop your own prompting questions to ensure that you learn all that is pertinent to the case. If the victim is elderly, infirm, or retarded, you need to establish those facts in the statement to justify a more serious charge.

You need not apologize for taking notes. You need specific information to fill out a burglary or lost child report, and no one expects you to remember all those details. But a person who is frightened in the presence of police officers is already anxious, and his anxiety may be heightened by the sight of a notebook. You may ease his mind with such a question as "Do you mind if I make a list of the things that were taken?" Or a comment: "Let me make a note of that so I'll be sure to remember the details."

This is the "velvet glove" approach to interviewing. You need a light touch when dealing with a citizen, especially one trying to be helpful. If you run into a memory block, real or feigned, divert his attention to another point, then work back to the blocked information from a different direction. Such a shift may give the witness a different trigger to his memory, or catch him off guard if he's intentionally evasive.

Be tactful in dealing with a witness. Don't pressure him over "discrepancies" in his statement, nor call his comment a "lie," even if you know it is. Instead, refer to "points" in his story, minor matters that need to be "clarified." It could be that the witness just doesn't want to admit that he doesn't know, or doesn't remember. It could be that he was in that motel with someone other than his wife. The employee may think his boss will have his hide if he doesn't give the police a complete and total picture of what happened, even though he was hiding behind the counter at the time and couldn't see anything.

A good interviewer reads body language. The witness who folds his arms across his chest and leans back is shutting you out, perhaps hiding something. One whose arms are open and leans forward attentively may be more eager to help or may be promoting a tall tale. Remember, too, that the interviewer can also telegraph thoughts and reactions by gestures and expressions that can be picked up by the person being interviewed.

17.2 Interrogation

When you set out to question a suspect, you can't count on his cooperation even if he appears cooperative. It can become a game of wits.

The principal psychological factor in a successful interrogation is privacy. When someone confides in another, he does so out of earshot of others. It's human nature. But other investigators want to take part, and you may even want a witness present. Just remember: a group of people crowding the suspect isn't conducive to a good interrogation.

In a Midwestern town, a citizen was being questioned about the killing of his wife. The husband's story was that he and his wife were riding in their car when they were robbed by a man who shot the wife when she called for help. Investigators were skeptical. The husband was questioned several times over the next twenty-four hours, but always with several investigators present. Later, an outside expert was called by the state's attorney. The expert selected a private room and excluded everyone else.

"From the moment the suspect entered the room, he showed signs of guilt," the expert said. "He acted as if he wanted to unburden himself. He wanted sympathy. Once he was alone with just one interrogator, he quickly confessed how and why he killed his wife."

In our headquarters, the interview room is small. It contains one table and a couple of chairs. No telephone. No windows. No pictures on the walls. There is nothing to distract the subject. A one-way mirror in the door lets others observe from outside. If your state laws permit, a hidden microphone may let observers hear or record the confession.

Conduct of the Interrogator

Psychologically, the interrogator wants to appear as one who is merely seeking the truth, not an inquisitor. It's better to keep pencil and notebook out of sight so you don't remind the suspect of the permanent nature of his statements. For the same reasons, it's better if the interviewer is in conservative civilian clothes rather than uniform.

Be tactful in your choice of words. Avoid "kill," "steal," "confess." Better are "shoot," "take," and "tell the truth." Don't say, "You're lying to me." Say, "You haven't told me the whole truth." Your language should be an idiom understood by the suspect.

Treating the subject with decency and respect can be rewarding. A prostitute was suspected of robbing a drugged victim. As she removed her coat in the interview room, the interrogator saw that a broken shoulder strap left one of her breasts exposed. He got a towel and draped it over her shoulder. He addressed her as "Miss" rather than by her first name. She wasn't accustomed to being treated like a lady, and she readily confessed the crime and named her accomplice. No matter how despicable the crime, a sympathetic and understanding attitude by the interrogator is far more effective than pressure tactics.

To avoid any taint of coercion, restraints should not be used in the interrogation room. The interrogator should not be armed. A guard can always be posted just outside the door.

Sizing Up Suspects

Evaluating a suspect to determine the techniques and tactics most appropriate is a skill you develop through practical experience. With a suspect whose guilt is reasonably certain, you might confront him with your belief, hoping to prompt a confession or at least an incriminating statement. If the suspect's guilt is uncertain, then you have to feel your way around.

HOT TIPS FROM OLD HANDS

Question the unquestionable. As a young patrolman, I learned a valuable lesson. I had stopped a car with New Jersey plates. It had been acting suspiciously in a residential area. The four male occupants all showed IDs with home addresses in Newark, New Jersey. Our dispatcher ran the car and occupants through NCIC but found no "hits," so I let them go.

Later in the day, I talked to an experienced detective. He asked if I had checked with Newark PD. I told him no, believing that NCIC was the great golden god of information. On his advice, even though the car and subjects were long gone, I called Newark police and found that two of the subjects had outstanding bench warrants for robbery, but the warrants had not been entered into NCIC.

Later in my career, I defined this lesson into a simple rule: "Never believe anything the first time you hear it!" Check it out.

Sgt. Frank Branca
Greenwich, Connecticut, police department

Among probably guilty suspects, those who commit crimes against persons are usually more emotional. They may have a troubled conscience. The sympathetic approach is likely to be successful. Those who commit crimes for financial gain are more likely to be unemotional. A factual analysis is better, using techniques that appeal to common sense and reasoning.

Interrogation Techniques and Tactics   Skillful interrogation is an ability a police officer develops over time through study and practice. It's nothing more—or less—than applied psychology. Questioning is really an interplay between two people. You have to establish a rapport with the suspect. Small talk can get him to talking. Then interject a question about one small point of the purpose of the questioning. You have to play it by ear.

There are a variety of tactics you can use, depending on the situation. Your air of confidence is important, and especially if guilt is certain, your confidence in his guilt. You can reveal some, but not all, of the circumstantial evidence that indicates guilt. If you point out a suspect's symptoms of guilt, he may feel he's betraying himself. Sympathy might help him open up. Minimizing the moral seriousness of the offense, particularly in sex cases, may encourage the suspect to talk. You might play one accomplice against another.

It's well worth your time to read up on interrogation and interview techniques. Because it is such a mind game, it helps you to understand the psychology of people. And that can help in more ways than just interrogation.

17.3 Touchy Subjects

Interviewing child sexual abuse victims is usually left to specially trained officers. But you deal with kids on the street. If a child runs to you for help, you can't turn your back. It's important that you understand the special concerns so that your initial actions won't jeopardize followup investigations.

Robert N. Parrish, Utah assistant attorney general, addresses this subject in a paper, "Interviewing Child Sexual Abuse Victims When the Goal Is Prosecution of an Offender." He was eager to include his concepts here "to get the idea across that it's not the same as other interviews and requires special training.

"Anyone who has interviewed children knows there's no perfect way that applies in all cases," Parrish says. "But many who are given this responsibility have no training in the special techniques of getting information from a child. They're frustrated because they can't get the child to 'open up' and discuss what may have happened to them."

Your objective is to get enough information to determine the probable validity of the child's statement while minimizing trauma.

"In this context, I'm defining 'interview' as a questioning of the child by one whose purpose is to obtain and preserve evidence of possible criminal activity," Parrish explains. "This is quite different from interviewing to allow diagnosis and treatment through therapy. What I say applies only to law enforcement. It's been my experience that a basic understanding of the nature of child abuse is fundamental to a successful interview. Many of the usual interview techniques lead to frustration. Specific training is imperative."

If you are faced with such an encounter with an abused child, your own discomfort could disquiet the child. You need patience. "I usually tell a child that I've already heard just about everything, that while I understand their embarrassment I will not be embarrassed," Parrish explains. "That usually puts the child at ease."

However, you can't believe everything a child says. If you say that whatever the child says will be believed, a defense attorney will call that a license to lie. Yet, you need to develop a reasonable belief that a crime has been committed before turning the case over to specialists. Better to tell the child you're there to help and you need to know everything that happened honestly and completely. By the same token, an aggressive cross examination will cause the child to clam up.

There has been enough false reporting of child abuse, particularly during a bitter divorce, to make people suspicious. You may have seen misleading statistics that 60 percent of all child abuse reports are unsubstantiated. But "unsubstantiated" may mean simply that an agency was unable (or unwilling) to find corroborating evidence. The best study of false reporting (*Journal of Interpersonal Violence,* March 1987) established only an 8 percent rate of fictitious reports.

Generally recognized factors that help validate a child's allegation include unusual or unpredictable details, descriptions of context, relating specific conversation, the child's mental and emotional state, child's knowledge of sexual matters and body parts, and consistency between interviews.

The bottom line is that validity of a child's account of sexual abuse is not an easy thing to determine, according to Parrish. But it is much easier when the interviews are conducted competently, when the child is given the chance to provide detail.

"The application of common sense and training in child abuse, in my opinion, usually allows a reliable prediction of validity or invalidity of a child's accusations," Parrish concludes.

18

Investigations

Some say a good investigator is born and not made. Others say the opposite. Frankly, I think both sides of the argument are right. Good investigators are born, but they can also be made *if they understand what they are doing.* It isn't just a list of procedures or following specific techniques. Investigators need a natural curiosity to recognize what could be an unusual lead. This means they must understand people, products, situations, and circumstances.

It's easy to see why a recruit doesn't go right into the detective division. Investigative skills are learned in training, to be sure, but they are fully developed only with experience. However, even recruits can influence the effectiveness of a detective's investigation by their actions at the scene and the reports they write later.

18.1 Crime Scene

As a patrol officer, you are usually first on the scene of a crime. And you learn a long list of things to do and not to do. You aren't expected to be a forensic scientist, but it would help if you understood some of the reasons why you can make or break everything that happens next.

The homeowner returns from the concert and finds his home in a shambles. You answer the burglary call. It's dark. You're met at the door, and the resident wants to march you all around to show you the disruption. A rear window was broken and entered so you go out and around to get a good look from outside. In the course of these seemingly innocent meanderings, valuable evidence could be destroyed.

Forensic Determinations Depend on You   Procedures you should follow at various types of crime scenes are part of your academy training. You need to collect evidence using techniques acceptable to your courts. You learn how to draw or diagram a crime scene, depending on how your jurisdiction likes it presented. Just be aware that the first officer to arrive at a crime scene is suddenly faced with awesome responsibilities.

This Allegheny County, Pennsylvania, detective is taking a plaster cast of a footprint found at a crime scene. **L&O.**

If there are victims, are they alive? Need first aid? Was a crime actually committed? Notify the dispatcher of your evaluation of the situation. Request medical assistance. Render first aid. And while you're doing all this, remember to preserve any potential physical evidence, such as footprints and fingerprints.

Once you've taken care of immediate needs, your purpose becomes to secure and protect the scene. Identify possible witnesses. Be aware that the perpetrator might return—or may never have left.

Until a supervisor arrives, the officer who was dispatched on the call is in charge. Establish a perimeter and direct spectators where to stand. Delegate this responsibility to a citizen, if you must, but keep big feet and curious hands out of the area you think might contain evidence.

Once you've spotted possible physical evidence, remember that responding backup units, supervisor, ambulance, paramedics, and investigators don't know where it is when they drive up. You have to be on hand to direct them and prevent its destruction. Normally a crime-scene investigator will survey the area to determine safe pathways where officers and medics may walk without destroying evidence. But if there's a need for medical attention before the investigator arrives, at least determine for yourself the least destructive routes.

The purpose of a crime-scene investigation is to reconstruct the events that led up to the commission of a crime. Significant evidence might be anything from a hair to an automobile, skin flecks under a victim's fingernails to the gun lying on the ground.

Even seemingly simple scenes can turn up surprising information. Lt. Robert L. Burriss is the forensic investigations unit of the Biloxi, Mississippi, police department. *Police* magazine calls him legendary. He illustrates some of the things a qualified investigator can learn from a crime scene.

After a local store was burglarized, Burriss swept the interior and found nothing. He took photographs inside and out. Even they showed nothing obvious. In one he noticed a dolly leaning against the wall outside the rear entrance. A dolly's not unusual, but outside? The owner confirmed that the dolly was kept inside. Burriss dusted it for fingerprints and lifted a perfect set. Eventually he made a match. Police followed up and found merchandise from the store in the home of the suspect. The "out of place" or "unusual" could be as simple as this.

A woman was found shot to death in an automobile. Her husband admitted he shot her but said it was accidental—they were struggling for the gun. Burriss worked the scene. He found blood spattered on the husband, nearly none in the car, and a few drops on the ground beside the car. Burriss wasn't satisfied. The next day he visited the funeral home and examined the body. A bruise had appeared on the face and another on her arm, as if fingers had gripped it. Burriss wondered.

The husband's story was that he had grappled with the woman over the gun. But that would occupy both hands, Burriss thought. He examined the car again. The blood inside was a soaking stain, rather than a spatter you'd find from a gunshot wound. A blood spatter had been found on the ground outside of the car. Burriss deduced the husband had pulled his wife from the car, shot her, then put her back into the car. Confronted with the evidence, he confessed. Burriss is convinced that crime scenes "talk" to him if he'll just look and listen hard enough.

Things begin to happen fast when you arrive at a crime scene. Burriss's advice is to compose yourself before going in, and log everything you do so you can advise the forensic investigator when he or she arrives. Of course, you must first determine if anyone needs medical attention and if the deceased is really dead. But keep people away, seal the scene as quickly as you can, and don't touch or move anything.

A murder weapon was given to one department firearms instructor, and he was asked to check it for functioning and safety. As it happened, that instructor understood that biological material can be blown back into the bore of a gun from a contact wound. Even though he wasn't asked, he ran a dry patch through the bore and filed it away for later reference. Then he performed the tests requested.

Like it or not, bullets can't always be matched to the responsible gun with a comparison microscope. The problem in this case was that the evidence bullet was badly deformed, and so there was no way to link the gun to the victim. There was a good chance of losing the case until the instructor heard about the problem in a chance conversation. He suggested an analysis of the dry patch he had run through the barrel. The lab found trace evidence of blood and tissue that matched the victim. If that firearms instructor had done only what was asked of him, that trace evidence would have been lost forever.

Shooting Cases

Lucien C. Haag of Phoenix, Arizona, was technical director and criminalist at the Phoenix police department crime lab for nearly seventeen years. Now he heads Forensic Science Services Inc., and consults all over the world. He has published more than sixty scientific papers, mostly concerned with exterior and terminal ballistics and the effects and behavior of projectiles. He is a past president of the Association of Firearms and Toolmark Examiners.

Haag is particularly interested in the reconstruction of shooting scenes. "My biggest grievance over the years has been the misplaced concern many officers have that the gun lying on the floor at a shooting scene is suddenly going to strike out and injure someone unless there's a mad rush to make it safe and unload it. That same officer has been walking around all day with a loaded gun on his hip, and it hasn't shot anyone unless he fired it intentionally."

In a Phoenix barroom, the man lay dead on the floor, one bullet hole in the body. Another person was standing over him, holding a literally smoking gun from which three shots had been fired. Of course, everyone else in the room had been in the bathroom when the shots were fired. On the scene, the responding officer drew a picture of the cylinder and cartridge locations.

The only witness both living and willing to testify was the suspect. He claimed the deceased was the aggressor who, intoxicated, had come at him with a broken beer bottle. The suspect explained that he had fired a warning shot into the ceiling, and another into the floor, and a third and final shot into the aggressor.

As it happens, bullets were recovered from the ceiling (a Winchester), the floor (a Remington), and the body (a Federal). According to the field officer's diagram, a Winchester case was in cylinder position one, a Remington in two, and a Federal in three. Other mixed unfired brands were in the remaining three. Haag says mixed brands are common in such shootings.

Knowing where the cartridges were in the cylinder could substantiate the defendant's statement. But what if the Winchester bullet had been recovered from the body? The diagram would have shown the subject had fired first at the victim and the other two shots were either wild shots or were fired to set up his self-defense story. If the responding officer had hurriedly opened the revolver and dumped the cylinder's contents into his hand, no one would ever know whether the guy was telling the truth.

"All officers need to understand the variety of firearms evidence that can be important, beyond the simple matching of a fired bullet to the gun that fired it," Haag says. "Given the great variety of ammunition, bullets and propellants used in shootings, there are ways to determine not only who fired a particular shot, but how the shooting occurred—who fired first, from which direction or position, how many shots were fired, in what sequence. Which shot was fired last was critical in that barroom case. Possible issues regarding ricochet or deflection can become a vital factor that doesn't emerge until later.

"Rather than just putting things in envelopes and routing them to the lab with the usual request to match the bullet to the gun, there needs to be much earlier communication between the investigator and the forensic firearms examiner. It takes this dialogue to pinpoint what the issues really are, and to determine how to prioritize analytical procedures," says Haag.

In another case, a man called police and said he had just accidentally shot his wife. Officers found the woman dead from a single gunshot wound to her chest. A Smith & Wesson Model 39 autoloading pistol was found on a nearby dresser. A loaded magazine was later recovered from under the mattress, after the husband told the police where to find it. The husband said that the pistol and magazine were always kept apart, that the magazine was not in the pistol when the accident occurred.

The husband explained that he got the pistol from a nightstand drawer when he heard a noise outside. He didn't think there was a cartridge in the chamber and had started toward the bed to get the magazine, when he must have inadvertently touched the trigger. Hearing his wife cry out, he immediately set the pistol on the dresser and rushed to her aid.

Understanding the mechanism of the suspect gun, an officer would know that the Model 39 has a magazine disconnector. If it were in good working order, it could not fire without a magazine inserted. Suppose blood were found on the top cartridge in the recovered magazine? Preserving that magazine just as it was found and getting blood samples of those involved would be critical. With recent forensic developments, blood traces can be matched with "almost fingerprint specificity" to a person. Suppose the blood traces were found on the second cartridge down in the magazine? The suspect obviously removed the live round from the pistol and put it back into the magazine before he placed it under the mattress and called police.

The careful diagramming of a shooting scene can be critical in determining just how far away the shooter was from the victim at the moment of discharge. The victim's garments can be tested for gunshot residue patterns—if the medics don't throw them away—and then a test of the gun at the distance claimed can produce a gunshot residue pattern that can be compared with the suspect's story.

There's a lot more to firearms evidence than what we see on cop shows on television, and it can involve many things other than the gun itself. When you are the first responder to a crime scene involving guns, you must anticipate the possible questions attorneys might raise to discredit the case. Getting the forensic expert involved early can help. If these questions come as a surprise when you are on the witness stand, it's too late to decide which tests you should have had performed to substantiate your case.

18.2 Counterfeiting

Counterfeiting of currency is one of the oldest crimes in history. With the convenience of modern photography and printing techniques, counterfeiting is again on the rise.

When a citizen is concerned about a bill he has received, the first person he is likely to ask about it is the patrol officer. You should understand what bills are in circulation and how to spot a counterfeit.

There are three types of U.S. paper currency in circulation today. Federal Reserve notes have a green seal and serial number and are in denominations of $1, $2, $5, $10, $20, $50, and $100. U.S. notes have a red seal and serial number and are in denominations of $2, $5, and $100. Silver certificates have a blue seal and number and were in denominations of $1, $5, and $10. Silver certificates, as well as $2 and $5 U.S. notes, are no longer being printed. The $100 bill is the highest denomination now being printed.

The best way to detect a counterfeit bill is to compare it with a genuine bill of the same denomination and series. Look for the red and blue fibers in the paper. Counterfeiters try to mimic these fibers by printing colored lines on the paper.

Compare other features, and look for differences, not similarities. The counterfeit is usually printed by a photomechanical process and is not as sharp as the real thing. It may appear flat, lacking the three-dimensional quality of genuine bills. In the portrait background, those lines form squares. On counterfeits, some squares may be filled in, and delicate lines in the portrait may be broken or missing. The portrait is lifeless and the background is usually too dark. Sawtooth points on the seal are usually uneven, blunt, or broken off. Serial numbers may be off color, improperly spaced or aligned. Border lines that crisscross are not clear and distinct.

Any counterfeit bill you find is contraband, so you must seize it. Then follow the policy of your department.

18.3 Undercover Concerns

Working undercover is a very special assignment only a few officers experience. But every police officer needs to understand that a sign of recognition could be hazardous to a fellow officer's health. If your department is running an undercover operation, every officer on that department needs to know just enough about it to avoid jeopardizing a fellow officer.

What happens if you stumble onto a drug buy by accident? You probably won't recognize an undercover officer, but if you do, *don't.* If he happened to be a classmate at the academy and you say, "Hi, Joe" on the street, he could wind up dead. Put him through the arrest procedure the same as the others to avoid blowing his cover.

One major city department, where headbands are a popular item of attire, set up a code using a particular color headband for each day of the week. In addition to visual codes, some form of silent signal is necessary. But it needs to change frequently; nothing remains secret for long.

18.4 Entrapment

If you, or someone acting for you, convinces an otherwise innocent person to commit a crime and then encourages him to commit it, that person is immune from prosecution for that crime. But giving a person who is already predisposed to commit a crime the opportunity to do it is not entrapment.

Suppose your informer knows that someone has access to heroin but does not sell it. The informer poses as an addict and convinces the person to get some heroin and sell it to him, and he does. That's entrapment because the informer would be considered a government agent. But suppose a certain person is suspected of selling heroin in a certain place. An undercover agent approaches him and asks to buy some "stuff." After taking the usual precautions, the suspect sells him some drugs. This is not entrapment.

However, some Supreme Court justices have asserted that the test for entrapment is based on the behavior of the police and not on the predisposition of the defendant. Under this concept, entrapment may be any improper police action aimed at inducing criminal activity by a person who would otherwise resist the temptation. One court held that any police activity that makes contraband available for purchase is entrapment, even if the purchaser is the one who suggested the sale. Check with your department counsel to learn what constitutes entrapment in your jurisdiction.

19

Dogs in Police Service

You've heard about guard dogs and dogs who sniff out bombs or drugs in seemingly innocent shipments. A police K-9 unit is a team of officer and dog who work patrol and support others. This may involve looking for the felon who fled into the woods or a prison escapee, searching a building for an intruder, or looking for a lost child. An officer with a dog provides capabilities far beyond an officer by himself.

Robert S. Eden, a constable with the Delta, British Columbia, police department, has trained dogs professionally and privately. He's a K-9 cop. One of his experiences shows how the team could virtually see in the dark.

Eden was working a stakeout at a drug drop in a highly visible area with a suspect who was wise to surveillance. There was no way to use manpower to cover the area. Only Eden and his dog were positioned inside the target area. The moonless night provided little light for observation. "Suddenly my dog lifted his head, ears intently forward. Obviously, someone I couldn't see was walking across the site," Eden explained. "The dog's head slowly panned left to right as he focused on the suspect's movements. At this point, backup was called and the apprehension was successfully concluded."

The officer who works with a dog will raise and care for him. Before even considering basic obedience training, the officer must understand how the dog relates to the family and how to read his body language. Then there are training exercises, tracking and area searches, aggression and criminal apprehension, and building searches. Eden's book (see bibliography) gives many useful guidelines.

19.1 The Dog and Your Family

The police service dog is not a pet, but a partner, with an individual personality. After all, a dog is only human. The bond between the man and dog becomes a partnership for life.

Canines have a pack instinct, and the pack has a definite social structure. Your dog will attempt to define his status within your family "pack." The dominate male of his pack is you, especially for a young pup. You establish this by training disciplines. But a young adult male may well try to challenge your standing. The dog will recognize the dominate female, the "mother" of the pack, your wife. He is instinctively protective of the young. I had a collie once who was a better baby-sitter than any teenager we ever hired. It's important to understand this pack instinct because the dog looks to you for commands. He'll obey your wife, but the kids should be only playmates—within reason, of course.

19.2 Dog's Special Talents

The dog is a loving companion. He seeks your approval. He's not a vicious guard or attack dog, but a working "police officer" who is caring and protective until circumstances require his aggression. He's also unique in the talents he can employ.

It's a common misconception that dogs have poor eyesight. Tests have shown they can focus clearly on objects more than 100 yards away. But dogs demand more than a single source of information, just like any good investigator. My dog will recognize me clear across the yard but he still approaches to smell my crotch to confirm the identification.

As Eden's nighttime example shows, it's also believed that dogs have far better night vision than humans. Their eyes contain a higher percentage of rods than ours do. They can detect the slightest movement that we'd never notice.

The animal's keen sense of smell and ability to identify scents specific to an individual are demonstrated by tracking dogs. The dog's nostrils appear as two long tubes in an X-ray but they are full of scroll-like passages lined with millions of receptor cells. The olfactory system of man has about one inch of area, the dog's nearly a yard.

Watch your dog at rest sometime. When he's alert, both ears may be very erect and forward. Sometimes one ear may be forward and one back, or both may be back when he's relaxed. This is sort of a directional antenna system. When both ears are up and forward, he is attentive to a sound in that direction. If one ear keeps moving to another direction, you can be forewarned that someone else is approaching. Dogs hear a higher range of frequencies than humans. Some say the dog has six times the hearing capacity of man.

Your dog "talks" with different kinds of barks, whines, yelps, and growls. A single bark may mean "What's that?" or "Hey, partner, come check this out." A steady, rhythmic barking is a warning of danger—or the approach of the mail carrier. If he barks several times and then is quiet, he's trying to communicate, then stopping to listen. If those barks are combined with a growl, he's detected a threat and he's getting angry. The hackles (hair above his shoulders) may stand up. A deep-throated growl shows anger or warning or perhaps fear. High-pitched yelps are reserved for excitement, playfulness. Crying or whining usually shows concern, fear, loneliness, pain, or injury.

The tail held high shows his dominance. He's exposing scent glands for others of the pack to smell. The tail tucked is submissive, hiding that scent gland. Tail straight out is a ready or danger signal.

Once you learn your dog's body language, the communication potential is surprising.

19.3 Arson Dog

There is another police service dog you may not have heard about yet. Until recently, there was only one in the world, as far as I know. In the previous chapter, we did not talk about the special concerns of arson investigation because this dog lets us explain both in one story.

Mattie is a black Labrador retriever. She came to the Connecticut state police through the Federal Bureau of Alcohol, Tobacco and Firearms (ATF). ATF forensic chemist Richard A. Strobel and dog handler Robert Noll had done a feasibility study, using a mixed-breed dog. With the collaboration of ATF, the New Haven County state's attorney's office, the state police forensic science lab, the Emergency Services Division canine unit, and the Bureau of State Fire Marshal, the Connecticut state police canine unit started an arson accelerant-detection training program.

Using traditional Pavlovian conditioning techniques, Mattie was "imprinted" with accelerant odors—flammable materials used to make a fire

Trooper Jim Butterworth lets Mattie cast about the fire scene to get her bearings and catch the scent of any accelerant that may have been used.

spread quickly. To this day, Mattie is never fed unless she scores a "hit." Of course, this means the handlers work her every day, in training if not in practice, to be sure she receives a proper diet.

I first met Mattie one morning when the unit was called out to a fire. One fire truck was still on the scene. Several firefighters were standing on the sidewalk in front of the burned-out store front as the black station wagon from the Connecticut state police K-9 unit was directed behind the barricades. Troopers Douglas Lancelot and James Butterworth entered the gutted store, listening as the fire marshall pointed out the probable place of origin of the fire. Lancelot suggested Butterworth bring Mattie around to the back entrance. Inside, I positioned myself where I could photograph the dog at work.

Mattie cast around the charred remains of what once was a shoestore. She was getting familiar with the area. Then Jim took her back outside and in again; her nose was working in earnest. This time, she paid close attention to several spots, but moved on until she reached the sill of the door leading to the showroom. She quickly sat and looked up at Butterworth.

"That's her indication of a hit," Lancelot explained.

"You got something, girl?" Butterworth said to Mattie. "Show me."

"She'll signal as soon as she catches scent of an accelerant," Lancelot explained. "But she isn't rewarded until she pinpoints the source."

The firefighters used an axe to lift the tiles. They took a sample of the under-flooring. But Mattie indicated the sample was negative when she checked it in its sample can. Mattie sniffed the area again, and indicated a spot just a few inches away from where the first sample had been taken. The firefighters took another sample that met Mattie's approval.

The fire marshal asked Butterworth to check the rear stairs in the foyer. Mattie found nothing on the stairs leading down, but she signaled a hit on the flight leading up to the second floor. She worked it over until she indicated just one spot near the right edge of one of the rubber treads. The fire marshal cut part of the tread and sealed it in a sample can.

"The big advantage Mattie offers is identifying samples to be taken for laboratory analysis," Lancelot said. "Normally, arson investigators will take many samples and that can be expensive at $150 per test. With Mattie, we might cut that number to a dozen, and she's been right every time."

Arson investigators may spend a week or more at the scene of a major fire sifting for clues. They look for char patterns and other indicators that might lead them to believe an accelerant was used, and where it had been poured. Mattie can find such spots in a day or two. We were in the rubble of the shoestore less than an hour, and Mattie identified a half dozen suspicious spots for sampling. And she frequently finds traces of accelerants in places where investigators would not usually look.

She has other advantages over the detecting instruments used by investigators in the field. While hydrocarbon detectors are sensitive to gasoline components in the parts per million range, laboratory scientists have confirmed that Mattie's sensitivity is even greater. Field instruments give many false positives because they also react to similar compounds that are not used as accelerants.

Mattie has not given a false positive yet. So far, she has been trained to identify paint remover, lacquer thinner, charcoal lighter, paint thinner, kerosene, naptha, acetone, dry gas, heptone, gasoline, no. 2 fuel, diesel fuel, gum turpentine, Heritage camp oil, transmission fluid, octane, and Jet A fuel.

Three handlers share duty with Mattie: Lancelot, Butterworth, and David Barger. Each keeps her for one week, and both handler and dog are on call twenty-four hours a day. She's the first dog I've met lucky enough to have three families.

Mattie became "operational" in September 1986, and she's been winning over doubting fire investigators ever since. The shoestore was the fifty-fifth fire scene she worked. Where investigations had concluded, there had been nine arrests. Two ended in convictions, and the other seven were still pending.

"I can't say enough good things about Mattie. We're very proud of her, and of the program," said Joseph Toscano, arson investigator on the New Haven state's attorney's arson task force. "All the different agencies are working well together."

In late 1986, Mattie was brought to the scene of a fire that leveled a company that manufactured wooden trusses. It was a "complete catastrophe," according to Toscano; nothing was left standing. That's the sort of situation that would take days of sifting to locate evidence. It took only a few minutes for Mattie to find traces of accelerant just inside the door. A disgruntled former employee was arrested shortly thereafter, and pleaded no contest to a charge of first-degree arson.

Early last year, a student set fire to his high school. Police had a suspect and a confession, but needed corroborating evidence. The boy admitted he had used gasoline and had spilled some on his pants. But those pants were home, starting the final spin in his mother's washing machine. Still wet, the clothes were brought to police headquarters and lined up with other garments. Mattie indicated a "positive" on those pants. "Even I didn't know she could do that," Lancelot added.

The black Lab was chosen for this job for a variety of reasons. While a German shepherd, normally associated with police work, could probably do it just as well, the shepherd's nature is more protective of his handler, so in a hazardous environment he might put all his energy into the safety of his partner. Also, following a scent to find a downed bird is the purpose of the Labrador retriever. Having a short, black coat helps too. She's easier to clean after rummaging through the soot and smoke of a fire scene.

As far as we know, Mattie was the first arson dog in the country, perhaps in the world. Inquiries about the program have been received from many states and from foreign countries, too.

I asked why arson dogs hadn't been developed before. "From what I gather, everyone was fearful that a fire scene would be too hazardous for a dog," Lancelot answered. "But it really isn't hazardous. You have to use some common sense when you approach a fire scene—not only for her, but for me. I'm holding the leash. She doesn't go anywhere I won't go."

After nearly two years, there was no indication that working fire scenes had affected her health. Dr. Joseph V. St. Clair of the Meriden Animal Hospital had examined Mattie and agreed, "She's shown absolutely no signs of ill effects. That's a happy, healthy dog—a beautiful dog."

20

Identification

Identification is an area of specialization in law enforcement. It's an area into which you're promoted when you become a technician. But every officer needs to understand how it's done because you provide the input.

You're the first on the scene of a crime. If you understand what can be accomplished with sophisticated identification techniques, you may recognize the need for a crime-scene technician. They don't come out for all the petty incidents you encounter. You may recognize the opportunity to lift a latent print that could be critical in solving the case. You may see the opportunity to have a technician do a composite.

You arrive at a robbery scene. The victim describes the robber. While your partner secures the scene and begins to get the information, you scout the neighborhood and spot someone who fits the description. This aspect of "identification" faces every police officer, whether you're a technician or not. What you do and how you do it can affect the outcome of the case.

20.1 Identification Procedures

Courts look very carefully at your identification of a suspect. First, they will determine if your identification was "unnecessarily suggestive." If, in viewing suspects in person or by photograph, you indicate to the witness that a particular person is the suspect, the court will consider your identification suggestive (*Neil* v. *Biggers*, 409 U.S. 188, 1972.)

The judge will look at the reliability of the identification based on the totality of the circumstances. "Reliability" considers such factors as the opportunity of the witness to see the perpetrator at the time of the crime, how much attention the witness paid at the time, the accuracy of his prior description of the perpetrator, the certainty the witness demonstrates when he is confronted with the criminal, and how much time passed between the crime and when the witness saw the criminal.

Most often, police use photographic identification and the one-on-one show-up.

Photo Lineup   When you show a witness photographs of possible suspects, you can avoid "unnecessary suggestiveness" by following a few simple rules. Never use only a single photo; use at least eight photos of persons with similar characteristics. The photos should not include names, numbers, or dates. Be impartial. Do nothing to lead the witness to pick a particular photo and never let witnesses view photos together. Once the witness has made a selection, have him sign the photo he picked and initial others in the lineup. Then write a report documenting the procedures you used, including identification of other officers or persons who witnessed the procedure. Save the photos so you can assemble the same array later in court.

Showup   There are times when you need to have a witness view a suspect one on one. While this procedure is "inherently suggestive," it may be used under certain circumstances. You collar a suspect immediately after the commission of the crime, and the witness says, "That's the guy." Or the witness is on his deathbed in the hospital and you need a quick identification to detain a guilty party or release an innocent person.

But because a showup is inherently suggestive, you must be particularly careful not to lead the witness. Never allow several witnesses to view the suspect together, or discuss the identification.

You need probable cause or the suspect's consent. If you have probable cause, he can't refuse to take part in the showup.

Lineup   You've seen enough lineups on television to know the same rules of reliability apply when you line up a group of suspects for a witness to view. You should also be aware that a suspect who has been charged has a right to have an attorney present during a lineup. The attorney, however, can't interfere with the procedures; he or she is only there to observe (*United States* v. *Wade,* 388 U.S. 218, 1967.) Any waiver of that right should be in writing.

20.2 Fingerprints

Whenever you pick up an object, materials from your skin are transferred to that object, leaving an image of the skin pattern of your fingertips— a latent print. Since no two people have the same fingerprints, those latent prints can be critical evidence. Because it is so often fragmentary, a latent print seldom provides enough information for a classification and file search. It may not help you identify the perpetrator when you have no suspects. But it often provides enough information for identification purposes when compared with the inked fingerprint of a suspect. Furthermore, some large departments now have the

Lt. Joel Kent of Windsor, Connecticut, demonstrates proper fingerprinting technique. You need to roll the fingers on the card with most systems. **LLOYD BURNHAM.**

Latent examiners Patterson and Krupowicz work with a computer. **L&O.**

capability to search thousands of fingerprints by computer to discover who left a single latent print at the scene of a crime.

Say you're investigating a burglary. The victim arrived home after the movie to find his home in a shambles. Dresser drawers are rifled. Some obviously valuable objects are missing. A back window was broken. Now, if you're part of a big department with a burglary detail, all you may need to do is secure the scene until the technicians arrive. More than likely, it will fall to you to do at least a preliminary investigation and part of it is to determine whether to call your identification technician.

Virtually anything the perpetrator touches will retain a latent print, but you are more likely to find one on such hard, nonporous surfaces as glass, metal, painted or enamel surfaces, polished or varnished hardwood. That's why you need to reconstruct where the burglar broke in—a likely place to find prints—and what he may have touched as he roamed the residence.

Sometimes holding your flashlight obliquely to the surface will reveal the presence of a latent print. When you find one, protect it, of course, but try to find out if it was left by a member of the household or the burglar. If there are a lot of likely prospects, the crime-scene technician will dust them all. He'll also fingerprint everyone on the scene to compare with any latents found, to eliminate those that aren't evidence.

A latent print is developed by dusting it with any of a number of special powders. Black, gray, and white powders provide a contrast with the background. The powder sticks to the moisture in the print and you can then lift the image with a piece of transparent tape. Latent prints on paper, cloth, and other porous material can be developed chemically.

It is sound practice to photograph a latent print first. Suppose the print smudges when lifted. Suppose the defense claims the image was altered. It's easy enough to photograph latents in place with a special fingerprint camera. It provides its own oblique light source, uses fixed focus to give an actual-size photo, and a frame on the front positions it precisely. When you shoot the picture, don't forget to put a label where it will be photographed at the same time. On this label, write an identifying number or letter, victim's name, crime-scene address, date and hour photo was taken, case number, and a description of the article or surface on which the print was found.

There are new techniques to developing latent prints on objects where powders would fail. An aquarium, the kind you put your kid's fish in, is used to hold the object. You break a pouch of Super Glue, drop it inside, and cover the aquarium. The vapors from the glue react with the print and develop it.

20.3 Photography

The camera can tell much more with a picture than you can with words. When you describe a scene, each listener visualizes it in terms of his own experience. When you can show a photograph, the viewer doesn't have to visualize. Photography is an important part of identification and investigation.

Police photography has specific requirements. Any photograph you take must meet certain tests to be admissible in court. Among legal precedents are the relevance of the object pictured to the point at issue, the impartiality of the image, and its accuracy in representation. Trial judges have suppressed photos of particularly grisly and gory scenes, or scenes that are distorted or poorly exposed.

It's common to include in the photograph labels and markers identifying the scene or giving a perspective of size. Make careful and detailed notes so you can identify the photo by case number, subject, location, date and time, light source, distance from camera to subject, height of camera above ground, type of camera and lens, exposure, film speed, name of photographer and witness.

20.4 Composites

A composite is a graphic representation of a person's description developed either with transparent films of facial characteristics or by computer using computer drawings or photographic components. The kits used by many police departments contain several hundred transparent films. Each film shows a single facial feature and the films are laid on top of each other to build a composite. With computers, the composite is built in much the same way but with computer images on a screen.

Most police officers don't really understand the psychology of developing a composite likeness from a description. If you think that a composite likeness is supposed to give you a "photographic" image of the perpetrator, you're wrong. "The composite doesn't tell you who the culprit is," says Identi-Kit instructor Frank Mauriello of Smith & Wesson. "It tells you who he isn't." Mauriello is "dean" of the Identi-Kit training program, and some of his war stories can exercise your imagination.

Frank checked into a hotel in a small Northeastern town where he was to conduct a class. The hotel had been held up the week before. But no one thought of getting a composite because the robber wore a stocking mask, which distorts a person's facial features.

Frank seized the opportunity to prove a point. He questioned the clerk, who had a general idea of age, height, build, skin tone, and major features (the robber had a moustache) but could not describe the man who robbed him. Victims suffer tunnel vision; they see only the gun or knife. Perhaps the horror of the situation hangs a curtain over the unpleasant memory.

Eyewitness accounts are notoriously unreliable, but the details are there. What the eye sees, the mind "photographs." The witness may be reluctant or unable to remember details of a culprit's description, but by using what the witness can describe, a skilled operator can develop a likeness.

Frank put the clerk at ease. He interviewed him in the hotel lobby rather than at the police station. He discussed general impressions, then put together several films (transparencies of facial features) to show the clerk a starting point. The clerk could not describe any specific feature, but he did get a feeling of what was wrong with the image. Frank swapped films to accommodate those feelings. Each time the clerk looked at the image, he felt something else was wrong. The more he looked, the more he recalled. More changes were made.

When the clerk thought the composite was as close as he could get, Frank showed it to the investigating officer. The officer raised his eyebrows and exclaimed, "Why, that's Joe Smith!" (name changed to protect the guilty). The suspect was brought in and quickly confessed.

The secret to developing a composite is stimulating the witness's memory. The hotel clerk remembered one tiny detail, the moustache mashed under the stocking mask. Then he remembered another. Recalling one memory makes the next one easier. Piece by piece, you can develop a composite of features that the witness would never have remembered without the programmed interview. You might develop a likeness that comes so close as to eliminate all the suspects but one, as Frank found with the hotel robber, but that's not usual. It usually lets you zero in on the most likely few, and that's really the purpose of the exercise.

Then, if your mug file is set up on the IDMO system, you can pull mugs that match the composite and eliminate all but a manageable number of possibles. In our hotel-robbery example, these mugs were in the officer's memory and the composite triggered a match.

The IDMO system is simply a classification of mug photos according to age group, race, and hair color. Once a composite is developed, you can easily pull the

With an Identi-Kit, the investigator can develop a likeness of a suspect in the home of the witness.

The computer can develop a composite likeness, store the data, compare your composite with others in file, and show them to you. You just might find a match.

mugs that fit the general description. In our operator certification class, Frank described a suspect from among a group of photos. Each student officer developed a composite as Frank further refined his description. Then each student had to pick out the photo that matched his composite. We all found the correct mug shot.

Another advantage that composite kits offer is speed. Once the composite is completed, you can transmit a series of letters, numbers, and slash marks on your teletype or telecommunications system that enable any other department with a similar kit to reconstruct the same likeness.

In another case, the Identi-Kit operator was one of the early responders to the scene. He immediately developed a composite and flashed the code on the statewide teletype net. In another town, some fifty miles away, the composite triggered a police officer's memory. They were waiting for the holdup man as he pulled into his driveway.

I live in a different town than the one I police. One night I heard the local dispatcher tell a detective that no composite kit was available. I quickly phoned in: "Mine's available." The detective called back and invited me to the scene.

A young man had broken through the screen door of the elderly man's residence, then grabbed the homeowner from behind and held a sharp object to his throat. The burglar marched the old man through the house, finding money in the sugar bowl and dresser drawer, then took the man out to the garage and tied him up. It was dark. The elderly man never caught more than a fleeting glimpse of the culprit.

Following Frank's teachings, I explained, "Let's just develop an image of how such a person of that height and build might look." Then we went through changes, each time getting closer to the victim's memory. After nearly an hour he said, "That's pretty close, but remember I didn't get a good look at him." Copies of the composite were distributed to patrol officers and the perpetrator was identified.

Hugh McDonald of the Los Angeles police department, who developed the Identi-Kit concept, once tried an experiment that stretches credibility to the limit. A woman had been raped and murdered in her home by an assailant who broke in through a bedroom window. There were no witnesses. Working strictly from physical evidence—the length of a footprint, height of the window sill—McDonald developed a composite and filed it away. Much later, a rapist convicted of a different crime also confessed to the one in McDonald's experiment. McDonald got the man's mug shot and compared it with his no-witness composite—Frank Mauriello says it was 60 percent accurate. This obviously isn't evidence but it shows what a skilled operator can do with just a little bit of information.

A composite should always be developed, even if the witness cannot give you a description. By probing the witness's subconscious mind, you can develop a much better likeness than you'd think. And who knows how many cases have been closed because someone recognized the composite published in the local newspaper?

20.5 Computer Identification

The days of spending hours leafing through mug books are numbered. How'd you like to have a computer cull through thousands of mug shots in seconds and display only those that meet designated descriptive criteria? Or develop a composite likeness from an interview with a witness; then store that image and case information on a hard disk? And then be able to search past cases for similar composites when you put in a new suspect?

All these things are possible with technology that exists today. A number of computer systems directly concerned with identification are already on the market today.

Doing an Identi-Kit composite usually takes me most of an hour interviewing the witness. Part of that time is spent thumbing through the transparent films portraying the various physical characteristics. Then you have to file them back in numerical sequence when you're finished, so you can find them the next time you use the kit. With a computer, you can do essentially the same process but the machine holds hundreds more selections of components and finds them far faster than a person ever could.

Mug files can be converted from your old photographs or created from new images read with a video camera. Corrolary data is added by keyboard. Then you can produce a photo line-up, wanted sheet, or other form that includes the subject's photo.

Three Computer ID Systems

ComPHOTOfit   With a software program called comPHOTOfit from Axiom Research Corporation, you can use your familiar interview technique and build the composite image on a video screen. The component parts—forehead, eyes, nose, mouth, and chin—are derived from actual photographs, mug shots, or from live people through a video camera. Then you can add moustaches, beards, eyeglasses, and headgear. The program comes with a standard data base but you can expand it with your own mug files. This way you can be sure that components characteristic of your local population are available to build likenesses. You can have a maximum of 999 entries in each component. Once the composite is the best the witness can make it, the image is digitized, coded, and stored along with whatever descriptive text you want to add.

The comPHOTOfit software has two main parts. The first creates the composite from the data base, using built-in software "tools" that let you customize the image however you want. The second puts associated case information into a user-defined area that is saved with the image in the database.

The image generated is virtually photo quality, after you blend out the section lines between the component parts or "paint" in moles and scars. Images are really black and white, but the software provides a pseudo-color function that closely approximates flesh tones. You can lighten or darken the tone overall or "paint" specific areas.

An image index function finds and displays the components that most closely match the description characteristics you type in. If your technique is to let the witness pick the component parts, you can show him a group to pick from. Or you can use the index yourself to build an interim composite for the witness to correct. With rapid scan, you can look at many variations of any one component.

This software doesn't support communications, but it operates on an IBM-compatible system. Using your own modem program, you can transmit a file of the image and text data by phone in a matter of seconds to another agency that also has a comPHOTOfit system.

Here's how it might work. You've got a preliminary composite, but suppose the suspect's nose is a bit off center. You can capture a portion of the face by outlining it with the "mouse" and move it wherever you want it. So you outline the nose, and move it. If the hairline isn't quite right, just use a "paintbrush" to erase part of the hair or add to another area. Put glasses on the image. But he wore them down on his nose, the witness says. Just move them.

The screen is split into two image areas. The one on the right is the working image where you create the composite. When it gets close to a good likeness but the witness wants to try something else, you can save it to the facsimile image screen. It's on this screen that imaging enhancing is done.

Then the witness frustrates your efforts by saying, "We were closer before." Rather than reshuffling the films in a traditional composite kit, just touch a key and retrieve the earlier version.

The system includes a search routine that enables you to find all other images in the data base using the same component numbers. This might tie your suspect into a previous case in which he was identified.

Edicon   Handling massive mug files and doing acceptable photo lineups can be a monumental task. But now there's the Edicon Mug Identification System. Images are input into the system by video camera, either by copying mug shots or taking a live picture. The image is linked with text data or graphics and is displayed on the screen.

"The image quality is exceptional," said John Doyle of Edicon. "This system is the first to produce images using IBM's enhanced graphics adapter display standard. It has been installed here at the Metropolitan Toronto Police."

Doyle opened a search routine and entered a last name. The screen displayed all the subjects with that name. Putting the cursor on the name, he retrieved the image in under three seconds.

But what if the witness doesn't know the name of the suspect he saw? If descriptive characteristics are entered, the system will retrieve all who match that description. Then you can reject or save the most likely mugs and produce a photo lineup. Once the witness identifies the suspect, you can isolate the individual and bring up associated information with the touch of a key. The text information can be printed out, and the mug shot can be printed using a photographic or color thermal printer.

The system can also print a booking sheet including physical description and the mug shot on a plain piece of paper. When you capture the subject's image, the system can use your departmental forms for entering text data. This eases the transition from paper and film. In a correctional facility, having a photo is important when it comes time to release the proper prisoner.

The Edicon system captures images with a video camera, either from your old mug file or directly from the live suspect. The image is digitized and stored on a hard disk along with the suspect's personal descriptors, criminal record, and fingerprint classification—and all this information can be displayed together on one screen.

The system combines standard components, including the video camera, an IBM PC, and color video monitor, that Edicon integrates with its proprietary hardware and software. As your needs grow, it can be networked with additional stations, all sharing one central data base. Access can be limited according to the needs of the substation. Using standard communications techniques, you can interact with another Edicon system over telephone lines.

The capacity of the system can be whatever you need. A 30 megabyte Winchester drive will store 3,300 images, a 250 megabyte drive will hold 27,700. Or you could go to optical drives to run your capacity up to more than 20 million. Price depends on individual requirements for hardware and customized software. A basic system capable of capturing and displaying color images, graphics, and text ran about $35,000 in 1987.

Instant Image   Using a different technology is the Instant Image Lineup from Royal Recovery Systems. Rather than digitizing images and storing them on a hard disk, photos are captured by a video camera and stored on a video disk in a video player-recorder. "This way, we can store 24,000 color images on one $100 disk," says Dr. Elliot Packer, president of the company. "And you can stack playback units to handle whatever volume you need."

Instant Image bypasses the digital steps by storing the analog signal directly on disk in a Panasonic TQ2026F videodisk machine. The recorder-player can be attached to your IBM-AT–compatible computer. Then you take or retrieve pictures by giving commands to the recorder through the computer's communications port or by using the recorder's front panel controls. Bypassing the digital steps lets the system record a picture in less than half a second. Retrieval is just as fast.

When a suspect is processed, the officer has an on-screen menu for entering name, address, Social Security number, and an elaborate physical description. The image is captured by video camera, and all is stored on the video disk with associated identifying key words and descriptive text. The text shows up on your computer screen while the photo appears on the color monitor. The system includes an unsolved-crimes data base. When you arrest someone who fits the description of the perpetrator of an unsolved crime, the system will pop it up and let you know.

A custom-designed pad lets even an illiterate five-year-old scroll through hundreds of photos that match the physical description. Images can be locked in and printed out on the spot for identification. And it prints an audit trail for use in court. "This is the only system that has actually gone through a jury trial as the primary means of identification," Dr. Packer added. "We had a lot of help from district attorneys in designing the system in the first place."

He made a point of explaining that surveillance tapes and tapes from bank robberies may also be the source of an image that can be entered into the system to generate a meaningful "wanted" photo. "We're also networking the system so a number of smaller towns can merge to work with one central system," Packer said.

Visatech   A shortcoming of composite kits is that it takes a couple of days of training and continual practice to be proficient with them. With a computer, once you read the instruction manual, you're ready to go. The program is in the computer. You just follow the prompts to complete a sketch.

Visatech Compusketch, developed with the help of a police artist, can produce 85,000 types of eyes and 14,000 different noses, rather than just the few hundred you have in a film kit. Don Sumner, president of Visatech, first showed me the system in 1986. It was originally designed to take advantage of the Macintosh's graphics capabilities. More recently, I talked with Steve Williams, an engineer who helped develop the system. "To the Macintosh version of the program, we've added a lot more detail," he explained. "You can now add forehead wrinkles, various kinds of blemishes and scars, and you can rotate those scars."

A major difference from other systems, according to Williams, is that the witness isn't shown a lot of images that tends to confuse him. When you develop a Compusketch image, an interview is part of the program, designed to reinforce the witness's memory, draw out detail, and avoid "leading" the witness or suggesting answers.

Tom Macris, a police officer for twenty-one years, is a sketch artist with the San Jose, California, police department. He has composed more than 4,000 sketches of suspects from witness descriptions over the past decade. His well-honed interview techniques are built into the program. "Not only does the interview program aid the witness," Macris says, "it relieves the operator of remembering all those details and perhaps overlooking something."

What Does the Future Hold?   You haven't heard the end of it yet.

Every cell in your body carries your personal genetic code (DNA); every one is unique, except for identical twins. It is now possible to literally take a "genetic fingerprint" and match it to an evidence sample. There have been a number of cases where DNA analysis pinpointed a perpetrator from among a group of suspects. In a Connecticut case recently, a prison inmate convicted of earlier rapes was charged with the burglary and rape of an elderly woman based solely on genetic matching of his blood with semen left on the victim.

Technicians can use a retina-scanning device made by EyeDentify of Portland, Oregon, and store in a computer the unique pattern of blood vessels in the back of your eye. Scanning just one eye makes chances of misidentification one in a million; scanning both eyes reduces the odds to one in a trillion.

"Identification by retinal pattern will never replace fingerprints," said Sheriff Bill Belt of Marksville, Louisiana. "People don't leave 'eyeprints' at a crime scene. But for identification of prisoners, it's a useful tool." Sheriff Belt's Avoyelles Parish jail uses the retina scanner and a data-base management system devised by Thomas W. Tubre of Data Security Systems Inc., Bunkie, Louisiana. It was the only such combined system in the United States, according to Tubre, as this was written.

One big advantage of computers is their ability to communicate. With words, it's easy. If you store a text file in pure ASCII format, it doesn't matter which word processor you use; all can read it. But if you store a WordStar file in document mode, printer control codes are embedded and only another WordStar user can read it, unless it is processed first to zero the eighth bit. If you have a data base created with one program, it could look like gibberish if you try to read it with a different data base program—if it can read it at all.

The computer identification systems described here are so new at this writing we can't say what compatibility there may or may not be among them in the future. But wouldn't it be great if a data file image of a wanted person could be transmitted by phone to other departments, along with fingerprints, genetic code, and retinal pattern? The mug systems described can share data with another of the same system. But there are a variety of systems. Developing a compatibility standard or a translation system to interface one system with another is definitely needed.

21

Going to Court

When you appear in court, you are completing the police process. You are probably the prosecutor's principal witness. It was your effort that precipitated the case. You are the one who did the ground work, and the legwork. But the whole case could depend on your preparation and your conduct in court.

Impartiality is important in every aspect of your job but especially so in court. If you let the case become a personal matter, it will show. It will influence the judge or jury in a way that's not favorable to you. Remember, the defendant violated the state's law, not yours. He offended the rights of society, not yours. The verdict is a victory or loss for the people of the state, not your personal triumph or defeat. Of course you feel satisfaction when your efforts achieve what you think they should, and you feel disappointment when they don't—but don't let it get to you.

You are a big influence on the outcome of the case. Your conduct, appearance, demeanor, impartiality, and convincing testimony can determine a decision even before the jury leaves the courtroom. But to get there in the first place, you have to prepare the case. After all, you, not the prosecutor, were there when it happened.

21.1 Case Preparation

Your preparation of a case for court really starts when you begin to investigate a crime. How you develop and substantiate information will be subject to review in a trial. You really write reports to inform a prosecutor of the facts, evidence, elements of the crime, its seriousness, and which witnesses can testify to what evidence. Knowing what essentials should be included in your report helps you to investigate properly at the scene to be sure you have the information you need. And that's the first step in case preparation. Reread the chapter on report writing.

To refresh your memory, your report must contain facts, not assumptions, conclusions, or opinions. It should list names and addresses of all witnesses, a summary of oral statements, and any evidence that may be excluded. You don't want to give the prosecutor any surprises. Knowing about it lets the prosecutor deal with it.

Your report should also include background information on the defendant, victim, and witnesses.

Statements establish a person's recollection of the incident and lock him or her into a particular version of the story. You take statements from a suspect as soon as you can. You take statements from witnesses at their convenience. Sometimes it's better if they have a chance to think a bit about what they saw, as long as there's no chance of discussing it with others. That may taint their memory.

In a major case, it's a good idea to work with the prosecutor even at this early stage to be sure the case is prepared properly.

21.2 The Trial

Under the Sixth Amendment to the U.S. Constitution, every criminal defendant has the right to "a speedy and public trial, by an impartial jury." The trial really is a fact-finding process, operating under strict and specific procedural rules that, theoretically, guarantee a fair trial. In a criminal case, the prosecution—you're part of it—must prove guilt "beyond a reasonable doubt" or else the defendant must be acquitted.

The trial may or may not involve a jury. While the right to trial by a jury is spelled out in the Constitution, a defendant may waive this right and elect to have a nonjury trial in cases where the facts are in agreement and only the law needs clarifying. If a case is emotional and confusing, the choice is usually for a jury trial. If defense counsel can confuse the jury and avoid a unanimous decision beyond a reasonable doubt, there's a good chance for success—from the defense point of view.

The trial process can be broken down into six parts. In a jury trial, the jury will be selected first, then each side makes opening statements, the prosecutor presents his case, the defense presents its case, then each side makes closing statements, and, finally, the judge or jury renders a decision.

You will most likely be a witness for the prosecution. The prosecutor will put you on the stand, and question you under *direct examination*. The purpose here is to bring out the facts of the case that are favorable to the state. However, you must be truthful and totally honest. If you avoid acknowledging a fact that is favorable to the defense, you can bet it will come out later and cast a shadow of doubt on all your testimony.

After the prosecutor finishes with you, the defense counsel has a shot at *cross examination*, and suddenly you're under the microscope. Defense will have read your departmental reports and if anything in your testimony differs from or adds to the facts contained in those reports, you'll be grilled.

You should anticipate cross examination. Time and distance are common questions. How long was the defendant under your observation? How far away when you first saw the defendant? How long did it take you to form an opinion of sobriety? How far did the defendant walk in the field sobriety test?

If any new information is brought out in cross examination, the prosecutor may *redirect* questions to you for clarification. And any time the prosecutor has a turn, the defense gets a subsequent turn.

The defense follows the same pattern in presenting its case, but remember, the defense must show only that there is doubt about the defendant's guilt. After the defense concludes its presentation, the prosecutor may attack any new evidence through *rebuttal*. By the same token, the defense may examine these witnesses or introduce new evidence in the process of *surrebuttal*.

21.3 Courtroom Conduct

Arrive early enough that you have a chance to relax, reflect on the case, and be available for last-minute discussions with the prosecutor. Depending on your department's policy, it may be advisable to wear a business suit rather than a uniform. The defendant will look much more presentable when he appears in court than when you arrested him. He may even bring his kids to show that he's a "family man." A court case can be a battle of appearances as much as an analysis of facts.

You must consider yourself "under observation" by judge or jurors whenever you are within three blocks of the courthouse, certainly while you're in the corridors or at a restaurant during recess. Jurors consider themselves as junior-grade Perry Masons, you know. Avoid horseplay, hilarity, recounting "them" (public) and "us" (cops) war stories. In short, conduct yourself in a confident and businesslike manner. Be particularly careful of conversations with attorneys. Something said in jest might unethically be used in cross examination to indicate animosity toward the defendant or weakness in the government's case.

When opposing witnesses are testifying, don't let your facial expression or body language indicate your disbelief. Some judges won't hesitate to reprimand an offending officer in the presence of the jury.

Presenting Testimony
In the witness chair, sit up straight. Look the attorney in the eye as if you care about what she's asking. Keep cool. Think. Speak slowly and distinctly, using proper English without cop jargon. Use plenty of "sirs" or "ma'ams" when answering the defense attorney. If you leer or smirk at the defendant, the judge or jury will see it.

Obviously, you must be impeccably truthful without exaggerating or understating the facts. Make sure you hear and understand the question. Under cross examination, don't shoot "panic glances" at the prosecutor, looking for help. If facts are favorable to the defendant, you must reveal them if you are asked. Yes, you can refer to notes. But anything you introduce in court can be held in evidence so bring only the notes you need, rather than your whole book of field notes.

Defending Against Attack
A defense attorney may speak quickly or fade out toward the end of his question to confuse you. He wants to make you appear uncertain or indecisive. Keep your own pace in speaking. If you don't understand the question, ask for a repeat or a rephrasing. Then answer the question. But don't volunteer information not required in your answer.

Don't rush into an answer. Let the attorney finish the question, then wait for a few seconds. If you need time to consider your reply, you can repeat the question. But be careful about doing that too frequently; it gives the impression that you're stalling for time while you concoct an answer. Don't be drawn into exaggerations; a drinking-driver defendant who was unsteady on his feet wasn't necessarily "falling down drunk." If you make a mistake, correct it before defense counsel points out your inaccurate answer.

There's a big difference between not remembering something and remembering that something didn't happen. The defense attorney may ask, "Do you remember the color of the defendant's tie that night?" You don't remember. But "Do you remember telling the defendant that the only reason he was arrested was because he was a wiseguy?" You never said that. Don't say, "I don't remember" when you mean to say, "That never happened."

Another trap is defense's sarcastic statement, "Of course, you've discussed this case before, haven't you, Officer?" Your answer is, "Yes, sir, I have." Proper preparation is acceptable and expected. "Rehearsal" is not. You may think the question refers to impropriety on your part but its phrasing really includes proper preparation.

Never offer an opinion unless you are asked. Then a short legal discussion may ensue between the prosecutor and the defense counsel. If the judge allows the answer, give it. A defense counsel may ask a sarcastic question, hoping to elicit a sarcastic answer. He may try to anger you in order to sway members of a jury. If you reply in kind, you prove his point. If you answer calmly and courteously, you gain the advantage.

Civil Actions

There is always the possibility of civil suit against an officer; nowadays it's usually for "excessive force," but it could be anything. If your pursuit caused damage or injury, an attorney will try to prove negligence or impropriety on your part. At times like that, it may be important to have your own attorney, rather than depending on your department or city attorney. Remember, his client is your employer, and it just could be in his client's best interest to throw you to the wolves.

Remember that your reports should include every fact justifying your use of force, what you and the defendant said and did. Sooner or later, a judge, jury, or Internal Affairs must decide whether force was used legitimately in self-defense or to preserve order, or was used maliciously and sadistically to cause pain and punishment to the offender. Now you wish you had demonstrated before witnesses your concern for the defendant's well-being. Unless the need for medical attention is obvious, ask, "Are you injured? Do you want medical attention?" Ask even if you know it will be refused. And include it in your report.

Civil suits are a threat, but they aren't always decided in favor of the "wronged" party. A Norwich, Connecticut, policeman who was sued for police brutality was awarded $500 by a federal judge. Officer Kevin McKeon and his partner Andrew Bartha were sued by a woman who claimed she was deprived of her civil rights when the officers broke her arm while subduing her.

McKeon filed a counterclaim saying he was the victim because the woman bit him and struck him several times during the incident. After a two-day trial in November 1986, U.S. District Judge Jose A. Cabranes ruled in favor of the police officer. "The judge took the opportunity to send a message to all law enforcement officers in Connecticut that they are no longer sitting ducks in civil rights actions," McKeon's attorney said.

22

Traffic

Traffic control and enforcement are fundamental to the police function. In a major metropolitan city, there may be a separate traffic division, but officers on the beat or motor patrol are still expected to enforce traffic laws.

When you consider that there are 171,653,675 vehicles in the United States and 3,861,934 miles of public roads, and that motor vehicles have killed more Americans than all the wars in which the United States participated, you can appreciate the importance of this concern. And despite millions of dollars spent in highway design and construction, the only force operating in the front lines of this motor mayhem is the police.

Tragedy on the street is so commonplace that even fatal accidents may not make the evening news. Yet, they can confront you with sights that test the strength of your stomach. While it may seem mundane, effective motor vehicle law enforcement can potentially save more lives than anything else you do.

22.1 Motor Vehicle Laws

There are "models" for traffic laws, such as the Uniform Vehicle Code published by the National Committee on Uniform State Traffic Laws and Ordinances, and a commonality among the traffic laws of all jurisdictions, but they can differ in detail. It's up to you to learn the specific laws that apply in your jurisdiction. My purpose here is to help you understand them. With that thought in mind, let's take a look at traffic codes.

All traffic codes are intended to promote the safe movement of traffic. Common sense is the basis for traffic laws. Essentially, these laws evolved in response to problems police officers identified in the past, and they change in response to deficiencies police officers discover during their daily routine. It may be a long legislative process to effect change, but police officers have more influence than they realize.

Perhaps traffic enforcement doesn't fit your image of a macho crime fighter. Most of what you deal with are infractions, punishable by fine rather than a term behind bars. Most aren't "crimes," but they are "law." They are your responsibility.

22.2 Rules of the Road

Of course, some vehicle statutes are crimes, particularly auto theft or drunken driving. But your involvement in enhancing public safety and preventing accidents most often concerns the category of *moving violations*. Whatever the wording of your state's code, you can be sure a number of moving violations are covered.

1. Failure to keep to the right.   As a rule, all traffic codes require driving to the right and delineate the exceptions: passing to the left, vehicle signaling a left turn, one-way street. But suppose you're passing a car traveling in the center lane of a three-lane roadway? It would be unsafe to cross two lanes just to pass on his left, so that's one of the exceptions.

2. Making an improper turn.   "Cutting corners," swinging wide unnecessarily, turning right or left from anywhere other than the rightmost or leftmost lane, most U-turns—all these are violations. If you cut a left turn too tight, a car turning right out of the street you're turning into doesn't have room. A driver swung way right to make a tight U-turn to the left, but the car behind didn't know that. The driver of the front car was at fault in that accident investigation.

3. Failing to obey a traffic signal.   Too many young and impatient drivers think an amber light means "speed up before it turns red." They forget that it really means "prepare to stop." The exception is when otherwise directed by a police officer.

4. Failing to obey a stop sign.   There's more to this *subject of stopping* than you might think. Stop at a stop sign, obviously, but where exactly? A limit line may be marked. At a marked pedestrian crossing, it's the near side line for approaching vehicles. If unmarked, it's the line extended from the edge of the crossroad.

5. Failing to obey the signal of an officer.   This law puts teeth in your traffic direction.

6. Failing to signal when stopping or turning.   The purpose of these laws is to require drivers to make their intentions known to others. But some motorists seem to think that signaling gives them some sort of right of way. It doesn't.

7. Failing to yield right of way.   Motor vehicle codes use many words to define all the conditions and circumstances that determine which vehicle has the right of way. You have to study your state's code anyway, so we won't spend the space to repeat them here. But you'll see that they boil down to common sense. The vehicle having right of way usually is the one on a thoroughfare, the one on the right, or the one that got there first. When New Hampshire found drivers racing each other to be first at the intersection, they changed the law. Now it's only the one on the right. A favorite question of one of my instructors was, "If a responding ambulance, fire truck, police car, and mail truck arrive at an intersection at the same time, which has the right of way?" Technically, it's the mail truck. Under the U.S. Constitution, nothing can impede the U.S. mail. Practically, the mail carrier gives way.

8. Operating a vehicle in a reckless manner.   Statutes vary in their definition of "reckless driving." Some are quite broad: "operation of a vehicle on any highway in willful and wanton disregard for the safety of persons or property." In my state, a driver who proceeds through a marked crosswalk *containing pedestrians* is driving recklessly. "Recklessness" is more than mere negligence. It is a failure to perform because of carelessness or oversight, or failure to act in a manner common to a "reasonable and prudent" driver.

9. Speeding.   In addition to exceeding posted speed limits, speeding statutes include such phrases as "reasonable speed," "safe speed," and "road conditions." A highway with a posted fifty-five mph limit could be unsafe at any speed above forty in a snowstorm, for example. Heavy pedestrian traffic could make driving at the posted speed limit unsafe. Study your state's laws to see just how such statutes are worded. Driving too slow can also create a hazard, and can constitute a violation.

10. Driving while intoxicated.   This is another area that differs widely from state to state. The trend is to use the roadside check as probable cause for administering a breath, blood, or urine analysis. Anything more than .10 parts per million blood alcohol is considered too drunk to drive. My state has an implied consent law. If drivers refuse the test, their license is automatically suspended for a time.

11. Operating a vehicle with defective brakes or other equipment.   Brakes, windshield wipers, horn, lights, and tires can all be considered safety equipment on a motor vehicle. You can be sure your state statutes define just what is required and what is prohibited. I enjoy enforcing these statutes because it gives me an opportunity to get an unsafe vehicle off the road, and it's an action usually requiring correction rather than a court appearance. It also gives you probable cause for a stop, which may lead to the discovery of a more serious crime. Many's the burglar who met his demise because his car had a burned-out tail light.

The conduct of pedestrians is usually covered in the traffic code. Such provision came into law recently enough that there is surprising uniformity across the country. There is also surprising uniformity of ignorance. As you study these statutes, you'll be impressed with the fact that what they really demand is *courtesy*.

Leaving the scene of an accident is one violation the public will help you investigate. Evading responsibility, as my state calls it, carries a social stigma because of the possible consequences. If there is personal injury, the hit-and-run driver may contribute to the victim's death by leaving him unattended, without first aid, without even calling for help.

Your traffic code is bound to require anyone involved in an accident to stop, identify himself, and render aid. But at what point does leaving become "evading?" Is one who leaves the scene to go call for help an evader? And what if the driver doesn't even know he was involved in an accident? The rear of a tractor-trailer hit the front of a small car. A passenger getting off the rear door of a bus caught her arm and was dragged. In both cases, the operator had no inkling of anything wrong.

22.3 Traffic Enforcement

The police function is only the beginning of traffic enforcement. Come to think of it, it's only the beginning of *all* law enforcement. You locate and apprehend violators. You prepare the evidence against them. But it's still up to the court to determine guilt and set a penalty. Then if the court or statutory programs demand a suspension of license, the licensing authority is the third part of this traffic-enforcement triumvirate.

The Point System   The point system, used in some states, allocates values to each conviction for a serious moving violation. If drivers accumulate a certain number of points within a set time limit, they could lose their license. In some states it's automatic. In others, the offender gets a hearing. But it's the licensing authority who does the accounting and ultimate revocation.

Suspension Check   Whenever you stop a motorist, you call in your location and the plate number. You ask for his license and registration. In my state, a driver *must* show his license. That's the one time you can force an offender to identify himself. Then it should be standard procedure to run a suspension check. If his license was suspended but he hasn't surrendered it, you have him for operating under suspension. If he says he left it at home, you can call in for a license check. If that comes back negative, you have him for operating without a license.

The point of all this is to keep unsafe drivers off the road. Former inspector Paul Weston tells of one vehicle homicide case in New York City that involved not only drunk driving but an operator whose license had been suspended for a previous vehicle homicide. It may be that the driver evading responsibility is already operating under suspension and doesn't want to get caught again.

> ## HOT TIPS FROM OLD HANDS
>
> **Checking ID.** If you're presented with an ID card that you don't think really belongs to the presenter (the ID is stolen or "borrowed"), get the presenter to sign his name on your notepad, and then compare the signatures. Information on the ID card can be memorized, but signature forgery is much harder. The signature in the notepad can also be used as evidence of intent to deceive if you pursue a criminal charge involving the false ID.
>
> *Officer Tim Dees*
> *Reno, Nevada,*
> *police department*

You can argue that "driver control" programs are really run by the licensing authority. That's true. But the licensing authority can act only on the basis of your actions. You are the key to a successful program, and it merits your assistance to make it work.

Fraudulent Licenses

There's another consideration when you ask for a driver's license. Because they are a popular form of identification when cashing checks or proving one is old enough to order a drink, driver licenses are a prime target for forgery. Kids have been known to split the laminate of a legitimate license to change the birthdate. Fraudulent licenses have been manufactured. It's much more difficult with the modern photo licenses, but we've never eradicated the mosquito either.

Fraudulent licenses can be a big business. New York City once assigned several youthful officers to go undercover and infiltrate known gangs of hotrodders. They told their story of too many speeding tickets and subsequent suspensions. Within two weeks, they found four men who trafficked in forged licenses. One of those

> ## HOT TIPS FROM OLD HANDS
>
> **Matching numbers.** Since NCIC will hit on soundalike names but only exact matches of numbers, most crooks will change one number in their date of birth or Social Security number in falsifying their identity. If you suspect this, try adding or subtracting one from the Social Security number or year of birth. The last digit is the one most often changed, and usually upward. Juveniles will decrease their year of birth, for obvious reasons.
>
> *Officer Tim Dees*
> *Reno, Nevada,*
> *police department*

defendants fingered another group specializing in "stand-ins" for non–English-speaking applicants. If there is anything suspicious about the license the motorist hands you, check it out.

Persons likely to have forged or altered licenses are the chronic offenders whose license has been suspended, high-point violators who may use a forgery to keep their rural license clean, and under-age youths who are either too young to get a license or can't afford the high insurance premiums. Ask for the date of birth and full name and address. An operator with a forgery may not remember the fictitious address; some even forget the name. An operator who borrowed a friend's license may not remember his friend's date of birth.

22.4 Integrity of Enforcement

Corruption in law enforcement doesn't begin with thousand-dollar bribes. It begins with fixing tickets. That's not to say there aren't circumstances where a ticket should be revoked. A town meeting in my community drew some 5,000 citizens to the high school auditorium. The crowd overflowed into the gymnasium where closed-circuit television was set up to show the testimony. Naturally, people were parked all over the place. There's an ordinance against parking on the grass but I considered the circumstances. I was assigned to work the meeting and I had ticketed only those cars parked in handicapped spaces. The sergeant had a cruiser come and ticket the cars on the grass. The chief later rescinded hundreds of tickets issued that night—except the ones for handicapped parking.

Your department surely has a policy on revoking tickets. Mine has a form that you can turn in with your copy of the ticket, explaining why it should be revoked. The supervisor may be approached by the violator and, after getting your side of the story, decide to revoke it. Once the ticket is written, it's out of your hands. Even our sergeant must complete a form to explain his reasons and that becomes part of the record. Those tickets are sequentially numbered in your ticket book. If one is missing, it will be detected by your Citation Audit System and you'll have to explain why.

22.5 The Next Generation

The clerk at City Hall will rejoice over getting rid of the task of deciphering a cop's scrawl on a parking ticket. In the future, the copy the clerk gets will likely be a computer printout. It could be even now.

With modern technology, the license plate number of an illegally parked car can be entered into a computer, which generates the ticket. **KET INC.**

Two computer ticket-issuing systems were introduced at an Institutional and Municipal Parking Congress in Chicago's McCormick Place. But several companies now offer operational systems, and more are almost there. TicketWizard is one of the original systems. K.E.T.'s Ticket Writer, Timelapse's Ticketer2, and IBS Traffic Ticketing System are all on the market. These systems consist of a portable computer and printer that do a lot more than just write tickets.

The host computer at headquarters loads each portable unit with the day's hot sheet, scofflaw list, and whatever else. As you make your rounds, you enter the violation, vehicle license number, and location. Repetitious information of date, time, and issuing officer are entered automatically. Then a keystroke starts the printer, and the completed ticket emerges, consecutively numbered. As the ticket is issued, the computer checks the license number against its memory bank and lets you know if it finds a "hit." And all this information is recorded in machine memory.

When you return to headquarters, you hook the machine up to the host computer and upload your daily activity. Electronic transfer of this data eliminates the need to send hardly legible copies of handwritten tickets to the tax collector's office, or wherever your tickets are collected. It's a data base that can be accessed to update disposition of a particular ticket and to compile reports for town officials.

22.6 Directing Traffic

It's usually not an efficient use of personnel to tie up an officer regularly directing traffic. A traffic signal works twenty-four hours a day and doesn't need relief to go to the bathroom. But there are circumstances—road construction, an accident,

An accident in a heavily traveled portion of a highway presents many responsibilities for the police officer. Once the injured are treated and the scene protected, preventing additional accidents and keeping traffic moving are important. **ED LESCOE.**

disaster, parade, or other special events—where you must step off the sidewalk, get out of the car, or do extra duty to make sure traffic flows as smoothly as possible.

There can be a certain satisfaction in suddenly finding yourself the "point man" in police contact with the public.

You'll get every question you can imagine. You are the target of everyone who is confused, lost, strayed, or stolen, and it's amazing how many motorists have no idea where they are. You must be polite, try to avoid sarcasm, and leave them thinking nice thoughts about you and your town.

Your purpose really is to expedite the smooth flow of traffic. You need to anticipate what's needed and accommodate it, while figuring a way for normal traffic to flow. You have to get crowds of sports spectators across the busy street or empty out the parking lot onto the thoroughfare without congesting normal traffic. Your assignment is to keep rubberneckers away from a disaster scene yet leave a route for emergency vehicles to get in. Talk about a balancing act!

I'll never forget my baptism in traffic direction. I was so young and green I hadn't yet learned the indifference that plagues veterans. It was on old Route 1 between Baltimore and Washington, a four-lane highway with two lanes in each direction, and only a double white line to separate the two; it had been dubbed "Bloody Mary" by the media.

One of a convoy of military trucks carrying ammunition had an accident and the fire chief had closed the road for fear of an explosion. Well, you didn't close that road for more than a few seconds without causing a major traffic jam.

The state trooper put me at the south end and another town officer at the north end of the accident area to close the road. But I knew the area. I motioned the first car in the right line to approach me. I gave him directions to turn right, go two blocks down, turn left two more blocks, then left again to get back onto the highway above the accident. And I asked him to go slow because a line of cars would be following him.

Consider that I had two lines of cars coming at me. So often, one line moves quicker than the other and drivers try to switch lanes, causing more accidents. I stood just above the turnoff and motioned one car from each line at a time. The drivers soon picked up on the idea they were taking turns, and it worked. Both lines progressed slowly, no one tried to change lanes, and everyone was happy.

Giving Good Signals   Directing traffic is part of basic training, but many officers seem to forget or become lackadaisical. Too many officers are injured each year while directing traffic, so pay attention to the cautions that cover your posterior.

You soon learn that a driver won't do what you want him to do if he doesn't understand your signal. I've seen officers, arm down by their side, meekly wave their hand or flap their fingers, and expect the driver thirty feet away to understand their gesture. In my experience, the rigidly formal gesturing taught in military police school is the most understandable.

First, on a traffic post, wear a reflective vest and reflective gloves. The traditional upraised hand to signal "Stop" is hardly noticeable if you're wearing black gloves at dusk. It's not only for your own protection, but it helps your case when you testify against the beatlehead who ran through your signal. Use decisive arm (not hand) movements. If you wave cars to pass in front of you, wave your hand in front. If they should pass behind you, bring your hand up and behind your head. If you want them to turn left inside of you, move your hand in that direction. If they should turn around you, sweep your hand around.

Stopping a line of traffic is a problem. Near cars don't have time to stop. So wave them through with your left hand held low as you point with your right hand at the car farther back in the line that you want to stop. You must get the driver's attention before you can give him a signal, and pointing purposefully at one particular car can be surprisingly effective. Stand on a safety island, if there is one, or between the lanes; makes it easier when you have to play the matador in a bullfight.

In my area, you don't see a brass whistle as part of the uniform any more. But it was a good tool in its day. Lest we forget, remember that a long blast on the whistle, coupled with the upturned palm, means Stop. Two quick blasts, with a wave, means start. And a series of three short blasts means "*Stop* before you screw up the whole detail!"

Directing Traffic After Dark
A reflective traffic vest and gloves are important during daylight. At night they're mandatory—but inadequate. Flares in a pattern to slow and shift oncoming traffic around an accident will be seen long before traffic sees you. Unless you're standing in their headlight beams—which is a place I don't particularly care to be—drivers may have a hard time seeing your reflective garments.

Use your flashlight to extend your signal. People interpret a horizontally waving light as a stop signal. When you point it, then raise it vertically like a come-on wave, they come.

In the West, where lonely roads run straight for miles, your warning signals need to extend much farther than the lonely flare on a city street. Flares, light sticks, flashlight, flashlight with a red baton, traffic cones, overhead floodlights, a parked cruiser with the flashing lights on, barricades with flashing yellow lights—use whatever you can get your hands on to protect yourself while prompting the passing cars to do what you want them to.

22.7 Accident Investigation

When two drivers are involved in an accident, each thinks the other was at fault. If damage is significant, you can be sure there'll be a battle. It could go to court. In many jurisdictions, accidents are so frequent they become an onerous chore, especially in bad weather. But citizens have a right to have their accidents investigated. True, many fender-benders are so cut and dried the two operators will exchange information, fill out their separate accident reports, and decline a police investigation. If that happens, you're lucky. But one who feels aggrieved is likely to want your investigation.

For the most part, the patrol officer's accident "investigation" is simply interviewing those involved and completing an accident report form. Larger departments will have a special accident investigation unit to do the more sophisticated reconstructions.

HOT TIPS FROM OLD HANDS

Chalk useful. Carry a piece of yellow lumber crayon in your pocket. This is useful for drawing lines on the pavement or sidewalk for field sobriety tests, chalking the positions of tires in accidents, marking evidence locations, and outlining bodies (just like on TV). This material is not expensive, and will not leak or otherwise ruin uniform material.

Officer Tim Dees
Reno, Nevada,
police department

Aside from the obvious purpose of clearing up confusion, accident reports provide the basis for accident-prevention programs. You might identify an unsafe road condition that needs correcting, an unsafe vehicle that you can get off the road, or an unsafe driver you need to cite for violation.

Essentially, your investigation reconstructs the accident far enough back in time to identify all contributing factors. This involves seeing the scene before vehicles are moved, interviewing witnesses, searching for physical evidence (debris), and measuring skid marks. You need to work backward from the point of impact to determine the path of each vehicle, find the point at which each driver perceived the problem, then fix the point where there was no escape. If you can fix the point of possible perception, where a normal person would have identified the hazard, you might learn something about the offending motorist or discover a view obstruction that needs to be removed.

Identify the initial behavior of each driver. Did he signal his intent? Did the pedestrian step out from between parked cars? Where did he jam on his brakes? Fix the point of impact, then the final resting place. This helps you to estimate the energy of the impact and that leads to an estimate of the speed. Computer programs are available to help you to reconstruct an accident, and you'd be amazed at what a skilled investigator can determine from these basic facts.

New York's accident investigation squad identified the "unlucky seven" contributing causes of driver failure: improper speed, failing to yield right of way, following too closely, driving left of center, improper turning, improper passing, and ignoring a traffic signal.

I've nearly been hit by an approaching motorist who didn't see my cruiser stopped in the middle of the road with the red lights flashing. Some people just like to play Russian roulette with a speeding car. Some may be venting anger after a fight with the spouse. Some may really be subconsciously bent on suicide. Some may simply be overconfident. Everyone thinks he's an excellent driver, and that could color the account of the drivers involved. Certainly there is an emotional impact on those involved, and careful questioning can lead to truthful answers. What's going on in a motorists' mind may be difficult to determine, but it could be crucial to a successful investigation.

Accident reconstruction seldom identifies mechanical failure as a causal factor. Is the blown tire a cause or a result? In a major fatal accident situation, it could be worthwhile to have the vehicle checked, the way aircraft accident investigators reassemble all the broken parts.

A modern trend in accident investigation is to be especially concerned with reconstructing the event. Enforcement action is a byproduct of the procedures used to determine the truth of what happened. A fatal accident is going to take more of your time than a fender-bender, certainly, but the procedures you use to investigate both are essentially the same. An advantage is that the minor ones become training for those where your testimony may be critical.

As you approach the scene, plan out where to put your car so the warning lights will protect the people and scene, let your headlights help illuminate the scene, and keep your radio where you can reach it without crossing traffic. Set up flares or whatever you need. Quickly survey the scene to determine what else may be needed and call for fire or medical response, if needed. Check *all* injured persons; identify those most seriously injured and attend to them first. Then look to make sure you've found them all; some may have been thrown clear.

Identify all operators and get their licenses and registrations. Ask bystanders to help. One may walk uptraffic with a flare to help avoid a subsidiary accident. Be careful of exposing them to a dangerous situation, though. You may be responsible if they are hurt. Injured persons should not be moved; bystanders could help reassure a victim lying on the ground while you're attending to someone else. A bystander may help you preserve areas where critical evidence will be sought later, and help prevent theft of personal property.

If one of the drivers is inebriated, put him under arrest. Handcuff him if that's department policy, and put him in the back of your cruiser. Don't let him eat, drink, or smoke until after the breath test. An "unlicensed" driver should be held until his record can be verified. He may be subject to arrest if you find he's operating under suspension, has failed to answer previous citations, or has no proof of identity. Remember that the person who appears intoxicated may be suffering a head injury, epilepsy, or diabetes and may need prompt medical attention.

In practice, a minor accident is customarily moved out of the travel lanes to clear the road once you've seen the setup. But a fatal one may require photography, and moving the vehicles could degrade the integrity of the investigation. If the accident is on a main thoroughfare at peak traffic hours, at least chalk mark the positions of vehicles and pertinent pieces of evidence before you accommodate the traffic.

In any case, you need to sketch the scene, noting positions of the vehicles involved before and after impact, landmarks, and significant evidence; measure distances accurately. In a major accident, the investigation will take on all the elements of a crime-scene investigation. Keep good field notes because you may have to testify in court.

The specific form of your accident report is dictated by your state and department policy and it's important. In basic training, you're likely to spend two full days just learning how to fill out that form and all that goes with it. And that's just the basic data for a more extensive investigation if it's a major accident.

23
Principles of Patrol

Patrol is the first line of defense against crime. The patrol officer does the day-to-day work that makes a law enforcement agency effective. Patrol is what controls most criminals. It is the basic function of police in protecting life and property and serving the public.

How well you patrol depends on your training, to be sure, but it depends even more on how you approach the task. If patrol is just something you have to do to get through eight hours, it can be a monotonous chore. If you are conscientious, patrol can be quite interesting. Every area has its own personality and problems. If you make the effort to know the people, analyze the area, identify and attempt to solve the problems, you'll find that your shift will pass quickly and you'll feel good about the job you did. The television show *Blue Knight* was about a cop on a foot beat. It was a popular show because of the human interest of the officer's involvement with *his* people, both good and bad. It works the same for you.

Patrol isn't necessarily pleasant. In fact, the word is derived from the French *patrouiller*, meaning "to go through puddles." That's basically what the cop on patrol does: goes through littered alleys, up rickety back stairs, sloshing through slush in winter and mud puddles in summer. I've heard that the word *cop* is derived from "constable on patrol."

No officer gets to know the beat better than the officer on foot. You chat with the residents, learn their habits and concerns. You move slowly enough to see what's happening and to detect when something is out of the ordinary. I'm old-fashioned enough to believe that walking the beat is the foundation of urban policing.

If you make the motor patrol and get to wear a leather jacket as you ride that motorcycle, you can still get close to people. Two wheels make you more mobile but you can stop to visit with the regulars on your beat on a personal basis.

The automobile became part of policing soon after it was invented, yet cruisers are relatively new to patrol work. Those first automobiles were kept at the stationhouse and responded to emergency calls. The use of automobiles to replace the beat cop in a defined patrol area did not develop until the 1920s. During World War II, a manpower shortage and the advent of two-way radio put an increased

<table>
</table>

> ## HOT TIPS FROM
> ## OLD HANDS
>
> **Joe Namath had the idea.** An excellent in-
> sulator for cold-weather uniform wear is
> women's panty hose. Wear one or two pair
> as the innermost layer of your outfit, with
> wicking (polypropylene or Duofold-type)
> long underwear on top, followed by the
> body armor and uniform shirt. Unless you
> are very secure in your sexuality (or are
> female to begin with), you might not want
> to start out dressing this way in the locker
> room on day one.
>
> *Officer Tim Dees*
> *Reno, Nevada,*
> *police department*

emphasis on the squad car. Some larger cities went almost entirely to motorized patrol.

In most urban areas now you'll find a mix of motor and foot patrols, and almost everyone would rather sit in a squad car than pound the pavement. Most smaller departments don't have large downtown areas or the manpower to make much use of foot beats.

Many police departments have "walk and talk" programs. Officers periodically park the cruiser and walk through a neighborhood, keeping in touch with headquarters by portable radio. This tactic combines the best of both worlds— foot and cruiser patrol. Flint, Michigan, recently experimented with a reinstituted foot patrol in the downtown area. Crime dropped and citizen satisfaction with the police skyrocketed. People's fear of crime was reduced.

Whether your patrol assignment is on shoe leather, two wheels, or four, the principles of good patrol work are the same.

23.1 Theories of Patrol

During the 1970s, police administrators became aware that a reevaluation of traditional patrol strategies was needed. With ready availability of federal funds, many studies were done, and many raised more questions than they answered. The Kansas City Patrol Experiment is an example.

Preventive police patrol was studied by the Kansas City, Missouri, police department during 1972 and 1973 with funding from the Police Foundation. Simply adding more units doesn't prevent crime, so different levels of patrol were tried and compared. One level, called *proactive,* put more than the normal number of units on the street. The *reactive* level restricted patrols to answering calls for service. The conclusion was that varying the level of preventive patrol caused no significant effect on crime or citizen evaluation of police service.

There are many patrol strategies because no single plan will work in all places all the time. Also, there are two distinct philosophies of patrol work. You may employ both at different times, depending on the situation.

In one philosophy, you wear a distinctive uniform and drive a car with a distinctive color scheme and a light bar with flashing emergency lights. The light bar is equipped with low-power "glow" bulbs on each side, "cruise" lights, so it is dimly illuminated at night. On foot, you walk on the curb side of the sidewalk, highly visible. The theory here is to make yourself as conspicuous as possible. Let the public know you're on the job and, incidentally, forestall contemplated actions by a criminal. This technique may be the choice when your purpose is to prevent crime or disturbance, such as at the high school football game.

In the second approach, while you are in uniform you drive an inconspicuous and unmarked car with emergency lights concealed on the dashboard and rear-window shelf. On foot, you walk next to the buildings, ducking into doorways where you can observe without being easily seen. When your purpose is appre-hension, you want to be unobtrusive. You want a perpetrator to make his move so you can grab him. This is your choice when you are suspicious of something or don't want to influence a situation. Even at the high school football game, you may duck behind the bleachers to watch some scruffy character hanging around the concession stand.

23.2 Avoid Obvious Routine

Humans are creatures of habit. You've analyzed your patrol area and determined a patrol routine that covers it effectively and efficiently. You hit the restaurant just before it closes for that last cup of coffee. The morning newspaper is delivered to the carriers on a certain corner at 4:30 A.M. You shun streets with potholes. Your routine works, so why change it?

Because a crook soon learns your routine and plans his actions accordingly. He learns that once you check the back door of the drugstore, you won't be back for at least an hour. That gives him plenty of time to make his entry and scoop up the narcotics. He learns that you always start your evening patrol in the less populated areas where good citizens will see you, then work your way toward the high-crime areas later in the evening. He's going to hit the high-crime area early in your shift or the residential area later.

A smart chief once told me, "Be systematically unsystematic. You want people to know you're on the job, but you never want them to know where you'll be next."

23.3 Helpful Techniques

Backtracking is just one technique to break a routine, and it works on foot or on wheels. After you've walked a particularly vulnerable area, turn around and walk it back the other way. On your walk back, duck into a doorway and wait for a while. Observe without being observed. Drive around the block and cover it again, this time cutting up the alley.

When walking a beat at night, you don't want to stroll down the street, trying every door, and flashing your light around at random. Even an inexperienced crook can keep track of your movements. It may seem obvious but it happens.

When you enter a dark alley from a lighted street, wait for a few minutes to let your eyes adjust. This gives you a chance to watch for movement of someone who saw you enter the alley. You might pass the alley entrance, then double back. Stand where you are shielded from the street so you aren't silhouetted against the street lights. Work your way through the alley by hugging the sides and ducking behind the dumpster. Use your light only if it's necessary.

There are some areas you simply can't reach when sitting in a squad car. Park it. Turn on your portable radio, put your stick on your belt, and hoof it into the walkway or onto the loading dock to check windows and doors. Remember to turn your portable off when you get back into the car to avoid feedback, presuming both radios are on the same frequency.

HOT TIPS FROM OLD HANDS

Hang your hat. If your car has a cage, where do you put your hat so that it's out of the way, yet handy when you need it? How about hanging it on the cage? We tried it and found a benefit we hadn't expected.

When we stopped requiring officers to wear hats in cruisers, we looked for a convenient location to keep them where they wouldn't slip off onto the dirty car floor. The cage offered a handy place.

Rig a hook that can't be removed by a prisoner, or use an adhesive picture hanger, so that your hat hangs just over the back of the passenger seat. We quickly realized that, to someone in a stopped vehicle, looking in the rear-view mirror to size up the situation, that hat looks like the head of someone sitting in the passenger seat. The officer appears to have backup right in the car and that could discourage someone from doing something he shouldn't.

Lt. Richard E. Bailey
Wethersfield, Connecticut,
police department

23.4 Know Where You Are

It may seem obvious, but you need to know more than just every street name and how buildings are numbered. You need to know the peculiarities of every street, road, or alley. Knowing where a high-crowned cross street creates a dip could be critical in a high-speed chase. When a car you're chasing turns into a street you know is closed because of road construction, you've got the advantage.

Or you're chasing a guy on foot and he ducks into a building. Where will he go in that building? If you know there's an unlocked door to the basement but a locked inside door to the interior, you can guess where he went when you don't find him in the lobby.

When you respond to an armed robbery at the liquor store, is there an escape route out the back? Or does this proprietor have a barred steel door that's never opened unless a delivery is being made? It would help you to know that in advance. Does a particular real estate office collect rents at the beginning of the month and stash the cash in an old safe? Such knowledge might influence that way you patrol at the beginning of the month.

Where are the businesses in your area that are similar to those being hit frequently in other areas? Where do they keep valuable inventory or large amounts of money? What are the most vulnerable potential points of entry? Is that particular business or residence equipped with an alarm system? If so, what kind? Does the system sense perimeter intrusion or is it a pressure pad at a vulnerable area inside? And where is the safe, jewelry box, or narcotics cabinet? At night, is there supposed to be a light on in the back of the store? Is that revolving yellow light outside a warning of burglary or does it indicate that power to the freezer is off?

The point is, there is a lot for you to learn about your patrol area. It takes a lot of time on patrol to develop this knowledge, but you can't be a good patrol officer without it.

23.5 Know the People

In his book *Police Patrol*, Richard L. Holcomb says, "If the law enforcement officers of this country had all of the information regarding crimes that the general public has, they could solve almost every crime committed."

You can't do a good job of patrol unless you know the people, know what they know, and have their confidence and respect. All that's been said previously about professionalism and public relations comes into play when you hit the street. Your skills in getting along with people directly enhance your performance as a police officer.

Good citizens of your community will likely never meet you, or you them, unless they become a victim of a crime. But when you investigate a burglary and discover Mr. Good Citizen doesn't know the serial numbers on items taken, you'll wish you had met him before so you could have given him good advice. You say that's the job of the community relations person? Not really. He's the one who's supposed to develop programs. But who has more contact, him or all the other cops in the patrol division?

Organized citizen involvement programs are used in some areas to extend the eyes of the police. Volunteers with two-way radios patrol their communities and report suspicious activity. Neighborhood Watch is a program that encourages residents to be aware of what's going on and report to police. But you should identify and keep contact with those who can help your patrol work.

There are many people whose jobs put them in good position to help you. It's worth cultivating their friendship. Delivery persons, anyone who covers a daily route, can be a second set of eyes for you. The newspaper carrier gets to know a daily route and recognizes when something is wrong. Hotel clerks, bellhops, cab drivers, and security guards could be sources of good information. Gas station attendants see a lot more than they talk about. Retirees who sit in the park most of the day become skilled observers, if only to salve their own boredom.

You know best who are the influential people in your area. Tip off the community relations person. When someone new moves into your neighborhood, stop in and meet them; see if you can help. Drop off literature you got from the community relations person. First impressions are the most lasting and those few minutes helping newcomers have lasting public relations benefits. Besides, you get the chance to size them up.

Even before computers, many police departments kept a card file on each business in town with names, phone numbers, locations of vulnerable entry, and sensitive points. Use the same idea on your beat. Every patrol area has locations where trouble is likely to develop. Identify those areas that have had the most calls for service, that have been held up before, or that are a type being hit more often in the region. It's a good bet you'll find taverns, convenience stores, liquor stores, amusement facilities, and such on the list. You need to know the proprietors and employees by sight, if not by name.

You need to know personal habits. If you know a store manager never opens before 9:00 A.M., someone moving around inside at 8 A.M. would be suspicious. If you know the owner goes to the bank night deposit box at 4:00 P.M. on the button, her absence may signal a holdup. If you know the clerks restock the shelves after closing time, activity inside then might not be suspicious. But if it is someone you don't recognize, it could be a burglar trying to look like an employee.

In the course of getting to know the people, get to know their vehicles. After a few weeks in a patrol area, you should know the cars that are normally parked on the street overnight. When you've developed this feel for your patrol, a car that doesn't fit will strike you as out of place and one worth looking into.

23.6 Directed Patrols

Your supervisor may or may not give you special instructions before you go on patrol. Squad briefing is to keep you up to date on recent events and special emphasis, not to tell you what to do. You're supposed to know that already.

On the other hand, some departments have developed sophisticated "directed patrol" systems based on computerized analysis of crime data that has proved more accurate than human intuition in determining where and when a crime will be committed. A certain portion of the force is held in reserve to answer calls for service. Other officers are assigned to "D-runs"—directed deterrent patrol assignments with specific instructions on where to be at a certain time or what patrol tactics to employ.

Officers can't be called off from D-run assignment to handle a nonemergency call. It has been found by experimentation that patrol is most effective when performed in uninterrupted blocks at least twenty minutes long. At the conclusion of the assignment, the officer fills out a brief report to provide feedback the crime analyst needs to revise or cancel the assignment.

To free up an officer's time and make directed patrol possible, many departments have developed alternative means of responding to nonemergency calls for service, such as handling some complaints over the phone and scheduling nonemergency calls for later response when a patrol unit becomes available.

23.7 Be Alert

Watch for Traffic Violations   Unless you are on a special assignment, traffic law enforcement is fundamental to patrol work, even if your department is large enough to have a traffic division. Besides, how does it look to the taxpayer when he sees you fail to act on an obvious traffic violation?

A smart crook isn't going to attract your attention with a minor traffic violation. But who said crooks are smart? A driver who has something to hide may even be *overly* cautious, and that should attract your attention. You may not catch many crooks through traffic-law enforcement, but you do make your patrol area a safer place for both motorists and pedestrians. Some studies indicate that crooks stay away from areas where the police practice aggressive traffic enforcement.

Traffic-law enforcement can be a tool for catching crooks. With *Miranda* and all the constitutional rights afforded a suspect, you can't force him to identify himself—unless he is operating a motor vehicle. In my state, and probably yours, motor vehicle law requires the driver to present his operator's license, or give his

A traffic stop is a common occurance, yet it can be dangerous. **L&O.**

name and address, when requested by an officer in uniform. Of course, you must have a good reason to make the stop, and a traffic violation or equipment violation can be just the reason you need.

Improve Observation Skills   It's human nature to see an area in terms of your own interests. A sign painter sees the signs; a salesperson sees the stores that sell her product. The vice squad detective may spot a prostitute two blocks away, but he won't notice a drunken driver unless he runs over him.

Learn to observe people, to note their differences and distinguishing features. Practice glancing at people quickly, then describing them. From your description could a fellow officer pick the individual from a crowd?

Some officers seem to have a sixth sense that tells them "that person is wrong." They have simply learned to observe details of dress, actions, mannerisms, and appearance. These details may be so minor they're meaningless, until they are viewed in context of the total picture.

Look for the differences—unusual acts, manner of dress, whatever. Someone paying inordinate attention to you might bear watching. One who seems totally indifferent to you may be trying to hide his own nervousness. Notice the driver who seems unfamiliar with the operation of his car. Does he appear to be the sort of person who would be driving that kind of car? A youngster driving a Cadillac may have a rich father—or he may be on a joy ride.

Sometimes you might want to become conspicuous, letting the suspicious person know he's being followed. Pull up as if you were going to stop him and see what happens. He may bail out and run, or accelerate, or quickly pull over to the curb. If he does none of these things, you can drop back and you haven't lost a thing. The honest citizen will rarely notice, but you can be sure a car thief will.

There are certain areas where people normally congregate. You can expect to find kids in front of the theater when the last show lets out, especially if there's an ice cream store next door. But what if the stores are closed and an individual is hanging around? Position yourself so you can observe him without being obvious. What's he looking at? Did he take notice of you as you passed? It could be he's the lookout for his partner jimmying the narcotics locker in the drugstore. If you do approach and question him, look for signs of nervousness, frequent glances in a particular direction. He may try to divert your attention or encourage you to run him in. That's a good time to check doors and windows. Look for marks on door jams or scratches on locks.

Around transportation terminals most people are carrying luggage. But does the quality of luggage fit the dress of the person carrying it? Watch for travelers being approached by people they don't seem to know. Look for youngsters who appear unfamiliar with the town and don't seem to have a destination. Does the person fit the profile or a drug courier, or someone on the lam?

Every time you make a good arrest, ask yourself, "What tipped me off that something was wrong? What attracted my attention?" By analyzing each situation, you'll discover the seemingly insignificant action or thing that didn't fit. If you have a partner, talk it over together. You'll find that the vague feeling you get when something is wrong has a sound basis in your observation.

Using the Spotlight   You seldom see a passenger car equipped with a spotlight nowadays, unless it's a police car. Driving through dark alleys, flashing the spotlight around, is a sure tipoff to any unsavory character. Use the spotlight the same as you do your flashlight when you're on foot—sparingly.

Get to know your spotlight. Practice pointing it at the spot you want to illuminate, then turn it on for just a second and turn it right off. Don't sweep the light
from one side of the street to the other when it's on. Shining a spotlight down the
block will warn a perpetrator many blocks away.

23.8 Situations That Call for Caution

Let's say you spot a car that doesn't fit the area where it's parked. You radio the
dispatcher for a motor vehicle registration check and it comes back "stolen." Do
you rush right over and start rummaging through it for evidence? Of course not.
Better to drive on by and position yourself where you can watch it unobtrusively.
Particularly if it was stolen very recently, the thief may be using it to hold up the
store. He may have stopped to pick up his girl. Advise the dispatcher what you've
got. Perhaps a plainclothes officer will want to stake it out. Once you're reasonably
sure the car has been abandoned, let the investigators do the rummaging. They're
trained to find evidence not obvious to you, since you don't recover stolen cars
every day.

What if, responding to an armed-robbery call, you find the perpetrator still in the
store with salesclerks and customers? Rushing in could be dangerous to someone
inside, even create a hostage situation. Better to wait a discreet distance away for
the robbers to come outside before you confront them.

Narcotics cases can be touchy. If you have a narcotics squad, they may work a
case for months without making an arrest. Many people are involved in this
business, with one level shielding the next higher group. If you rush in and bust the
pusher, you could blow the case of an officer who was using the pusher to identify
his distributor. If you come across a drug transaction and can discreetly check by
radio, do it; get the expert's advice.

Emergency Calls   Let an accident happen in the northbound lanes, and
the southbound traffic ties up with people rubbernecking. Well, police officers are
people, too, and perhaps even more curious than passersby. That's why it needs to
be said, "Don't respond to an emergency call unless you are dispatched to it." The
assigned officer doesn't need a pack of police cars causing congestion. The officer
may need to get an ambulance or fire truck to the scene.

But when you are dispatched on an emergency call, remember that your first
responsibility is to reach your destination safely. It's little consolation to the accident victim who's bleeding to death that you would have arrived sixty seconds
sooner if that drunken driver hadn't pulled out in front of you and caused a crash.

Treat every emergency call like an emergency. "Routine" is a threat to the police
officer. The seventh response to a particular alarm that's always false just might be
real. You can't assume anything. Every emergency call is an emergency until you
determine the facts.

If you can, avoid approaching where you'll be seen from some distance away. In
the city, use a parallel street and cut over at the last possible intersection. If it's a
holdup, burglary, or prowler call, cut your siren several blocks away and extinguish
your lights before you'll be spotted from the destination. No point in telling the
suspect you'll be there soon.

Note the registration numbers of vehicles or persons departing as you near the
scene. When you arrive, stop a little way down the street. Wait a second, size up
what you can see. Is someone waiting in a car with the engine running? Is some-

one running off in the opposite direction? If nothing attracts your attention, identify the best approach route.

Have a plan. If you're working with a partner, it's critical that each of you knows what the other is going to do. Talk about it. A poor plan is better than no plan at all.

23.9 Hazards

What most people would simply avoid is just part of the job when your job is to protect the public. You can't avoid hazardous situations, so you'd better understand them and know what you should and shouldn't do.

Electrical Hazards   It's important to recognize that there is no safe level of electricity. The shock from 120-volt house current can kill just as much as a 115,000-volt transmission line.

You may be sent to an automobile accident where the car hit a utility pole and knocked the lines down. A rotted tree limb falls and breaks the wires. And you know the havoc a storm can raise. A fallen wire may flail around and spark all over the place. But it may lie quietly, giving no indication that it is "hot." Stay at least ten feet from any fallen wire and assume it is live.

Obviously, the first thing to do on arrival is to call in and ask that the utility be notified. Give the location and, if you can get it safely, the pole number. Set out flares and keep yourself and other people at least 100 feet away. If it's raining, wet ground increases the hazard. Keep people away from metal fences, highway dividers, or anything else that might conduct the electricity outside of your safety perimeter.

Like lightning, electricity will seek the ground. Keep yourself and others from between downed lines or between a wire and the ground. When a fallen wire is draped over an automobile, you can presume that the metal shell of the car is hot. If the car is occupied, tell the occupants to stay where they are. As long as they remain inside the vehicle, they don't complete the circuit to the ground. If they must leave the safety of the car's interior, as in the danger of fire, tell them to jump completely free of the car before they hit the ground. Don't touch the car and the ground at the same time.

If a wire has fallen on a victim, don't try to move it off with a tree limb. If wood is moist, it could conduct electricity. A long, dry rope may be used. Try to move the dangerous part of the wire while leaving other parts in contact with the ground. That reduces the danger.

A writhing wire may be stabilized by rolling a spare tire onto it. If you can, leave it to the utility crew with proper equipment.

Hazardous Materials   There is so much being carried in tanker trucks, you never know what you might face in a highway accident: gasoline, chemicals, radiological materials. When you reach the scene of an accident involving hazardous materials, help is only a radio call away. Your dispatcher should have a copy of the U.S. Department of Transportation's "Hazardous Materials" Emergency Response Guidebook (DOT-P 5800.2). It lists the code numbers posted on the diamond-shaped placard on the exterior of the truck and listed on the shipping papers, and the code will tell you exactly what the substance is. With each entry is a guide number that refers you to the back of the book for an outline of potential hazards to health, fire or explosion, and recommended remedial actions including type of fire extinguisher, how to handle a spill or leak, and first aid procedures.

Explosives and blasting agents are not listed by number, but a guide sheet is provided for Class A, Class B, and Class C explosives.

CHEMTREC, the Chemical Transportation Emergency Center, with an 800 number you can call for immediate advice, is open twenty-four hours a day. It's a public service of the Chemical Manufacturers Association at its offices in Washington, D.C. They can usually provide hazard information warnings and guidance when you can tell them the identification number or name of the product, and the nature of the problem.

The National Sheriff's Association (NSA) has instituted a new information service called HAZMAT; it puts the guidebook information into NSA's computer data base, which is accessible through the National Law Enforcement Telecommunications System. When you call in the ID number off the placard, your dispatcher can send a message query addressed to NSA's HAZMAT system and receive in seconds appropriate instructions for emergency action.

HAZMAT and CHEMTREC work together to give the first responder a fast identification of the material, define the hazards, and explain the actions to be taken until hazardous materials units can respond. Since the data base is updated frequently with current information, it may be more accurate—certainly more up to date—than the printed guidebook.

But what do you do until you know what to do? Call in the number off the placard. Keep unnecessary people away. Stay upwind and out of low areas. Isolate the hazard area and deny entry to everyone except trained HAZMAT units. You may need to wear protective clothing or breathing apparatus. Do not walk into or touch any spilled material. Avoid inhaling any gases, fumes, and smoke even if no hazardous materials are involved. Evacuate the area endangered by a drifting cloud. You don't know what it might be, so don't assume it's harmless just because you can't smell it.

Reporting Hazardous Conditions

As the only government representative who travels the highways and byways of your area around the clock, you're in the best position to note and report various hazards and attractive nuisances. In fact, you may face the prospect of a lawsuit for "failure to protect" if you just drive by and do nothing.

It's up to you to ask your dispatcher to notify the proper agency in case of streetlight outages, unprotected manholes, or icy spots on the road. It's up to you to remove vehicles parked in hazardous locations, assist stranded motorists, or help a confused elderly person get home. If you allow an intoxicated person to wander the streets and he gets hit by a car, you may be liable. Besides, you make friends for your department when you aggressively pursue a helping role in the community.

24

Patrol in Modern Times

The impact of computers on patrol operations has been as dramatic as the introduction of two-way radio. With two-way radio, you could let the dispatcher know where you were when you stopped a vehicle on the road. Now, with computers, the modern dispatcher can advise you in seconds if there is a potential danger associated with that vehicle.

24.1 Computers Go Afield

Mobile data terminals (MDTs) extend access to all that instant information residing in police data bases right to you, via a computer terminal right in your patrol car. You don't have to wait for someone else to key in your query, then read to you off the screen. You can punch up your own registration check and see the display on your own screen. And computers communicate at digital speeds—a lot faster than talking.

In San Jose, California, Sgt. Aubrey Perrott sits in his patrol car next to a stack of black boxes topped by a keyboard and monitor. He types in a few letters and immediately sees the status and location of all the officers in his district. He can also call up a summary of the night's events. He can run a check on a vehicle's plate number, tapping directly into the state's motor vehicle records. "You really feel naked without it," Perrott said when he had to share it with another supervisor. "It's like forgetting your gun."

Digital systems for mobile communications got their start in the 1970s, most with the support of the Law Enforcement Assistance Administration. But those early MDTs were neither reliable nor easy to use. Host computer systems were rather inflexible. When LEAA funds dried up, the manufacturers deemphasized MDT products. In more recent years, the continuing miniaturization of electronic equipment made possible small, rugged, self-contained, and easy-to-use microprocessor-based MDTs. They're finding their way into police cars all over the country, but not just because of their direct access to timely police information.

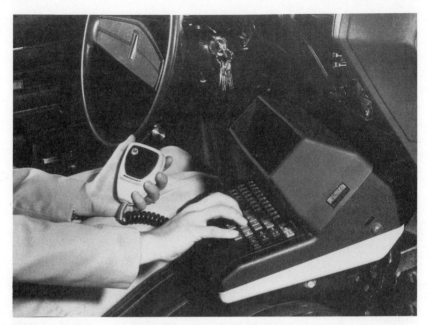

With mobile data terminals, there is access to mainframe computers by radio. **L&O.**

Computers talk faster than people. You can handle some five to ten times the traffic on one radio frequency with digital communication as you can with voice. Also, digital-burst transmission requires a computer to read, so interception on scanners is futile.

Typically, about half of your radio traffic consists of routine status reports and acknowledgments. Commonly used messages can be stored in the MDT and transmitted by a single keystroke. Fill-in-the-blank forms are stored in the machine to facilitate filing field reports, immediately and right from the field. Free-form messages can be transmitted between mobile units or to other offices on your system. If you're away from your car, the dispatcher can still send you a message. It will be stored or displayed in your terminal until you read it and clear it.

Stockton, California, installed a mobile data communications system from Mobile Data International. Forty patrol cars, already equipped with voice radio, were equipped with MDTs operating on the same frequency. When a call comes in, it is displayed on the screen. The officer acknowledges by pushing a status key: Enroute, At Scene, In Service, Traffic Stop, Check Out, Meal Break, and Returning to PD.

David Yamada, director of planning in Stockton, said the most noticeable effect of the system was a tremendous drop in voice traffic and fewer followup queries. Certain calls, such as in-progress calls, were still made by voice to alert other units in the area. "Voice backup will always be necessary," said dispatcher supervisor Audrey Smith. But she feels the terminals are good for rapport. Officers in the field can converse through the keyboard where they might be reluctant to chat over a voice channel.

With predefined forms, the officer can complete a field report on the terminal and transmit it in digital-burst form back to the host computer at Headquarters. All this input during the shift is automatically assembled and can be printed out by the computer. There's no staying overtime to complete your paperwork.

Because license checks are so much easier, many more of them are done. In one twenty-four hour period, Stockton officers made a total of 1,620 data-base inquiries. In another agency that went to mobile data communications, data-base inquiries went from a monthly average of 500 to more than 80,000 after the system was installed.

"Patrol officers are more efficient now," Yamada added. He summarized the effects of the system as reducing radio traffic, creating cost efficiencies in the dispatch area, saving report filing time, increasing the number of arrests and recovery of stolen property, reducing response time, and improving supervisory techniques and morale.

Talk about miniaturization. Would you believe you can pull a computer out of your pocket, key in a message, and transmit it to the stationhouse without being in your car or near a telephone? The key to Motorola's Portable Data Communications System is a portable computer terminal that weighs twenty-eight ounces and measures 7.5 by 4 by 1.3 inches. It has a two-line display and fifty-nine-position keyboard with full standard typewriter arrangement plus a numeric keypad. It contains an 800 MHz two-way data radio, internal antenna, telephone modem, and intelligence beyond many personal computers.

Of course, we're talking a system here, but it can be adapted to a local, campus-size area or a major metropolitan area. And metropolitan area networks can be linked to provide nationwide coverage. Being realistic, you could set up one 800

Lt. Debbie Johnson, head of special investigations in Lakeland, Florida, uses a terminal at headquarters to update a criminal history file.

MHz repeater station on a high point of ground in town, and every foot patrol could carry its own portable data terminal. If they should get out of radio range, they can accoustically couple it to a telephone.

24.2 Some Other Experiments

You don't need major metropolitan budgets to take computers into the field. It's been done using inexpensive general-purpose machines such as the Tandy Model 100 and Commodore C64.

In St. Petersburg, Florida, Sgt. Maurice McGough gave twenty officers Tandy portable computers. His idea was to relieve the tedium of manual report writing. Officers typed in reports while on patrol, then hooked the machine to a telephone and sent the reports to headquarters. The project worked so well that more than 200 officers now use them.

Officers are given an eight-hour training course, and they are encouraged to take their computers home to learn more applications—like games for the kids. The officers report they spend less time creating better reports and they enjoy doing it. They've developed other uses on their own: radar logs, a daily schedule with court appointments, or a surveillance notebook.

In a Lakeland, Florida, experiment, each of the department's twenty-four marked patrol cars were equipped with Commodore 64 computers at a cost of about $500 per car. It all started when canine handler Joseph Salvatore bought a C64 and developed a program with the help of eighteen-year-old Steven Atkins, whom he met through a local Commodore users' group. Their program can be loaded by disk into each machine with all the information from the daily briefing session. House checks, car hot sheet, descriptions of up to 25 wanted persons, 14 local street maps, and a phone directory are stored in each car computer.

In St. Petersburg, Florida, reports are completed right in the cruiser. Laptop computers can also be taken back to the station to bring field notes up to date. L&O.

"It didn't take long before everyone was fighting over the test car," Salvatore says. "They all wanted it. A lot of what a police officer does is manipulate data. Before, it's done by hand and radio. Using a computer, we cut routine radio transmissions by 70 percent and leave the radio free for emergency calls."

24.3 Computer-Aided Dispatch

The dispatcher scribbles on cards to keep track of calls for service. Then the officer writes a report, duplicating much of the same information. A detective's followup requires more paperwork, again repeating much of the same information. If the chief wants a summary of activity in a particular neighborhood, you can spend days shuffling cards.

But not with computer-aided dispatch.

The emergency phone rings. The caller describes a situation, gives a location, and identifies himself in response to the dispatcher's queries. As the caller talks, the dispatcher types on a keyboard and the information is entered into a form displayed on the computer screen. A priority is assigned to the incident, and the dispatcher touches another key. The computer automatically assigns a case number to the call.

If there are a number of minor calls waiting, the new call is queued in priority order on the dispatcher's screen at the radio position, if there are separate telephone and radio operators. If it's a high-priority call, it comes right up in front of the radio operator, and a police officer is dispatched. The time and unit number responding are keyed in to the form on the screen by the radio operator.

But suppose there have been previous calls to that same address. When the form is shifted to the radio operator, the computer checks its records and displays any information that will aid the responding officer. While this is going on, the radio dispatcher is looking at a status display that shows which units are in what areas and whether they are available, en route, or on another call. As the complaint screen comes up, it may even tell the dispatcher which unit is nearest to the incident location.

The responding officer calls in when he arrives. He advises the dispatcher when he clears the call and what action he took. This is also entered into the incident record.

But that's not the end of it.

All this information is already in the data base. A detective can call up the case number on his terminal and immediately have all the information available. The detective's report need only add the new information developed. Records division calls up the same data and checks it. If the chief wants a report, Records can search the data base by addresses and, in minutes, print out a record of all burglaries in that area, for example. A summary of activity for that shift, or any designated time period, can be compiled just as quickly.

Computer-aided dispatch can include such sophistication as mobile data terminals (MDT), digital status units (DSU) or status message units (which are DSUs tied in with an MDT), and automatic vehicle location.

24.4 Vehicle Tracking

Nautical navigation charts added a new set of grid lines in recent years and ships have a radio receiver that displays numbers. This is LORAN-C, a global network of low-frequency, high-powered transmitters that provide long-range navigation (LORAN). This system also covers more than three-fourths of the U.S. land area.

A LORAN receiver hears signals from two or more transmitters, and measures the difference in the time signals from two geographically separated transmitters arrive, translating that into distance from the location of the receiver. The intersection of two or more of these hyperbolic lines of position is the location of the receiver, accurate to one-eighth mile.

For police, the system offers greater capabilities than simply navigation. In a vehicle tracking system, a control console at the dispatcher's desk polls the vehicles by radio. Vehicles respond with current information on their position, and a computer translates this information and displays it on a city map or in a list.

In one system, this polling process takes less than two seconds for each vehicle. So, if ten units are being monitored, their positions are updated every twenty seconds. In another system, position reports are issued whenever the push-to-talk button is keyed. But these data bursts do not interfere with normal voice use of the radio.

The officers may have a separate status transmitter, so they can send any of a set of predetermined messages even if their voice radio fails. Such time-consuming voice messages as signing in, acknowledging a call, arriving on scene, clearing a call, returning to base, or "HELP," can be sent in nanoseconds with the touch of a button.

Besides radio positioning, one system also calculates its position using precise dead-reckoning techniques, taking input from the speedometer and a heading sensor. If you're in a fringe area for LORAN and lose the radio navigation signals, the system continues to function.

The Irvine, California, Police equipped twenty-five marked cars with a vehicle tracking system and found it accurate to 60 to 100 feet. Officers needed no training because it's all automatic. Dispatcher training required all of one hour. And the system has reduced response times by 7 percent for emergency calls and 19 percent for routine calls.

24.5 Stolen Cars That Tell on Themselves

Ken Nason and his wife of Northboro, Massachusetts, in the Boston area, had been burglarized several times before. They felt violated in their own home. And the burglaries had never been solved. In the last burglary, the burglars crept into the bedroom while the couple was asleep. They took Nason's wallet and car keys. Nason awoke later to find his Nissan gone.

"I called the Northboro police to report it," Nason said. What happened next is enough to warm the cockles of the National Auto Theft Bureau's heart.

In Massachusetts, when a stolen vehicle's identification number is entered into the state crime computer system, the computer automatically checks to see if that vehicle has a tracking device installed. Nason's did, so the computer automatically activated it.

Just fifteen minutes later, a Massachusetts state trooper about forty miles away heard the signal on the tracking device in his cruiser and he homed in on the signal. He found the car in the drive-in line at a hamburger stand. One of the two young occupants had Nason's wallet, driver's license, and credit cards in his pocket.

Nason had installed a LoJack unit in his car. It is a homing device that broadcasts a coded signal when it is activated by a computer signal over a discrete radio frequency. Any cruiser with a tracking device will hear it from a distance of five to seven miles, depending on terrain, and the device points to the signal's direction.

The system became operational in Massachusetts in July 1986. The units cost $595, but generate a 20 percent insurance discount. Through April 1988, 137 vehicles have been recovered in an average of ninety minutes using this device. The fastest recovery time was *seven minutes* after the report. Roughly one in three recoveries results in an arrest.

In Massachusetts, the system consists of five transmitting and receiving stations positioned to cover the entire state. These five stations are controlled by one small control box at state police headquarters. When a stolen vehicle is entered into the crime computer, it automatically checks the database of LoJack-equipped vehicles, which is updated daily. If a match is made, the computer automatically transmits a signal, activating the device in the stolen car. An officer cruising in the area receives the signal on his tracker. A distinctive code number is displayed, the compass shows the direction, and the signal strength meter gives an indication of distance.

The officer calls in the code by radio. When the dispatcher enters a query into his terminal, the screen displays the description of the vehicle, when and where it was stolen, the owner's name and address. Now the officer knows what to look for. When he finds it, he calls in a "locate" and the dispatcher deactivates the unit.

25

Crisis Intervention

A good part of police work is dealing with conflict of one kind or another. Since a quarter of American families sometimes have violent arguments, this obviously includes family disputes and domestic violence. But isn't a robbery also a crisis? It certainly is for the victim. It's no wonder that the term *crisis intervention* has become such an important part of police training.

It can happen anywhere, anytime, and to anybody. From your point of view, it could be more a matter of restoring order than enforcing law. The cause may be a subject of love, property, of honor, and it's something over which you have no control. It can bring out the worst behavior in an unpredictable, emotional, and perhaps dangerous situation.

25.1 Be Wary of Simple Domestics

As a police officer, you can easily become a target. Sixteen percent of fatal assaults on police, and 32 percent of all assaults, occur during domestic-violence calls. Among homicides of females, 41 percent are due to domestic violence. If you have to take the husband down with your nightstick, it isn't unusual for the wife to attack you in his defense.

It's policy in many departments that two officers are sent on every domestic disturbance call. Wait for your backup. You're going to need a partner. Plan for your survival. Find out as much as you can about where you're going. The dispatcher should advise you if a potential threat exists, but perhaps another officer, whom you can reach by radio, has been there before if you haven't. Have a planned response to threats and mentally rehearse your plan. Then, if forced to, you can respond to an attack quickly and decisively.

Obviously, keep the dispatcher and other units nearby informed. As soon after you sign off as you can, update the dispatcher on the situation. You may find a subject waiting out front to give one side of the story first—or to ambush you.

Be as cautious as you would approaching any threatening situation. Avoid announcing your arrival to the neighborhood with spotlights, slamming car doors, or loud knocks on the house door. Check your surroundings. And take your flashlight; you may need it inside.

25.2 Handling a Domestic Crisis

Before you can solve a problem, you have to know what the problem is. When you step into a crisis situation, you must first learn what upset the balance before you can resolve it. The procedure is *analyze, advise,* and then *act.* Establish that you are in control.

You may find people who believe you cannot enter without permission. Assure them it is your duty to investigate. Someone may accuse you of being sexist or racist. Assure them you're just doing your job impartially. If one party continues a protest or an argument, you might distract his attention by changing the subject. Just getting the name, address, and phone number into your notebook may be distraction enough.

If both parties are in the same room, let only one talk at a time. Stop violence by separating the warring parties. That's why two officers should respond to any domestic call. Then you can cool down the combatants and begin to learn what caused the problem. For obvious reasons, don't take the female alone into the bedroom. Children, or anyone else not involved, should be sent where they won't witness what's going on.

HOT TIPS FROM OLD HANDS

Keep your guard up. Back in the 1940s, before SWAT teams, hostage negotiating teams, and all that, a former neighbor of mine (the late retired chief of Patterson, New Jersey police, Marinus Ritter, then a sergeant) responded to a domestic quarrel/husband-armed call. Several other units were on the scene and could see the couple through the front windows of their second-floor apartment.

Ritter planned to go around back and surprise the husband from behind. As he was climbing the back steps he heard a sound on the landing above him. He looked up, right into the barrel of the husband's shotgun. With very few options, he said the first thing that came into his head. "I hear you're having some trouble with the missus." The remark totally defused the situation. The husband turned over his weapon and nobody was hurt.

I heard the story many years later when Ritter was making the point that you can't ever let your guard down on a domestic call. And also that a little communication without a massive show of force can be effective—although that certainly wasn't his plan at the time. Sometimes you have to rely on your instincts to see you through.

John Price
Former Assistant Prosecutor,
Passaic County, New Jersey
(now practicing civil law in Hawaii)

An episode of conflict follows a pattern: action and reaction. There is always a cause, but don't settle for the first thing you're told. There are likely to be underlying causes the people don't want you to know or don't even recognize themselves.

Show concern but get the combatants talking. Even more important, *listen.* Now's the time to find out what you need to know to resolve the situation. When one spouse shoulders all the blame, find out how others are involved. If one person points a finger of blame at the other, get him to think about something else, divert his attention. If the couple has a past history of domestic violence, you can bet the underlying problem hasn't been solved. Get them to tell you about previous attempts at resolution and why they failed. Then you won't waste time on futile efforts.

To further the resolution process, after the two parties have calmed down, have them talk to each other. When people argue, they hear only what they want to hear. Reasoned arguments fall on deaf ears. But inflammatory comments are readily heard and responded to in kind. With you controlling the situation, let each tell his story in front of the other. Again, only one talking at a time.

Because of "selective listening," you'll need to point out similarities and discrepancies in their stories. Of course they disagree on certain points, but there'll be points on which they do agree. These points of agreement are building blocks for further agreements. This enables you to concentrate on the real problems. If the problem is some insignificant irritation, the resolution may be easy. If it is a serious matter, understanding it is essential to its solution.

25.3 Reaching a Resolution

The situation climaxes when you reach the point of calling for a remedy. But rather than imposing your will, help the combatants reach the conclusion you want. Let them reason it out themselves. Listen to their plan carefully to detect faulty or incomplete reasoning or unacceptable methods.

If you think their plan is unworkable, you may have to recommend outside help. This is where you need to know what social services your community offers to its citizens. Refer the people to the place where they can find help, and be specific. "Get a lawyer" or "See a priest" leaves an unresolved conflict waiting to explode again.

The later you enter the sequence of events, the more likely that an arrest will need to be made. But put it in terms of punishing the act, not the person. Arrest—usually of the husband—should be the last resort. In some states, however, it's mandatory if there's evidence of assault.

25.4 Strategies of Solution

There is much more to becoming adept at crisis intervention than we can discuss here. There are many different types of domestic disputes and no two cases are ever the same. In some departments, it's an assignment for specially trained teams. But in most, it's up to you. To hit the highlights, here are a number of strategies you might use to resolve a dispute, any dispute.

You can create competition by pitting one individual's emotion against the other's intellect. You can cause a collaboration by creating a win/win situation between both parties. Compromise is often seen as a lose/lose situation, but it can be a winning negotiation. You can avoid the problem by taking one of the parties away and ordering him not to return; that just may be the resolution handed down by a court order. Or, best of all, you might find an accommodation that satisfies both parties' needs.

Reaching the best solutions usually takes more of your time. You solve the problem. You achieve an accommodation. You advise on a course of action that will enable the people to solve their own problem. However it works out, your aim is to engender in them a trust in you as a sage counselor, rather than just a shoulder to cry on.

Your own demeanor influences how people, particularly under the stress of a conflict, view you. Be forceful, but not belligerent. Speak clearly and decisively. Maintain poise. Avoid profanity. Of course, never be demeaning or intimidating.

When you advise people of an appropriate behavior or a corrective course, they aren't going to do it just because you told them to. You have to sell them on the idea. Your powers of persuasion may be taxed but you have to convince them of the benefits of following your recommendations. Of course, one benefit might be avoiding arrest. In my state, a new law requires the officer to make an arrest in a domestic disturbance if he finds evidence of abuse, assault, or a chargeable offense. But normally, in 43 percent of all misdemeanor calls and 52 percent of all felony calls no arrest is made.

If a situation is moving toward a resolution, you can use your discretion in overlooking an alleged violation as a way to promote that resolution. You may have the power to require social service intervention, but it works better if you've made the people more receptive by making them want it. You do that by identifying good reasons and helping them to reach those conclusions on their own. All people have needs. If you can give them a face-saving way to meet those needs, you might prevent the conflict from breaking out again.

25.5 Arrest Works

In a 1977 Kansas City study, researchers found that where a serious felony or homicide occurred in the home, police had been called in previously in 85 percent of the cases, and had responded five or more times in half of them. They concluded that just calming things down and getting the husband out for the night did not break that cycle of violence.

A study by the Minneapolis police department and the Police Foundation found that where police made an arrest, the recidivism rate was only 10 percent, where they attempted mediation it was 18 percent, and where they simply separated the warring couple for the night it was 24 percent.

The report of this study encouraged states to pass laws that permit you to make an arrest on probable cause if you believe that an assault took place within a short time before your arrival. You don't need the wife's complaint or even her testimony. A battered wife in Connecticut won a million-dollar "failure to protect" lawsuit against the town of Torrington, so our law leaves the officer no discretion. An arrest on probable cause is mandatory. Some department policies mandate arrest even where state law doesn't.

"Battered wives have been fearful for years, concerned about reprisals if they sign a complaint," says Earl Sweeney of the New Hampshire Police Standards and Training Council. "I don't favor taking away an officer's discretion but studies show that an arrest seems to break the cycle and is the preferred resolution."

26

Threat Response

In the Old West, the law enforcement officer was "made" by an oath, a badge, and a gun. Nowadays you don't become a police officer without completing an extensive academic and skills program. But how far away are we from the Old West mentality, really?

By the time you complete the police academy, you have been schooled in the judicial system, constitutional law, criminal law, penal code, human rights, laws of evidence, laws of arrest, search and seizure, and warrant application. Then you get into the specialties of investigative techniques, crime scene, interviews and interrogations, taking criminal statements, fingerprinting, developing informants, accident investigation, auto theft, preparing a case, courtroom demeanor, crisis intervention, handling domestics, and techniques of patrol. And then there are the subjects you might call "practical police skills," the skills that arm you to handle a situation. This usually includes some forty hours on firearms, forty hours on emergency medical, and perhaps twenty-four hours on defensive or pursuit driving.

But how many hours are devoted to unarmed defensive tactics? Probably no more than a dozen in all. Yet knowing defensive techniques can save your life.

Bob Dana was a dedicated officer in Boston. He was top in his recruit class. He was eager to attend every course and seminar he could, often at his own expense. He was a competitive shooter and firearms instructor. Early one morning he stopped a car that had been speeding. A local officer pulled in behind to back him up. They found a stolen television in the car. Bob attempted to handcuff the suspect. There was a struggle. The suspect grabbed the local officer's gun and shot Dana in the neck while Dana was trying to draw his own weapon.

Nothing in that situation justified deadly force—until it suddenly turned sour. In seconds, it was over, and Dana was dead. We'll never know for sure, of course, but might it have turned out differently if Dana's training in handcuffing techniques had been as thorough as his firearms training?

26.1 A New Perspective on Training

Andrew Casavant of the Midwest Tactical Training Institute polled his classes about their ongoing in-service training. How many receive unarmed defensive training? Usually none. How many are trained with their impact weapon? Perhaps two out

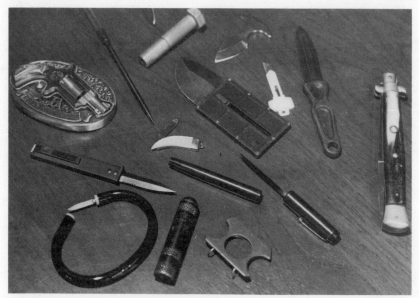

Remember that a variety of clandestine devices could be used against you. These are just a few from the collection of Dr. Kevin Parsons.

of forty. How many have ever had to use their guns? Usually none. But ask how many have had to physically subdue a subject or handcuff a struggling suspect, and almost all the hands will go up.

It stands to reason that you will be called on to exercise control over a subject in nonlethal situations many times more than you will ever have to resort to the ultimate measure of control: deadly force. Yet the emphasis in training is heavy on firearms but light in other control techniques.

Are we perpetuating the badge-and-gun mentality? If training emphasizes public relations on one hand and firearms on the other with too little time spent on responses in between, how are we arming the officer? If we spend forty hours in firearms training and then, at a different time and place, spend fewer than a dozen hours on all the other threat responses, how will the officer respond when the situation goes beyond talk? Even firearms instructors are concerned. "If we stress the gun in threat response training, are we predisposing our officers to *always* respond with the gun?"

26.2 Why Defensive Tactics?

The concept of defensive tactics makes sense. If you can employ simple procedures to exert control over a subject without resorting to impact weapons or firearms, you won't need to use the more forceful devices.

Threat response is not a black-and-white picture. It's a linear graph that passes through many shades of gray, depending on the force exerted against you. Officers need to know instinctively what is the appropriate response between the two extremes of a polite request and pulling the trigger. They need alternatives. If a defensive tactic can avoid the ultimate defensive force, it's a better choice than the gun.

Isn't it better to grip a reluctant subject's arm in a way that convinces him to comply, rather than bashing him with a baton? A physical response is likely to induce greater aggression, more injuries, and higher potential for civil suit. Isn't a quick reconciliation preferable to a brawl? If someone grabs your gun, isn't it better if you have it back in under two seconds? That's the value of learning and practicing nonlethal-force techniques. You may be able to resolve a situation with a simple grip on the guy's arm that causes him pain, before he pushes you into a knock-down, drag-out fight.

There's also a very practical reason for keeping the response level low. Dr. Kevin Parsons of the Justice System Training Association explains: "As the power of the police instrument increases, so do the chances for a lawsuit." When you pull your gun and fire, it means that all other control techniques were inappropriate, or were tried and failed. It means that the only way you could stop the aggressor's felonious assault was to shoot before he caused death or grievous bodily harm.

26.3 Continuum of Force

Threat response is a continuum, a graduated use of force dictated by the subject's degree of resistance.

At the bottom of the ladder, your very presence on a scene is a forceful influence. The way you stand, the image you project can influence a situation. Put your hands on your hips and stick your nose in the air, and you exude dominance. Stand relaxed, chin down, and you appear supportive.

When you say something to a suspect, you are exercising oral control, a form of force depending on your tone of voice. Verbal force begins with your request to a subject. It progresses to an order, then to an ORDER! Finally, you explain the consequences if the subject doesn't comply with your polite demands. These are successive rungs working your way up the ladder of force. When you touch a subject, you get into the next level of force—unarmed defensive control techniques. This can be a very unobtrusive grab of the guy's arm that appears passive but gives you a measure of control, such as walking a suspect from a position of advantage. It can escalate to a pain compliance technique, such as a wrist or thumb lock.

Higher up the ladder are the impact weapons. Your weapon may be as passive as a short stick on your key ring, but, when you know how to use it, it may enable you to control someone much stronger than you. The baton is seen by the public as a standard of police equipment, from a twenty-six-inch stick you carry on patrol to the thirty-six-inch riot baton that looks more threatening. The side-handle baton is used on all the television shows because it is more effective than a straight baton.

Using nonlethal weapons, a variety of chemical agents and electronic devices, escalates the level of force. Finally, the response of deadly force against the threat of deadly force from another reaches the outer limit.

When lethal force is justified, you think first of your gun. That's the usual response to a deadly threat. But consider this: *any* force you apply that results in death is deadly force. If you smash a suspect's head with your baton and he dies from a brain concussion, that's deadly force. If you apply a bar arm choke hold on a struggling suspect and he suffocates, that's deadly force. The term *deadly force* really refers to the result rather than the implement.

Of course, different devices are perceived differently. Your baton is considered nonlethal even though you can easily kill someone with it. Your gun is considered lethal even though only one in five police shootings results in death.

26.4 Appropriate Response

As a police officer, you need to be concerned with the application of force appropriate to the threat. Sooner or later, you will have to explain your actions in court. Invariably, the court will use "reasonable force" in judging a complaint. According to police trainer Massad Ayoob, "the judgment of the reasonable man" is a standard of the American legal system. Each case is decided on its own extenuating circumstances. It isn't all one-sided any more, either. That's why properly presented truth is your strongest weapon in court.

Remember that twin objectives of the use of force are to achieve and maintain control. Force response must be appropriate to the level of resistance or aggression exerted against the officer.

If you tell the subject in an authoritative voice to get into the back seat of your cruiser and he just stands there, your level of force is ineffective and puts you in jeopardy of losing control of the situation. If a subject curses you with a foul mouth and you zap him with a stun gun to punish him, that's excessive force. You are justified in using only that force necessary to resolve the situation.

26.5 When to Back Off

It's also part of threat response training that there's a big difference between backing off and backing down.

If you know the subject to be a skilled fighter with an aggressive personality, you can figure that eventually you might have to escalate to deadly force to resolve the situation. In circumstances like these, it makes more sense to back off and try to defuse the situation—providing it doesn't expose others to injury.

If you are facing a deadly-force situation with no chance of winning, you'd be stupid to proceed. When you can't control a subject or a situation, you can de-escalate your response. You can disengage, step back, move to cover to wait for backup. Then you become a trained witness, reporting information, noting details and descriptions.

In summary, threat-response training is a wide variety of actions, ranging on a continuum through body language, verbalization, commands, passive restraints, active countermeasures, nonlethal weapons, and firearms. An overemphasis on any one part of this continuum puts the officer at a disadvantage, leaving fewer alternatives.

26.6 Complacency Kills

Defensive techniques go beyond the one-on-one personal attack. The core issue is attitude. The one thing that threatens you most is complacency. Avoid the routine, remain alert, be in at least condition yellow at the best of times. One training film shows officers responding to a bank alarm for the umpteenth time. It had been a false each time before, so the cops were complacent this time. Two were discussing where to go fishing for the weekend when the robber came out of the bank and blew both of them away with a shotgun.

Lt. Carrol Hogue of the Los Angeles County sheriff's office tells of another common scenario. A crime is committed. Everyone on duty knows the crook and where he lives. So a half dozen cars roll. If it was your call, you're probably the last to arrive. Now, all the other times this subject was arrested he never resisted.

No one gets hurt. The crook winds up in custody and everyone takes an assist on their log.

But suppose this time is different. Perhaps he's fed up with being hassled by cops. Perhaps he's thinking the judge is planning to put him away. You can't be sure how a person will react, even if you've seen him react compliantly a thousand times. If you anticipate compliance, you could be injured or killed when surprised with an attack.

Okay, so we have several officers at Schmoe's house. But it's your call; you are the one who was sent. Even though there are no sergeant stripes on your sleeve, you are in charge. Any time two or more police officers are involved in the same situation, *one must take charge.* And your planning must be more than "You take the back and we'll go in the front."

You need to contain the suspect, to maintain the status quo. Two officers can watch all sides of a house when they are at opposite corners. If another officer assigns you a containment position, you must not leave that position unless relieved or cleared. The minute you leave, you can bet the crook will escape through your abandoned position.

Once you're put in position of masterminding an operation, you assign people to watch other avenues of possible attack, you determine what the next move will be if the subject slams the door in your face, or attacks. Once inside, you decide who's going to do the handcuffing.

Consider the alternative and you'll see why I group this "strategic function" under defensive techniques. If six guys surround the house and each acts on his own, who knows what the other guy is doing? If one conversed with the suspect last week and learned he was at the breaking point, who's he going to tell? If the subject attacks one of six independent buys, how'd you like to be the one wrestling

---

HOT TIPS FROM OLD HANDS

Fear is normal. No one knows how they'll react to danger until they're in it. This may cause anxiety, but consider this: fear is a normal response to danger and all normal people will experience it. Courage is the ability to cope with fear, and use it to your advantage. When danger is perceived, your body sounds an alarm: a knot in your stomach, goose bumps, hair rising on the back of the neck, or a little voice in the back of your mind.

Listen, because that sensation is your best friend, and you become wiser through experience. Controlled fear, in the presence of danger, will help keep you alive by heightening your physical and mental ability.

Panic results from the inability to control or cope with fear. It leads to disaster. If you find you cannot control fear, seek other employment because you're a threat to your fellow officers, the public, and yourself. My primary responsibility when I was on patrol was to return home safely to my family, and fear helped me to accomplish this.

Charles Bruni
Former patrolman, Augusta, Georgia,
police department; deputy, Richmond County,
Georgia, sheriff's department;
and supervisor, Augusta College police

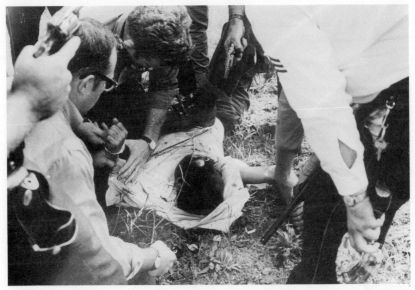

A task force of officers ferreted this felon from the woods. You seldom have this much help in effecting an arrest. **ED LESCOE.**

around on the floor while five excited cops point guns at the two of you? If no one's in charge, who's watching residents other than the suspect? Or covering the back of the officer involved in the scuffle?

Such a scenario as this should be a "snatch and grab." Once you have left, any resistance or belligerent assistance from friends or relatives of the subject will end.

"Complacency, familiarity, and routine are our deadly enemies," Lieutenant Hogue says. "One of the best ways to guard against them is assessment, planning, and assignment. Determine what you want to achieve and assess the hazard it presents. Formulate a plan to confront those hazards yet meet your needs. Assign specific people to specific tasks. Never hope or assume that someone will cover your rear—make sure. Your and your partner's safety is too critical to be left to chance because you failed to accept your responsibility."

26.7 Officer Survival

This, too, is a matter of attitude. Survival is really everything that you do. When you make a felony stop, you do it in such a way that you will survive if something goes wrong. When you search a house for an armed adversary, you use techniques that minimize your exposure to danger. When you go on patrol, you wear your body armor. You take care of your equipment and know that it will function when you call upon it. Survival is simply a matter of doing all things right. If you do your job properly, the way you are trained, you do it in ways that prevent mistakes.

Survival is a frame of mind. It means being aware of the little signs that signal danger, of being alert, of knowing what you're up against. To improve your odds, identify and evaluate the hazardous situations and critical areas you might face.

Identify the dangers presented by past cases in your jurisdiction: ambush, barricaded subjects, hostage situations, vehicle stops. Identify the signs and signals that should give you cause for concern. Doing this helps you develop a survivor's attitude.

Too many of us grow up in policing with the attitude that "it'll never happen to me." It's not a question of "if" you will ever confront a serious situation requiring a drastic response. It's a matter of "when." If you develop an attitude of watching for the worst while dealing politely with citizens, and being ready to act when you must, then you're well on your way to surviving.

27

Defensive Techniques

Defensive tactics—proper physical, unarmed response to resistance—are vitally important. It's not an overstatement to say that your lack of appropriate skills can cut your career short. Either you fail against an aggressor, or you respond with "excessive force," and the lawyers do you in. Don't get the idea that you can learn any of the techniques discussed here simply by reading. You must learn them "hands on," under the guidance of a qualified instructor.

27.1 Handcuffs

Police officers are helpful, friendly, concerned. They are protectors and rescuers. But there is one time when an officer must impose—when an arrest must be made. Then it doesn't matter what the other person thinks or wants. If that other person doesn't want to be arrested, it could mean a fight, unless the officer gets the person restrained in handcuffs quickly and efficiently.

Technical Reports   I won't use up space on a technical evaluation of handcuffs. In 1982, the National Institute of Justice (NIJ) reported on tests of seventeen models of double-locking handcuffs; later, three new models were tested. You can get the consumer product list and the metallic handcuff testing report from the NIJ's Technical Assessment Program Information Center (call 1-800-24-TAPIC; in Maryland and metropolitan Washington D.C., call 301-251-5060).

Modern Types   There are two principal types of handcuffs made today: chain-linked and stiff-hinged. Smith & Wesson offers a line of traditional chain-link handcuffs that comply with NIJ standards. Peerless produces a stiff-hinged model, connected with two bicycle-chain–type links. They fold to fit your handcuff case, but they don't twist. Hiatts of England offers a Tri-Hinge model that's as rigid as they come but folds flat to fit a standard handcuff case. Both the Peerless and Hiatts stiff-hinged cuffs allow a more expedient method of handcuffing a suspect; we'll get into that in a minute.

Connecticut Probation Officer Ed Dalenta, a qualified defensive tactics instructor, dem-
onstrates fending off a blow. His next move took the wind out of the aggressor's sails.

Handcuffs have four principal parts: the swinging arm, the fixed arm, the locking mechanism and ratchet, and the chain or hinge. The traditional handcuff with a chain is the easiest to escape from. It can be broken by persons with some strength, a high tolerance for pain, and some know-how.

Officer Tim Dees of the Field Services Bureau of the Reno, Nevada, police department is writing a paper on handcuffs, and he offers some cautions against complacency.

> Handcuffs of traditional design may be defeated by inserting a narrow piece of metal as a shim (the metal bristles that fall off of street-sweeper brushes are a favorite) into the slot on the locking mechanism where the swinging arm enters it. You can force down the pawls that hold the swinging arm in place. Double locking the cuff prevent this in some models, but makes no difference in others.
>
> Crooks sometimes conceal a homemade or real handcuff key. Keys are pretty much universal in design. Watch for a ballpoint pen that has a key in place of the push button on the top or a small piece of metal attached to the end of the refill.
>
> These methods are explained here to help you select handcuffs, and to encourage you to not rely on them too heavily. Despite the manufacturer's claims, no handcuff is completely escapeproof.

An advantage of the hinged cuff is that it provides better security against lock picking, and against a prisoner bringing the cuffs from back to front by forcing them under his rump and feet. When this first happened to me, I told the prisoner to put them back where they belonged. He did—easily.

"Handcuffs seldom require maintenance, but they do work better when broken in," Dees adds. "The action of handcuffs is likely to be rough when new. Simply

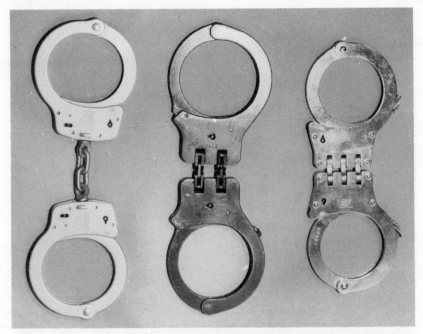

The three types of handcuffs you see carried by police officers today are, from left, traditional chain link, double bicycle hinge, and tri-hinge.

ratcheting the cuffs through a few hundred times is usually sufficient to wear away the burrs. You can also use some powdered graphite to lubricate the teeth and hinge, but don't use too much. You'll have it all over you every time you use the cuffs. Liquid lubricants should be avoided for the same reason."

27.2 Handcuffing Techniques

Everyone has a favorite technique for handcuffing a suspect. What's best in any given situation depends on how cooperative the suspect is—or isn't. Just remember; there are three times when police officers are vulnerable while handcuffing a suspect: (1) when they get into an unsafe position, (2) when they don't have the subject under control, or (3) when they relax too soon.

Get in the Habit of Double Locking
You can help to prevent both escapes and lawsuits by developing the habit of always double locking the cuffs whenever you apply them. Double locking prevents movement in either direction. If a prisoner sits on the cuffs and ratchets them down on his or her wrists, pain and injury can result. You may be held liable. The prisoner is likely to say that you put the cuffs on too tightly out of negligence or malice, and you'll be at a loss for a defense. Adjust the cuffs around the wrist just tightly enough to prevent escape. Be careful with very small people, particularly women with tiny wrists. Then push the small pin into the double-locking pin hole or slide it in the slot, depending on the brand of cuff you carry.

Capt. Robert Lindsey demonstrates how to keep a subject under control while putting on handcuffs.

When the cuffs are removed, the key must be turned in both directions to release first the double lock, then the locking pawls. This seems like a lot of trouble, but it goes quickly with practice.

Proper Search and Cuffing of an Armed Suspect   You spot a
suspect who fits the description of an armed robber, in an area where you'd expect him to be after holding up a store. You don't want to take any chances. Because the suspect is considered armed and dangerous, you need to get him into a controllable situation *immediately;* you're justified in covering him with your gun.

A popular technique that's effective and reasonably safe is the one developed by Robert Downey and Jordan Roth of the California Specialized Training Institute. If the suspect stops after your command "Police, don't move," tell him, "You're under arrest. Raise your hands high." Immediately assume an alert position at a safe distance. Keep him facing away from you. Making him "stretch for the sky" will lift his clothing to reveal weapons tucked into his belt. Even a concealed gun under the tightened shirt should bulge. Order him to turn a full circle *slowly,* so you get a good look all around.

Then command him to spreadeagle on the ground with his face away from the direction you plan to approach, and spread his feet. Put your gun back into its security holster before you approach. Then you can get a knee into the nape of his neck and immediately apply a wrist lock. Once you have control, you can cuff his wrists behind his back.

"Never struggle," says Bob Lindsey, former captain with the Jefferson Parish, Louisiana, sheriff's department. "If he resists and you've lost your control hold, *create distance* for your own sake, and start over."

My department firearms instructor, Frank Starnes, likes a variation of this technique. Once a subject is prone, instead of spreading his feet, Starnes has him raise his feet off the ground and hook his right foot over his left calf.

Approach from his foot end, still covering him with your gun, and apply an ankle twist. Now you can reholster, and grab the heel with your right hand. Just a little twisting pressure convinces him that you can cause him pain if he doesn't comply. But don't cause him so much pain that he'll try to get away.

You could do a quick patdown at this point, if you wish. Just be careful when twisting his foot. Too much pressure could break his ankle. Command him to put his right hand to his back and cuff it, then do the left hand—keeping some pressure on the toe of that foot to maintain control. Then you can stand him up and do a proper frisk.

Suppose you find the gun he was reported to have. Don't stuff it in the front of your pants. There's not only the potential for a damaging accident, it also keeps the gun within the suspect's reach. If you've got a backup, hand the gun to that officer. At least put it behind you, if you're sure it's safe.

Cuffing an Unarmed Suspect

You had the suspect "reach for the sky" and turn slowly, and you spotted no weapons. But the ground's muddy so you decide to cuff him standing up.

One popular technique is to command him to spread his feet slightly and put his left hand behind his back and his right hand behind his neck (mirror image for left-handed officers). Now you can reholster to get your gun out of the way while you approach—from a different direction than the suspect last saw you. But be alert. If he flinches, *create distance* as you go for your gun.

Get a wrist lock, a pain compliance hold, on the arm behind his back. Now you can control him while your right hand cuffs his right wrist up behind his neck. Keeping control, you bring his right hand behind his back and cuff his left wrist. Now you can walk him to the car while keeping that wrist or finger lock.

Speedcuffing

Jim Marsh of the Chicago police department teaches speedcuffing. First you "load" the cuffs, pushed nearly all the way through. With the loaded cuffs in your strong hand and the subject's hands behind with thumbs pointed down (as he were getting ready to dive), you can push the top cuff onto his right wrist from the little-finger side, quickly swing the bottom cuff under, and clamp it on his left wrist. He's cuffed in less time than it takes to tell it.

Rigid-hinge cuffs offer another simple and speedy technique. With the subject in that diving stance and the loaded cuffs in your hand, moving parts down, just push the cuffs down. Both cuffs engage respective wrists at the same time.

The Wall Is Passé

Capt. George Armbruster of the sheriff's department of Lafayette Parish, Louisiana, has researched handcuffing techniques extensively. He agrees that the technique developed by Downey and Roth is far superior to the old "assume the position against the wall" approach.

When the subject is leaning against the wall, you don't have him in a control hold. So you hook your left foot around his. He can kick you off balance as easily as you can trip him to the ground. He can push off from the stationary object and be in a struggle for your gun before you have a chance to draw.

Sgt. Gary Klugiewicz shows his blanket hold. It affords surprising control over the subject's arm. **DAVID PATRICK.**

Klugiewicz likes this escort position. His right hand controls the wrist as his left hand prevents the elbow from bending. If the subject resists, you can force him to the ground by simply bending over. **DAVID PATRICK.**

27.3 Physical Restraints

Principles of Control   John Desmedt, of the U.S. Secret Service, teaches a course called Principles of Control. His class demonstrates principles that are basic to all defensive tactics. One has to do with body tension. When you're tense, it doesn't take as much to push you over as when you're relaxed. "When you tense your body, you become less stable," Desmedt explained.

Desmedt believes that strength is concentrated at the center, and he has an effective demonstration. One partner stood with his arm straight out to the side, his hand in a fist. The other could push the fist down easily by pulling down on the first. At the forearm, it takes more effort. At the elbow it's very difficult. At the shoulder it's next to impossible. Push against a straight arm and you can easily push a man over. But let him bend his arm and it's not so easy. The bend creates an energy "sink" that drains off part of the energy of the push, and brings his fist nearer to his center.

Desmedt also demonstrated the power of distraction. With a student's hands clasping his shoulders, Desmedt couldn't lift them off by grasping the wrists. Then he slapped one arm and immediately moved the other hand away. He distracted the student's concentration by making him focus attention on an apparent attack.

Compliance Holds and Come-Alongs   In a confrontation, the people you face are in one of three frames of mind. The "yes" person is compliant. He shows you his driver's license when you ask for it. He gets out of his car when you tell him to. Or he drops his gun when you've got him covered. He may not be happy about it, but he's cooperative.

The "no" person resists, tells you to commit an unnatural act on yourself, takes a combative stance, indicating he's going to fight. You must deal with him in a more forceful manner. Then there's the "maybe" person. He hasn't made up his mind what he's going to do. He's the passive resister. He's debating with himself whether to comply or fight or run.

Compliance holds are applicable to the "maybe" person. They may be used when you feel you have an advantage in size, strength, skill, or backup support. They're intended to help convince the subject to do what *you* want him to do.

Blanket Hold   If the subject is passive, grasp his right elbow with both your hands, thumbs up. Most people are right-handed. It's safer if two officers each take one of his arms; but if you're alone, odds are his right is his strong side. This is a gentle grasp but it gives you good control of that arm. He can't elbow you or backhand you. If he tries to run at that point, you slip into the escort position.

Escort Position   Slide your right hand down to the suspect's wrist and get a good pincer grip between your thumb and middle finger. The opposing thumb and middle finger make the hand's strongest grip. Bring his hand close to your center, as you continue the grip on his elbow.

There are variations of the escort position. Some recommend twisting his hand under, so the back of his hand is against your hip, and hooking your other thumb under his armpit. Some don't recommend this because the subject may drop his shoulder down from your left hand or, if he's double-jointed, bend his elbow. In any case, you lose control.

Let's say you're holding the subject's right arm, your left hand on his elbow and your right hand locking his wrist. He starts serious resistance. Quickly bend forward with force, and the subject goes forward. But let him to the ground gently; you don't want to write all those long reports to explain his injuries.

Notice that this scenario gives you a sequence of events, events that you can explain in your report as justification for using increasingly forceful measures. Control is not a fifty-fifty proposition. It's all or nothing. If you have half control, you have no control.

While this escalation is happening, keep telling him in a stentorian voice, "Sir, calm down. Don't hurt yourself. Stop resisting. Drop the knife. Don't make me do this." Should he grab your holstered gun, as you chop his hand away, shout, "Sir, let go the gun!" Your explosive verbalization adds force to your chop, and lets witnesses know he threatened you.

If you lose control, duck behind him where he can't reach you. Then create distance, so you can draw your baton or gun.

Come-Along   There are many variations of come-alongs applied with both hands, one hand, or a baton, but they all boil down to one simple principle: anchor his elbow and bend his wrist—the common wrist lock. Any way you can anchor his elbow and bend his hand down with your force against his *knuckles*, you've got control.

I've seen them applied many ways, but the point is to jam his elbow into your lowest chest, grab his hand, and bend it down. Depending on the pressure you exert, it's either a come-along or pain compliance technique to "stabilize" a person and encourage his cooperation. It's part of an overall system, steps along the continuum of force, that can flow from a gentle touch to excruciating pain, depending on the resistance or aggression exerted by the subject against you.

Pressure-Point Control   Pressure-point control has graduated from a distraction technique to a system providing a high degree of control. It requires little skill, strength, or size to be effective and takes very little effort on the part of the officer to apply.

An anatomy book shows you many points on the body where nerves, bones, and muscular hollows are so situated that they are vulnerable. These are points to which many of the defensive techniques with a short stick or baton are directed. But some are vulnerable to your hand.

Bruce Siddle of PPCT Management Systems has probably studied pressure-point control more than anyone. What he can do with what appears to be a simple grab is astonishing. This could be quite a technical medical subject but he makes it simple—something you and I can do.

Touch Pressure Points   There are many places where a forceful touch can induce pain. One is the inside of the upper arm between the biceps and triceps muscles. Another is that muscle leading from shoulder to neck: place fingers or thumb into the depression above the collarbone and opposing digits on the other side, and squeeze. Touch pressure points are best used on "maybe" people, so they are a form of come-along. If you can't get his wrist, a one-hand hold at a touch pressure point may do the trick.

Three Points for Quick Penetration   When a subject actively resists, you need to grab a point that quickly convinces him to do what you ask. There are many potential points of vulnerability, but what can you grab in a fight? What can you get quickly and surely? And how many different holds are you going to remember anyway? To satisfy these questions, the experts emphasize three accessible points: behind the ear, beneath the jaw, at the base of the neck.

To find these points instinctively, you must be personally trained by a qualified instructor and experience the exercises, so we won't discuss it further.

Pain Is Relative   Pain compliance is an alternative you might use, but it is not a sure thing, as different people have different tolerances for pain. A subject high on drugs may not even feel pain. Your pain compliance technique may not work. When it fails, by definition, he is no longer a "maybe" person. He's a "no" person that requires force higher up the continuum—and you can explain to the judge why you had to use a higher level of force to gain compliance.

There is another restraint that you've probably read about in the news, but there's so much misunderstanding about pain compliance restraints involving the neck, you'd better be informed of the facts.

27.4 Carotid Neck Restraints

When you are facing a husky adversary, especially if he's bigger than you, it requires *technique* to restrain him, rather than brute strength.

I once saw a film of a 125-pound female police officer restrain, take down, and cuff a 210-pound construction worker. She started with a kick into the backs of his knees. Then she got her arm around the guy's neck—all the way around. Her elbow was in front and her hand extended back behind the guy's shoulder. Her other hand came up and clasped that hand, palms together with fingers wrapped, not interlaced. Then she pulled. Her hip hit the guy's butt, broke his balance to the rear, and she had him under control.

She was using the lateral vascular neck restraint, originated by Jim Lindell, physical training instructor for the Kansas City, Missouri, police and third-degree black belt in judo. This system was developed to control violent subjects. It's not a combat tactic. One basic hold can be applied in three levels of effect and you rarely need the third level. And it eliminates the hazards of the old choke hold.

Danger of the Bar-Arm Choke Hold   With all the publicity given to liability suits lost after a perpetrator died as a result of being restrained by a choke hold, only a reminder should be needed. But, incredibly, I hear that some police-

A class learns the proper neck restraint.

men are still being taught the bar-arm hold. Let this word to the wise be sufficient: *never use a bar-arm choke hold.*

A bar across the front of a subject's neck—whether it's your forearm, flashlight, or baton—can damage his windpipe, break the hyoid bone (Adam's apple), crush the larynx (voice box), and bring dire consequences to both him and you. You are justified in using only the degree of force necessary to effect the arrest. If the suspect dies, you used *deadly* force, whether you meant to or not.

When an aggressor gets his arm around *your* neck, get your chin into the crook of his elbow immediately. You are avoiding a bar arm and protecting your airway.

How It Works   In the lateral vascular neck restraint, your arm must be around the subject's neck so that your elbow is in front of his chin and your hand is behind his shoulder. Clasping your hands together without interlocking enables both forearms to form a straight line.

This restraint works by the scissors effect of your biceps and forearm bearing on either side of the subject's neck. When you squeeze the two together, it hurts. The carotid arteries run up the sides of the neck carrying a blood supply to the brain, so you have to be careful.

The degree of force exerted is increased both by the angle of your arms and amount of pull. If you exert too much force, the subject could lose consciousness in just a few seconds. But there's still very little chance of causing permanent injury—if you are trained and the restraint is properly applied. Improper application can cause death.

This is *not* the "sleeper" hold of judo, but its severity can be increased if you're not careful. When Lindell was demonstrating the technique at a defensive tactics seminar, he raised his elbow with his arm around a student's neck and explained how that increases the hold's effectiveness. But he cut short his talk as he lowered the officer to the mat—his demonstrator was out like a light.

The restraint can be applied from any position, right- or left-handed. It can be used to exert varying degrees of force, and it can be relaxed immediately when resistance ceases. While you should practice using the technique from both right and left sides, you are well advised to favor using your weak arm around the subject's neck. This puts your gun side away from the suspect and your dominant hand can be quickly freed if you should need it.

The lateral vascular neck restraint is effective and safe when its purpose and function are thoroughly understood and when the technique is properly used by the officer. In most situations, it should be used *only* as a last resort before physical violence.

Safety
While there are many kinds of neck restraints, Lindell limits his teaching to this two-arm carotid restraint. It's the safest for the subject at all levels of control, and it provides the officer with a sequence of one application that can be adapted to different situations.

As long as you can clasp your hands behind the subject's back, you can be sure that the arm is properly positioned on the sides of the neck. If you have to reach to the side of the subject's neck, your forearm may be forming a bar across his throat. Only with proper arm position can you break his balance with the same encircling action as you step to the rear, and maintain a safe distance between you and the subject as you maintain control.

A properly applied neck restraint can have the effect of protecting the subject's neck from injury. Your arm and head act like a cervical collar preventing lateral movement. When your head presses against the back of his head, your arm positioned under his chin allows only enough pressure to control backward movement but not enough to move his head forward. "When you have this 'neck brace,' you know you've applied the restraint properly and achieved the safe and protective potential inherent in its correct use," Lindell says. In fourteen years of use by police and some federal agencies, there have been no deaths or serious injuries. Yet a 120-pound female officer can easily control a 200-pound man without having to resort to a baton.

Medical Concerns
If you should ever render a subject unconscious, immediate relaxation should revive him in five to twenty seconds without any help from you. Loosen his collar and tie to aid his normal breathing. In the off chance he doesn't revive in thirty seconds, start approved methods of resuscitation *immediately* as a precaution. If a subject has been rendered unconscious, when he revives he should be informed that medical attention is available to him and, if he asks for it, he should be taken to a medical facility.

Legal Concerns
The question has been raised in several states, "Does the carotid neck restraint constitute deadly force?" The answer is cloudy.

You now know the difference between the lateral carotid hold and the frontal bar-arm hold. But they look a lot alike. The Minnesota Police Officer Standards and Training Board researched the legal aspect and found two relevant cases.

The first case reached the U.S. Supreme Court: *City of Los Angeles v. Lyons,* 1983. Lyons sought to enjoin the Los Angeles police department from using the neck restraint in the future. The court denied the injunction because, it said, Lyons could not prove that he was likely to be subjected to the technique again. But the court characterized the hold as "use of deadly force" and implied that Lyons might have been successful had he sued the city for damages.

McQurter v. City of Atlanta, 572 F. Supp. 1401 (D Ga. 1983) came out of a federal district court. McQurter had resisted being handcuffed. One of the officers used his flashlight in a choke hold to the front of his throat and subdued him while other officers cuffed him. Testimony indicated that once he was manacled, there was no possibility of McQurter's escape. But the officer then shifted his position to the safer carotid neck restraint, tightening when the subject struggled and relaxing when he was quiet. For fifteen minutes before the wagon arrived, McQurter was motionless, apparently unconscious. No one checked him. He was taken to a hospital and put in the detention area. It was some time before hospital personnel noticed anything wrong with him. He was dead.

The court held that once he was cuffed, further use of the neck restraint was unnecessary. Then the court said, "No one could have believed that the use of deadly force was necessary to prevent an escape, death, or serious bodily harm." The city, superiors, and four officers at the scene were held liable for showing deliberate indifference to the serious medical needs of the subject.

Those who teach the carotid neck restraint caution against excessive application. They know the difference between "restraint" and "deadly force." But history proves that people have died from a bar-arm choke hold that looks a lot like a carotid neck restraint, and judges and juries paint with a broad brush. Now there is legal precedent that naively lumps a safe control technique in with one that has caused death.

Unless you're thoroughly trained and practice regularly, *any* neck hold can be dangerous. For this reason, some departments prohibit their use. If your department has such an SOP, of course you must follow it. If it doesn't have such a policy, be sure you know what you're doing before you use any of these techniques.

27.5 Active Countermeasures

Sgt. Gary Klugiewicz, defensive tactics coordinator for the Milwaukee County, Wisconsin, sheriff's department recruit training academy, is nationally known for his Active Countermeasures course. It's a system of blocks, punches, and kicks that turn violent resistance into control. Of course, Gary makes it look easy. He's a third-degree black belt in U.S. Kyokushin karate and placed ninth in world-class competition in Japan. It's taught by demonstration, explanation, and repetition—realistic simulations—as he puts students through the exercises and drills that make them well practiced in performing these techniques.

Realistic simulation is important. If you received some defensive tactics training in the academy, didn't the instructor warn you about breaking your partner's fingers? And do you think your partner is dumb enough to really resist your efforts? You had to hold back. You indicated where you'd strike with the baton, rather than actually striking. The minute your partner felt pain, he slapped twice—the universal martial arts signal to stop. The techniques you were learning could potentially do damage to the person on whom you applied them.

The first time I saw Klugiewicz's seminar on Active Countermeasures, with the participants padded better than football linemen, I decided it was time for me to shoot some photographs. But the difference between really applying a technique and just going through the motions is surprising.

Decentralizations   In court, you refer to "decentralizing" the subject. "Takedown" is cop talk. When a subject actively resists or attacks, he's not cooperating; he's a "no" person. He isn't going to voluntarily assume a handcuffing position. You have to put him there.

Like most defensive tactics, there are many different techniques, variations on a theme. But a takedown—decentralization, that is—must provide for the safety of the subject, by protecting his head and neck and controlling the speed of descent. It's got to work whether you do it fast or slow. Grabbing a subject's hair or head and twisting him to the ground may give you control of his head, but what does that move do to his neck? Whiplash!

An obnoxious drunk would be "directed" to the ground more carefully and slowly than someone trying to smash your face. But you still must know how to do it right. If you do a full body slam on a guy, smash his face into the concrete so hard he breaks his neck and dies, the court will call it deadly force. Not only does that open a whole new can of worms in justifying your actions, but your conscience must live with it for the rest of your life.

These techniques must also be practical. The classic rearward takedown is probably still being taught, but it has been found that it wasn't being used on the street. It might work when done fast, but it doesn't work when done slowly.

Now Klugiewicz teaches one basic principle that satisfies the requirements and works from whatever grip you've got on the guy. You can apply it hard or soft, fast or slow. When the subject's off balance, you can stop halfway for his safety. Simply bring the subject to your center and bend over as if you were reaching for your right foot with your left hand (assuming you've got his right arm).

Three Levels

The secret of delivering a forceful blow is to translate force through fluid shock waves to motor points of the body. A punch, for example, doesn't stop on contact. To demonstrate, Klugiewicz had me hold my left arm out and hit the mound of my forearm with my right open hand. It looked like a karate chop, retracting immediately. "Everybody hits like that," Gary said. "There's no power. This time secure your arm by putting it on the table, and hit it again, but let it sink in." What a difference! My arm *hurt*.

A boxing parallel might be the difference between a jab and a punch. Rather than pulling back, you imagine the target a bit beyond where your fist hits. You want to transfer the kinetic energy from your hand through fluid shock waves to the subject's internal functions. It's the same principle with a bullet, or a baton.

Stunning Technique

When someone grapples with you, that's an assault. Remember to call it an assault. Can you strike him? Of course. But the guy is hyped up, drunk, emotionally upset. If you punch him once in the head, it likely won't do any good. You need to divert his attention, take away his ability to resist. "I 'direct' him to a wall, squad car, tree, bridge abutment—any hard object," Klugiewicz explains.

Body Slam   When someone slams into a hard object, it creates a dysfunction. It can knock the wind out of him. When someone hits backward into a wall, it's really a spread-out diffused strike, disrupting the synapses of the brain. You can prove it to yourself. Stand about four inches from the wall and ask your wife to push you forcefully backward. When the back of your shoulders hits the wall, your eyes stutter and you feel quite shaken up.

With one undamaging blow you have accomplished more than multiple blows with your portable radio or baton could have produced. "We found that many officers have done this instinctively," Klugiewicz says. "And you can do it vertically or horizontally with a much lower propensity for damage."

Diffused Strike   Using these fluid shock waves to cause trauma on the body, you can addle a subject without really hurting him. If you break his bones, you'll have to write a long report. So you want to hit the places where it won't do heavy-duty damage.

Klugiewicz laid the inside of his forearm at the base of my neck, the same place we discussed in pressure-point control. Then he pulled his arm out six to eight inches and slammed it back with modest force. That was enough to cause me some discomfort.

"This diffused strike is like a mobile wall stun," he explained. It's not like a chop-

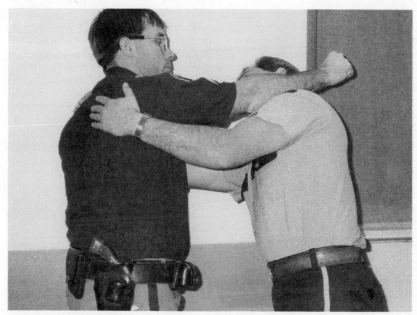

The diffused strike is used to stun an attacker with virtually no chance of doing him harm. **DAVID PATRICK.**

and-retract that does little, or punching "through" that winds up pushing the subject backward. It's a relaxed boom that lets everything rest into the subject. When you do it right, you can feel the vibration in the subject's body. It's comparable to the energy dump of an expanding bullet going into ballistic gelatin. "You don't need a lot of techniques or a high skill level if you learn to hit properly using fluid shock waves," Klugiewicz added.

Unarmed Blocking and Striking   When the guy attacks, your ready position is like the boxer's stance—hands up by your face, elbows tucked in. Swing side to side to guard against chest attacks. If he swings high, pop your arm up, block, and retract. Abdominal strikes can be deflected by dropping your elbow. If he swings low, swoop your arm down, around and back up.

But don't just stand there and box with the guy. Your purpose is to end the confrontation as quickly as possible. One block is all you should ever need. Once you've blocked his attack, you counterattack with a hand or leg strike, wrist lock, diffused strike, baton, or gun—whatever is called for.

A vertical punch to the suspect's jaw (like a left jab with the fist held vertically) stops his forward momentum, makes him bring his hands up, and sets him up for a reverse punch (like a strong right punch) to the lower abdomen to stun him. Then you can direct him to the ground and cuff him, effecting the arrest with a minimum amount of force.

Besides your fists, you might block or strike with your forearm, front or back side of the elbow, knee, or foot. A front kick aimed at his lower abdomen might keep him away. If he's already too close, it's a knee into his abdomen. That'll do it every time.

Purposes   Active countermeasures are what you use when you have to. They're for when you need to regain lost control, or can't reach your baton or firearm. Countermeasures can give you the opportunity to grab your baton or gun if the situation calls for it. And they give you a "weapon" to use when the situation no longer is appropriate for impact weapons.

They can defend you against an assault. They can distract the assailant. They can stun the subject to disorient him. They can impede him when his legs are knocked out from under him. They can stop his attack. They can enable you to control an aggressive subject and manage him into a position where he can no longer threaten you.

I was surprised how few fundamentals Klugiewicz employs in his Active Countermeasures system. And how many ways those few principles can be used to defend yourself. "We don't want multiple techniques that you won't remember," he explains. "We want multiple applications of a few effective techniques you *will* remember."

28

Defensive Devices

The police officer is given authority beyond what the law allows an average citizen. You are allowed to impose your will on an uncooperative subject who is violating the law. Because of this, you are exempt from the legislative prohibitions against many weapons.

There are a lot of things on the police market, so many it's confusing. You can't evaluate your need for such items unless you understand something about them. Your department will probably issue you a baton, but some law enforcement agencies don't use them. You'll need a flashlight, but what kind? You might even find saps or blackjacks still in the hands of old-time cops. To give you an understanding of devices you may encounter, we'll lump a lot of things into this broad category.

28.1 "Humane" Devices

Society has long looked for something that will help police restrain a subject without causing harmful effects. Some are rather colorful and some somewhat less than humane. Tear gas was developed back in World War I; the rubber bullets used in Northern Ireland today are an attempt to be "humane" in riot control. This search has produced a variety of devices designed for a police officer's personal use, but the simple fact is that a panacea has yet to be found.

For the officer well trained in defensive tactics, most nonlethal devices are "crutches" that shouldn't be needed. But they could be a help to officers less confident of their own physical skills. Some are designed to work against multiple adversaries.

The subject is an unarmed, but violent, mental patient, or a person under the influence of hallucinatory drugs and flipping out. He really doesn't know what he's doing. You don't want to kill him, but you must get him under control. Net the poor fish. *Captur-Net* takes a lesson from the purse fisherman. Two officers can fling the net to entangle such a subject and get him under control.

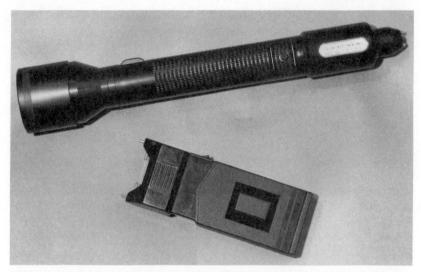

Of these two electric devices, only the Nova XR-5000 (bottom) is available today. In fact, it is even being used experimentally for shock treatment of snake bite with promising results. Above is the Source, flashlight on one end, electrodes on the other.

The *stun grenade* will get someone's attention with a loud bang and bright flash but no harmful shrapnel. It serves its purpose in tactical situations, but you're not likely to have one in your pocket.

Then there are electric devices used by some departments. Stun guns made the news in recent years, usually in an unfavorable light. The *Source,* no longer made, had a flashlight on one end and short electrodes on the other. When it was pressed against an aggressive subject and turned on, the pain-producing shock caused a retractive reflex. The *Nova XR5000* is designed to incapacitate a combative subject by inducing muscle spasms. It produces a high-voltage current that causes loss of muscular control, leaving the subject dazed but conscious.

Writer Tony Lesce tested these devices. He found them nonlethal and confirmed that they basically work as claimed. But he raised more questions than he answered. Electricity can be unpredictable when wet. Sparking can ignite combustible vapors. And it's too easy to misuse or abuse it.

These devices can be used only in close contact. There is another, the *Taser,* that can shoot electrode darts into a subject some thirty feet away, and zap him with an incapacitating jolt.

28.2 Chemical Devices

You're more likely to come into contact with chemical agents, so you should be familiar with them. All chemical-agent devices are color coded, to tell you what's inside. The names of the chemicals are next to impossible, so most people call them by abbreviations. Red means CN, blue is CS, yellow is HC or smoke, and gray means practice items. Violet is CR, a new chemical agent not used in the United States. You probably will never use DM (color coded green), which is a sickening agent used by the military. The two you're most likely to see are CN (red) or CS (blue).

What are they? During World War I, the U.S. Army spent a lot of time developing an inoffensive chemical agent suitable for training the troops with gas masks. The substance they developed was chloraceteophenone; just remember it as CN. That's tear gas, a lacrimating agent, color coded red. (It's not really a gas, but a fine powder "dust" that is carried by something else: smoke in a grenade, or liquid in an aerosol container.) When a person is exposed to it, his tear ducts flow, his eyes smart, and his eyelids try to close. A burning sensation is felt on moist skin. Get away from the gas and the effects soon dissipate. Flushing with water helps. There are no adverse aftereffects and it's relatively easy to clean up an area after exposure.

In 1960, the U.S. Army adopted a new chemical agent called orthochlorbenzalmalonontrile. Remember it as CS, color coded blue. It is more potent than CN, an irritant that's more effective than CN against a large mob. The effects of CS include extreme burning sensation of the eyes, flowing tears, involuntary closing of the eyes, coughing and chest tightening, sinus and nasal drip, extreme burning sensation on areas of moist skin, such as the face, armpits, and groin. If you use it indoors, it's more difficult to clean up than CN.

But a different characteristic becomes important when you put these substances in an aerosol container.

Aerosol Sprays

When the big controversy over "Chemical Mace" made national network news, I witnessed some and read many reports of tests by law enforcement agencies evaluating a variety of aerosol devices. They all reached similar conclusions.

CN vaporizes much more readily than CS. Yes, the milder of the two produces a quicker reaction when sprayed in a stream into an aggressor's face. From among the various manufacturers, you can get either CN or CS in an aerosol device.

A simple test proved it to me. I put a piece of cellophane tape under each eye, so I didn't feel the burning sensation. Then I smeared a drop of CS spray on one. It took twenty seconds or so before the vapors hit my eye. I tried it with CN under the other eye, and it closed in a second or three. Obviously, the better choice for an aerosol spray is CN, and it's the least likely to bring undesirable consequences down on your head.

First Aid

It's probably your department policy that if you gas someone, you have to provide first aid. Fortunately, common-sense practices apply to both CN and CS.

Remove the subject to a clear area and face him into the wind. Don't let him rub or scratch. This only pushes the particulates deeper into the skin. This treatment is usually enough if exposure isn't severe. Flushing the eyes with cool, clear water will speed recovery, but tell him to use ten times as much water as he feels necessary. Always remove contact lenses before flushing the eyes.

If his clothes have become contaminated, have him take them off. But be careful; you can pick up the agent on your hands and contaminate yourself. Normal cleaning will restore his clothing. Obviously, don't use any creams, salves, or dressings on irritated skin. That just traps the agent and prolongs its effects.

Exposure to chemical agents makes it seem as if you can't get your breath. That's a psychological effect on normal people. But if someone is showing signs of severe or prolonged effects, difficulty breathing, severe chest pain, or contamination of wounds, get medical help.

28.3 The Short Stick

Yawara, as an art, dates back to seventeenth-century Japan. Jujitsu schools of that time included the short stick among its weapons with tactics so fierce it became known as "seven inches of sudden death."

Such severe martial arts tactics and weapons have no place in police service. Even though the police officer may use the Yawara strictly as a defensive weapon, it is seen by the public as a martial arts device. But from this, there has evolved a system that can be used with a device that appears less intimidating. That's why I don't call the short stick a Yawara.

Frank A. Matsuyama was looking for an alternative for the traditional sap and billy. His Yawara was a seven-inch piece of plastic, 1¼ inches in diameter. The ends were rounded with four metal spikes embedded near the tip and butt. Grooves aided gripping while the spikes discouraged adversaries from trying to grab it.

Most Yawaras today are made either with rounded ends or with a steel ball on each end. More than a dozen varying designs have been popular over the years, although all have a relatively thick grip, limiting them to thrusting, striking, or blocking techniques. Dr. Keven Parsons, in his book *Techniques of Vigilance*, says the police Yawara was popular on the West Coast in the early 1950s.

It isn't unusual to put a fob of some kind on your key ring. A short stick is a handy device that you can tuck into your belt and keep the keys safe and accessible. The restroom key at the gasoline station is usually on a stick, so the customers don't lose it; same idea.

Why would you want to keep your keys on a short stick? Let me tell you a story.

A Defensible Defensive Device   When I attended a Kubotan instructor course at the Smith & Wesson Academy, John Peters of the Defensive Tactics Institute told of an officer who was sued for brutality after taking down a particularly boisterous resister. The judge told the officer to bring the weapon he used into court. When the officer appeared the next day, the judge didn't see anything in his hands and became irritated.

"Where's your weapon?" the judge demanded angrily. "Did you bring it?"

"Yes I did, your honor," the officer replied.

"Well, let me see it."

With that, the officer put his key ring on the table. It had a six-inch stick on it, with six grooves that apparently provided a grip. When the officer explained that this indeed was the weapon he used to subdue the aggressor, the judge used colorful language in throwing the case out of court.

Why It Works   The short stick is a pain compliance device in police use. Bone is living tissue, sheathed in a sensitive membrane. There are a number of points on the body where the bone is close under the skin and pressure against the resistant bone with a hard object produces pain—*plenty of pain*. That's where the short stick comes in. Like other pain compliance techniques, the short stick isn't an absolute solution. It's an alternative to more severe force, and it may work in some situations.

Six basic techniques are taught, and they are all variations of two simple moves: a squeeze and a poke. And there are any number of ways and situations in which you can apply short-stick principles.

Protesters lock their arms and lie down, face up, across the entrance to the defense plant. The edge of the stick under a protester's ear lobe convinces him to

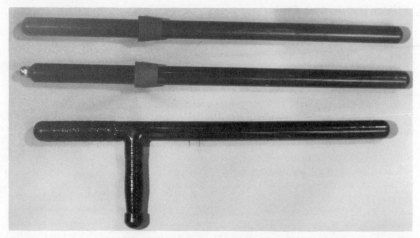

Batons come in a variety of configurations including the straight stick (top), a straight stick with a metal ball at the end for better jabbing (center), and the popular PR-24 (bottom).

sit up. A motorist gets a death grip on the steering wheel and refuses to get out of his car after you've opened the door. Slip the stick over his wrist, then step back as you grind the stick into his radial bone. He'll come with you and gladly lie face down on the street.

If someone grabs you in a bear hug from behind, you have several options. Bounce your head into his face. Swing your hip out of the way, as you chop your hand or stick down and back into his groin. If you can't move your upper arms, the pen from your shirt pocket or short stick from your belt poked into the back of his hand encourages him to get his hand away from you. If he gets you in a full-Nelson hold, you can still reach the back of his hand. As he loosens his grip, swing the stick into his lower abdomen. If he gets you in a choke hold, tuck your chin into the crook of his elbow to protect your airway and poke the stick into the muscles and tendons of his forearm. The short stick isn't an impact weapon, but if it's the only thing in your hand when someone kicks at you, sidestep as you snap it down onto his shin.

If you learn how to use it, the short stick can be a very effective tool in dealing with unarmed combatants. Then, when you are brought into civil court for using excessive force, the judge may think someone's trying to kid him when he sees your key ring.

28.4 Impact Weapons

When Sir Robert Peel established the world's first organized police force in London in 1829, he armed them with truncheons, a stick that carried over into the New World as the police baton. The baton has been part of police equipment ever since there have been policemen. History classifies the baton as an impact weapon, that is, a club with which you bash someone's head—but the way police use it today, it's not.

Historic Impact Devices   The short billy club was the traditional truncheon for police officers in the early days. But it is best suited for an overhand swing onto a person's head. Its range is short if you try to jab with it, and it really isn't long enough for the techniques you learn today.

The blackjack is a lump of lead on a springy handle covered with braided leather. Its flexibility gives it a snapping action that increases the momentum of the blow. It's designed to deliver a knockout blow to someone's head, and that could have dire consequences.

The sap, or slapper, is a lump of lead between two layers of leather. It's more rigid than a blackjack and, theoretically, less likely to crush a skull. Its effectiveness is in striking bone, such as ankles, shins, or wrists. It's handy for close-in fighting. You'll find saps still being made and sold—and even carried by police officers today. But show one to a judge and what will he think?

You may also find sap gloves for sale where they haven't been banned by police administrators. This is a leather glove with a pad of powdered lead over the knuckles. Frankly, the best use for sap gloves is to protect your hands when using a two-hand riot baton. But the public is likely to put them in the category of brass knuckles—a thug's weapon, not a police officer's.

Palm saps have a similar problem. This is a leather-covered pad of lead that covers your palm, with a strap around the back of your hand. A slap in the face with one feels like a hammer blow.

I classify all these devices as "historical," because that is where they belong—in history. They are bound to be construed as weapons of aggression, even if you use them defensively, because society sees them that way. None of these devices is considered "defensive," and most cause severe bleeding wounds that require stitches to close.

On the other hand, your baton is backed with a training program of many techniques for controlling a subject, blocking his attack, or hitting him in places you can't reach with a sap. Its very design shows its suitability for many things— except hitting heads. It's not a club. After all, the object of nonlethal force is to gain compliance, to control a combative subject—not to knock him senseless.

Your baton has many uses, and your instructor's lesson plan shows this. A straight stick is obviously not designed for bashing heads. It's a lever, jabber, blocker, and many other defensive things when you must take it to court.

Straight Baton   Roland Ouellette of the Connecticut Law Enforcement Training Institute gave us a quick review of basic techniques with the straight baton when a local labor dispute threatened to erupt into a strike. They show some of the many ways you can use a stick defensively.

A right-hander wears the baton on the left, like a sword. With your left hand on the grip, you can punch it straight ahead into an aggressor's abdomen. Or you can draw it with your right hand like a sword, if you want to intimidate someone. You can be more subtle by putting your right hand behind your back, using the left hand to lift the baton and push the grip back to your hand, and you've got it where others don't easily see it. Holding it like a sword puts it into view. It's less intimidating to hold it upside down with the blade up behind your arm. It's hidden, but readily available.

Lift your hand and clasp the baton horizontally under your upper arm, like a riding crop. While it is more visible, this ready position still isn't a threatening presentation of a baton. But you can deliver a devastating blow from this position.

Have your partner hang his or her stick about three feet in front of you. Slowly, flip your stick forward as you extend your hand, but be careful that you hit your partner's stick rather than the hand. Retract your stick after the blow is struck.

Speed up your action each time you try this. Get a real flipping motion. The tip of your baton travels a lot faster than your hand. With practice, you might even knock the stick out of your partner's hand.

Also, from that hidden-carry position, your baton is ready to block an aggressor's punch, parry the pipe he swings, or stop his kick to your groin. If he punches at you, simply bring your hand up, with the baton against what is now the outside of your forearm. There's a nice hard surface for his fist to crash into.

If he swings a piece of pipe with his right hand and you've got your baton in your right hand, bring it across in front of you, pushing your left hand at the tip of the baton. The baton is now at a forty-five-degree angle. Grip farther forward than the tip, so his bludgeon glances down your baton and, you hope, swings into his own shin. Keep your lower left hand open to keep your fingers out of the way.

If he starts to swing a kick up between your legs, flip the tip of the baton to your other hand and extend your arms. His shin meets the stick before his toe touches your genital area.

You can move a person back by holding the baton as though it were a pool cue, jabbing it through your left hand into his abdomen. But retract it quickly to keep him from grabbing it.

An arm lock is more effective when you put your baton under his wrist and over his upper arm. As you raise the grip, you can increase pain.

You can do the lateral neck restraint with the baton. From the hidden carry position, make a "V" with the stick and your forearm. Whip the baton around his neck, making sure your hand is to his front so you don't crush his windpipe. Reach behind his neck and grab the tip of your stick. Putting pressure on both sides of his neck, between your baton and your forearm, induces pain. (See the earlier discussion of neck restraints for cautionary information.)

Obviously, there is much more to baton technique than this. We're simply showing examples of the different ways one can be used. You're not going to become adept at any of these techniques without actually practicing them under the supervision of a qualified instructor. And never, ever hit a person in the head with any kind of impact weapon unless it's a situation where you're justified in using deadly force! Remember, too, that even a chop to the collarbone can result in death, if the collarbone splinters and punctures the trachea or larynx.

Side-Handle Baton
The side-handle baton was developed in 1971 by Lon Anderson. It is everything a straight baton is, and more.

Holding the side-handle in the ready position, you can jab the short end into a person's abdomen. The block that you can do with a straight baton can be done with the side-handle baton, and your hand is out of the way. That flipping strike is really devastating when you spin the side-handle baton using the handle as a pivot.

The handle gives you leverage, much more so than a straight baton. The baton come-along holds are easier to do with the side-handle, providing an extra dimension, like a shepherd's crook. It is so effective that Massad Ayoob, director of the Lethal Force Institute, says, "It is unwise to hold this instrument in other than the ready position, since the handle gives so much leverage that whoever is holding it pretty much has control of the weapon."

Using the side-handle baton is so different from a straight baton that we recommend specific training and certification before you're allowed to carry it. And now there's an expandable model of Monadnock's PR-24 side-handle baton.

Expandable Baton
Batons are an acceptable and effective tool for the police officer. But what's a plainclothes officer to do? It isn't very convenient to conceal a twenty-six-inch stick under your coat. Dr. Kevin Parsons recognized this

need. James Rohan, then an instructor at the Federal Law Enforcement Training Center in Georgia, had experimented with expandable martial arts tools but none met his criteria for police service. The two met at a defensive tactics seminar, and together they developed an expandable baton now called the ASP Tactical Baton.

The expandable baton has the advantage of appearing less intimidating than a long stick hanging from a ring on your belt. With it collapsed, you can use it to do the short-stick techniques. When you need an extended strike, a flip of the wrist extends it, even as you swing.

If you swing overhand, snap your wrist so the baton extends to the front. You can do the same thing if you swing backhand. I don't particularly care for the outward swings to open the baton, up or to the side, because they leave your baton out of action until you bring it back; but they're handy if an aggressor is standing toward your strong side.

Once opened, it stays open. It's designed to be rigid against a soft surface like a body. You can do the jabs that you would with a straight baton. To close it, you have to kneel and slam the tip down on a hard surface.

Lieutenant Rohan now runs the Containment and Emergency Response Team of the U.S. Capitol police. He's commander of the Recruit and Advanced Training Section of the Training Division. Even though his first thought was a concealable baton for plainclothes officers, he's found advantages for uniformed officers as well. A police department in my area has adopted the ASP as a primary baton. Officers always have it with them, where they might be tempted to leave a long stick behind when they get out of their car.

Targets and Nontargets   There are vulnerable parts of the body you must avoid with any impact weapon. The head and neck are always off limits. Avoid the solar plexus, where a hard strike could cause internal injuries. Kidneys and groin are highly sensitive areas that should not be struck with a hard object. Avoid the spine. From the neck to the tailbone, a concentrated blow to the backbone with a baton could cause permanent injury. Avoid striking joints, such as elbows and knees, with the baton.

There is less likelihood of damage and a high probability for effect if you strike motor points. Medical research has identified many areas of the body where nerves are clustered under a thin layer of muscle but over bone. There are points at the top of the calf, on the upper forearm, inside the forearm, and in a four-inch circle on the inside and outside of the thigh. Striking these areas with your fist, flashlight, or baton causes a temporary motor dysfunction (like hitting your funny bone) that incapacitates the subject for a few seconds, giving you an opportunity to immobilize him with handcuffs.

If motor points don't work, you can always aim for the traditional joints. But you can tell the judge that you tried to subdue him humanely before you smashed his knee, the next step on the force continuum.

28.5 Proper Use of the Flashlight

The driver pulled his car over to the curb when the siren signaled him to stop. According to testimony, the motorist resisted, scuffled with the two officers who had stopped him, and consequently, was subdued with their flashlights. The subject later died.

Obviously, beating someone about the head is not a proper use of the flashlight. It also isn't proper use of the police baton. But if the flashlight is in your hand, you can bet your sweet patoot it will be used as an impact weapon.

Officer Tom Lepore utilizes the police flashlight hold while examining a car.

A Touchy Subject The flashlight in police service is becoming a contradiction—a necessary piece of police equipment that is falling into such legal disfavor that some police chiefs have prohibited the long, aluminum-body lights. They've also eliminated any training in the proper use of a flashlight. Their theory is that if their officers use only simple flashlights and aren't trained in their proper use, they avoid liability should the flashlight be used to inflict injury.

A light source is a necessity. If you have a flashlight in your hand when someone jumps you, you've got no choice. Are you going to drop your only light source to grab your baton? Of course not. You'll smash that plastic two-cell, or whatever else is in your hand, into the guy to buy time so you can grab a better weapon. That's the way life is.

The flashlight is nothing more than a short baton or a big *Kubotan* when it is employed as a defensive device. Flashlight techniques are essentially the same as baton or short-stick techniques. Misuse any of these devices and you may be liable for using excessive force. It's well established that lack of training can incur liability. If officers are issued a proper flashlight and are trained in its defensive use, the department can show a positive liability defense.

Flashlight Holds No one has to tell you how to hold a flashlight civilian style. But cops also use a different kind of hold, for two reasons: (1) You want to look *down* the flashlight beam, as when looking into a stopped car or dark basement niches, and (2) you want the light to be "cocked" and ready for defensive use. So the police officer holds the light backward—with the weak hand, palm up, so that the barrel of the light rests on the shoulder as you aim the beam through the car window.

Retention Techniques   Let's go back to the interview position, with the flashlight in your hand in the police hold. Since you're in a lighted area, the light is off. But you gesture, pointing the end cap toward the subject. He grabs it, more than likely with his right hand, toward the tail end of the barrel. There are several things you can do.

Grabbing what you've got with both hands, rotate your hands and light in a small clockwise motion. The subject's wrist will bend as the tail of the light points upward. Continue the circular motion until the person's hand is palm up. Forcibly push the tail end of the light down against the subject's wrist, prying the light from under his thumb.

Or you can grab the tail end with your other hand and spin the flashlight like a propeller through the weak point of his grip—his thumb. Or you can grab the tail end with your other hand and, as you step forward with your weak-side foot, flip the head of the light down into his groin or stomach.

Or, say he grabs the tail end so you can't. Grab the barrel of the light with your other hand, palm down, so both hands are holding it the same way. Slide your leading hand forward and cover the subject's thumb, then force it into the light. This should cause him enough pain that he'll want to let go. But keep your grip. Forcibly point the light downward as you step back, bringing the subject to the ground. Keep his arm straight by pulling upward on the light. To get him ready for cuffing, walk toward his feet as you keep pulling up on the light. When he's on his stomach, bend his arm at the elbow and kneel on his shoulder, as you maintain the thumblock and apply the handcuffs.

Caution   There are many variations of the techniques you can apply with your flashlight (or baton). Most instructors I know concentrate their training on just a few techniques that are easy to remember and more natural in their response to a situation. But most cops don't get a chance to practice what they learn in too-brief training classes. You need techniques that will happen *naturally* when you need them on the street.

Be careful when you apply any defensive technique. There's a fine line between pain compliance and a broken bone. That's why you shouldn't read a book and then apply a technique, without being trained by a qualified instructor.

29

Weapons Are a Responsibility

The police officer uses many tools of the trade. Manufacturers are always coming up with new ideas and new products to put on the market. But whatever the weapon, whatever the device, there are some things you should keep in mind.

29.1 Mental Preparation

How many firearms instructors have preached that the handgun is simply a tool of the trade? That odds are you'll never need to use it? Do you believe that?

"An officer was called to a situation where there was known danger. He heard shots fired. He continued moving in, the gun still in his holster. The killer saw him first. The officer died with his gun still strapped in its leather."

Massad Ayoob, director of the Lethal Force Institute, tells that story to prove a point: if you're mentally unprepared to exert deadly force, your gun is no weapon at all.

Society has put us in position as its protector, using whatever force is necessary and justified. That means you may have to kill. The shooting decision isn't made by the officer. It's a reaction to the circumstances presented to the officer by the assailant. You shoot only to stop "the aggressor's felonious action that endangers himself or another," but the aftermath is a death by *your* hand. It doesn't help to think words like "may," "if," or "maybe." It's a matter of "will," "when," and "likely."

Never Give Up   When you played hide and seek as a kid, or cops and robbers, the rules of the game were that if you were tagged, you gave up. It's a good bet that you have an ingrained instinct to lie down and "die" if you lose. When you participate in shooting scenarios during officer survival training and don't shoot a hostile target, you are scored "dead." We continue to play by the same old rules of the game. But we need to add a new consideration.

I've seen stats that say four out of five shootings do not result in incapacitation. That's why we teach "double tap." Odds are that, even if you are shot, you can take out the shooter—*if you are mentally prepared to be shot.*

Take Offense   It's offensive if someone shoots you, so *take offense*. Get angry. After all, that shooter has tried to deprive you of everything you hold dear. As long as the offender holds a gun and is capable of pulling the trigger, he'll keep trying. You have no alternative. You must stop the aggressor's felonious act in the way you were trained.

The person shooting at you doesn't care about you, your spouse, or your children; he doesn't care about the consequences of his act. He sees you as an obstacle preventing his escape. Removing the obstacle is a natural thing, according to his primeval instincts, to ensure his own survival.

29.2 A Matter of Training

Firearms training is changing. Shooting techniques that the FBI teaches today are not the same as they taught up to 1980, according to Special Agent Bill Vanderpool of the FBI Academy Firearms Training Unit. Teaching methods and shooting techniques are changing so rapidly that a group of trainers formed the International Association of Law Enforcement Firearms Instructors. Yet how many departments send their firearms instructor back to school to learn what's new?

Consider the question of stance, as an example. If you are interviewing a suspect, you use the "interview position" taught in defensive tactics. If the suspect draws a gun, a quick movement of your arm puts you into the Weaver shooting stance faster than you could assume the old hip crouch position. And you can

Cathy Lane, a former Dallas police officer, demonstrates the Weaver Stance. She and her husband Jerry now run the OffShoots Training Institute.

deliver an aimed shot. If the attacker is far enough away that
you would move into the old
point shoulder position, that's
slower than simply bringing the
gun up into the Weaver stance.

If you can deliver faster, better-aimed fire with this new
technique, why clutter your
mind with learning two different positions? One will do both
jobs—better.

In fact, even the Weaver
stance taught today is slightly
different from what was once
taught. The "ready" position
was once taught as simply
dropping the handgun some six
inches. But that keeps it in your

HOT TIPS FROM OLD HANDS

Smoothing the draw. Buy a can of silicone spray and keep it in your locker, or wherever you store your sidearm and holster. Occasional spraying of the inside of the holster will make for an easier draw, and will retard rust and corrosion on the weapon itself. The can will probably last you for years.

Officer Tim Dees
Reno, Nevada, police
department

---

line of sight, and instructors found students still suffering "tunnel vision." Dropping
the gun a bit lower breaks that spell and lets the brain scan. It makes the officer
more alert.

Officers are still taught hip shooting with the shotgun: from a "port arms" carry,
straighten the left arm to level the gun and fire. But from the new shotgun "ready"
position, the gun can be mounted at the shoulder faster, and deliver a quicker,
better-aimed shot that hits its mark. Which would you rather use?

In a stress situation, you will react the way you have been conditioned to react by
your training. So training needs to instill the habits that keep you alive on the
street.

Firearms training is now conducted on a "hot" range. As soon as you empty your
handgun, you immediately reload, then check your target and scan for other
threats before you holster a *loaded* gun. You may have to "top off" a cylinder after
you've fired only a couple of rounds. You're taught to use cover. Tactical courses
make you decide how to get from one place to another safely. Stress courses teach
you to cope with the confusion you'll face on the street.

Of course there is still a very big difference between training and real life. When
you don't know where the threat is or how many there are, your tactics aren't as
clearly defined as they are on the firing line. There is no "target area" where all
your shots are directed. But if you are confident of your ability to use that gun
effectively, you will be much better prepared to face a "different" situation on the
street. You can afford to take a split second to carefully evaluate a threat before
pulling the trigger.

29.3 New Look at Shotgun Training

It actually happened.

The radio call put cars on the lookout for a vehicle used in an attempted armed
robbery. State police chased a car matching the description. City police stopped it.
They surrounded the vehicle. One city officer was holding his shotgun while
another checked out the occupants. The shotgun discharged—accidentally, as the
Firearms Review Board later determined. But that city is supporting the "victim" for
the rest of his life because the victim wasn't the culprit.

The shotgun is a patrol weapon, used by the patrol officer, rather than being relegated to specially trained tactical units. Yet in many departments shotgun training consists of little more than a demonstration in loading and unloading, shooting five buckshot at a silhouette and five birdshot at hand-thrown clay targets.

Training like that cost the city above more money than a good training program would have cost in twenty years.

We teach recruits shooting techniques with the handgun: proper grip, positions, sight alignment, trigger control. Yet we expect everyone to know hot to shoot a shotgun. We tell them to use the old military "port arms." We run trainees through an abbreviated course using silhouette targets and think that's sufficient. *Wrong.* New shooting techniques enable you to use the shotgun effectively, efficiently, and safely.

Are officers trained with slug loads? How often do you expect a patrol officer to need slugs? Slugs penetrate like you wouldn't believe. An aggressor behind a brick wall isn't safe. Several apartment walls seldom stop a slug from a shotgun. Do you think patrol officers should use slugs? Of course there are requirements for slug loads. But 00 buck can do virtually everything the patrol officer needs to do.

And what about shooting techniques? Not everyone in recruit class is a skeet shooter. It's not uncommon today for a recruit to have never fired a shotgun. They need to be taught from the ground up.

I mentioned skeet shooting purposely. The newest police shotgun techniques come from skeet shooting. John Satterwhite, nationally known competitive shotgunner now with Heckler and Koch, said that the "ready" position employed by the international skeet shooter enables officers to get off a fast, effective shot even under adverse conditions.

Bring a shotgun up to your cheek, pull it back into your shoulder, and point it at something. Now drop the stock down to the level of your strong forearm. That's the ready position. Notice that you are looking at the target through the front bead sight. From that position, notice how quickly you can mount the gun and get off a well-aimed shot.

In a shotgun instructor course, we were thoroughly exercised in properly mounting the gun from the ready position. We learned that the subconscious mind works one-third faster than the conscious mind. Mounting, aiming, and firing took much less time when we simply mounted the gun and fired; the subconscious mind took care of sighting the gun.

Then a low-light exercise proved it. On the indoor range, there was barely enough glow to tell where the target was. No way could we see the sight. Yet from the ready position, everyone in the class put every shot into center mass every time. To accomplish this, you need only learn how to properly mount the shotgun, and practice it enough to make it habit. We spent half a day learning the carry position, the ready position, and the loading position and then mounting the gun—before a shot was fired.

The first exercises emphasized individual skills. Then they became more complicated. In a vehicle gun mount, your shotgun is probably kept with the magazine loaded, action closed on an empty chamber and the safety on. The gun may be cocked. We loaded our guns in this "car-condition carry" on the command "fire," more than half the class couldn't rack a round into the chamber. You've got to release the action to open it when the gun is cocked. A cop on the street better have that idea ingrained into the brain if that shotgun is needed in a hurry.

There are techniques for loading the police shotgun that enable officers to keep their attention directed to the source of a potential threat. In the ready position, simply open the action. That's the "loading" position. If you've run the gun dry, you'd better get a couple of shells into it *fast.*

Jerry Lane demonstrates how to mount a shotgun. From this ready position (left) *raise the elbow to bring the gun into battery.*

"Combat loading" accomplishes this without interfering with your ability to shoot. Hold the gun in the loading position with the weak hand on the fore end while you grab two shells with the strong hand. It isn't difficult to know by feel that you've got the shells pointing the right direction.

Drop the bottom shell into the ejection port and, with the weak hand, close the action. You could fire at this point if you had to. Then roll the other shell down to the underside of the receiver and insert it into the tube through the loading port, maintaining target acquisition. Now you've got two shots available. If time allows, you can now hold the gun with the strong hand and insert additional rounds into the magazine with the weak hand. All the while, you can watch the target and react with a shot if necessary.

You're watching a suspect, standing in the "interview position" with the shotgun at ready. Suddenly, from one side, an accomplice steps out from behind cover and raises his gun. Must you shuffle your feet around so you can shoot? That takes too much time. Simply look at the target, pivot your whole body while mounting the gun, and fire. It's virtually as fast as shooting to the front.

You can get some real practice mounting the shotgun using the conventional clay-target games, but for a different purpose. Satterwhite said the FBI Academy uses the skeet field to develop a trainee's reaction. We had only a trap field available so we shot from very unconventional positions. The students quickly understood the concept of "leading" a moving target.

These are just highlights of what shotgun training should include today. It's much more than just being able to load, unload, and dump a load of buck shot onto a silhouette.

29.4 Realism in Training

The concept of firearms training goes far beyond the basics taught on a conventional range, just as defensive measures must be learned by actually applying them as if you mean it. And computer technology is a growing part of this "realistic simulation."

At a demonstration of the Firearms Training System (FATS), I stood before a movie screen. In my hand was a revolver, like the one I wear on duty, but equipped to fire only blanks and a light beam. The computer projected a scenario just as if I were there.

The ambassador stepped out of his house, flanked by two agents assigned to protect him. He walks briskly along the sidewalk, past a man dressed in light-colored pants and a short-sleeve shirt. Suddenly the man turns, reaches under his belt, and grabs a black metal object, which he points at the ambassador's back. Two shots ring out. The man is hit in the back of the head and in the side, fatally wounded by the agent—me—reacting to what he sees.

"Congratulations," the instructor said. "You just killed a tourist." It seems the man was aiming a camera. But thanks to computer capabilities, the next time that scenario is played, it could be a gun he's pointing.

A suspected drug dealer is holed up in an apartment. "Police, open the door. We have a warrant for your arrest," one agent shouts as he bangs on the door. No response. The door is kicked in and the officers make their way cautiously down a hallway and into a bedroom. The suspect is hiding in a closet.

"Come out with your hands up!" shouts an officer. The suspect braces his back against the wall of the closet and brings up his pistol, ready to shoot the first cop he sees.

An officer, kneeling on the floor, forces the closet door open. Suddenly exposed, the suspect sees no one and takes a step forward. Instantly, a second officer grabs his hand and slams him to the floor. No shots are fired. No one is injured.

"Good work," the instructor commented. "Let's try it again."

Computer-controlled videotape simulations can be amazingly realistic. But simulations can also be played in person. I visited the Orange County sheriff's department simulation range near Orlando, Florida. There were three blocks of building fronts laid out in a "U" shape, and different scenarios were being acted out in different locations.

At one, we were told a suspect was

In a class on handgun retention, James Lindell takes the gun away from an "aggressor," wrenching it from his hand.

inside and that there could be others in the room. We approached the door, past the carousel slide projector aimed through a hole in the wall. A female sergeant was testing our judgment in making a shooting decision.

As I stood in the door, a scene flashed onto the screen: a man holding a woman as a shield, with a knife at her throat. I might hit the hostage. Even if I shot the scumbag, his knife could do her serious harm. "Oh, s——," I said without thinking.

"Oh, s—— is not a proper response," the sergeant said as she marked me wrong.

At another part of "Survival City," a team of two officers had to take a barricaded suspect. At another, the officer used his car for cover. And the scenarios played out in reaction to the trainee's actions. They could go any way, according to what the trainee does.

Sometimes a scenario is set up to prove a point. In an officer survival course, I was given a gun loaded with blanks—checked and rechecked by the instructor—and a flashlight. The instructor set up the situation. "You've been called on a 'man with gun' complaint and you can't wait for backup. There's none available." That wiped out the first rule of survival—wait for backup.

The door led to a long hallway with a stairwell at the far end; the hallway was dimly lit. Boxes, a garbage can, and scraps of building material littered the way. There were many places where one could hide. Each man in the class had to work his way from cover to cover, flashing his light only as needed. I won't say who forgot to look behind the cover he just left, but I wasn't the only one.

The last cover before reaching the stairwell was an electric generator below a wall-mounted metal box. Then there was thirty feet of open area going straight into a light you couldn't turn off. The stairwell was dark. A man could have been standing there and you wouldn't see him. Flashing the landing revealed nothing.

From that point on, the story is different for each student. One almost made it to the top of the stairs, but most were surprised before they reached the landing. Only one "survived," but only because he refused to go any further. He didn't get his man but he lived to fight another day.

"I admit we set up a no-win situation," the instructor said. "But that's part of the decision process that faces every officer on the street." Fact is, such scenarios are supposed to make you think. They put you through situations you must evaluate, then react. If you've done it in training, you should be able to do it when the situation is real.

29.5 Keeping Control of Your Gun

Firearms training is more than simple shooting skills. *Making the shooting decision* is a critical aspect of firearms training. But what about making sure you've got your gun in the first place?

Gun Grabs Are a Threat   Gun grabs are a concern of anyone who is armed. According to the FBI Uniform Crime Reports, 106 officers were killed in 1979—17 of them with their own guns. The total number of officers feloniously killed declined steadily from 1979 to 1984. In 1984, the total of 72 was the lowest since 1968. But 12 of those 72 were killed with their own guns.

In Kansas City, Missouri, in one eighteen-month period, there were nine cases of officers disarmed. One officer was killed. One was shot in the leg. One was brutally beaten by an assailant who later killed a cab driver with the officer's revolver. "We evaluated and classified every case we could get a history on to determine how they happened and to develop a training program to respond to the most frequent circumstances," said James Lindell, physical training supervisor for the Kansas City police.

Lindell, a martial arts expert, is lanky and lithe. His graying hair belies what he can do to you with just his hands, arms, and feet. But Jim is expert enough to know that not all men behind the badge have the physique or motivation to become black belts. Experimenting with different martial arts and by trial and error, Lindell developed a simplified system aimed at defending the officer's revolver. Personal defense is a natural consequence.

Years ago, the Kansas City police adopted Lindell's initial revolver-retention system, and it continues to evolve and improve. For the first five years, in some thirty cases of disarming attempts, not one was successful. In the next five years, five officers were disarmed, but incident review determined that none had used personal defense, their weapon, or handgun-retention techniques. Fortunately, none was injured, but each committed some procedural violation or was physically outmatched by a much stronger aggressor. The fact that none of these five used any of the defensive skills they learned in the academy states a strong case for at least annual refresher courses.

When Lindell conducted an instructor training class in my area, I jumped at the chance. I figured if I could do it, anyone could. Most of the officers in class were younger and more athletic. But ever the gentleman, Lindell didn't look at me when he said, "Martial arts aren't the sole answer, but these principles can be applied to procedures that the average officer can easily do." He must have been right: I passed the course.

I won't try to summarize Lindell's 81-page training manual. You can get that from Odin Press, Box 11688, Kansas City, MO 64138. And you'll be surprised how easy it is.

Three Simple Steps

The Handgun Retention Course boils down to three simple steps: (1) secure the gun, (2) position, and (3) release.

The assailant is intent on grabbing your gun; the *gun* is the target. So the first thing to do is to secure the gun in the holster with one hand as you position yourself in a way that provides protection and the leverage that is more than the attacker can resist.

Keeping it simple, Lindell applies just five techniques that respond to virtually all the possible attempts to grab a holstered gun. If your gun is drawn, there are just four techniques you need to know, and they virtually ensure that you will keep control of your gun in your hands. Even if the assailant has the drop on you, or gets your gun out of the holster, there are three techniques that, in hardly more than a second, will turn the tables.

These simple three-step procedures use wrist locks (jujitsu), blocks (karate), and throws (judo). But you don't need to know the physics of body mechanics, leverage, or nerves to apply these principles.

The secret is to first learn the fundamentals properly, then practice, practice, practice. It's like drawing the revolver. With practice, when the occasion arises, a well-trained officer's response just happens, without conscious thought.

One of Lindell's students tells a story. "I felt the grab on my gun and the next thing I knew, the guy was on the ground, and my gun was in *my* hand aimed right at his temple." *That's* training!

Handgun retention is as much a part of firearms training as is sight picture, trigger control, and the Weaver stance. There are other effective systems developed by well-known instructors. Judging by what I've read, Lindell's method is the simplest. It develops natural reactions. It's the most easily done by a cruiser or desk-bound police officer who is not working out in the gym every day. And that suits me to a tee.

29.6 Keeping Your Shotgun

The detective has good information that the wanted man is in that warehouse. He warns, "He's armed and dangerous." The sergeant rolls up with another backup unit. Exits are covered. The building is supposedly clear of innocent bystanders. But the man you're after isn't one to flush easily. "Break out the shotguns," the sergeant says.

Now you are faced with doing a building search in a honeycomb of aisles and passages that interlace the pallets of crates and boxes on the warehouse floor. Or a tenement hallway, with every door a threat.

"That's one of the four situations where an attempt to disarm the officer with a shotgun is likely to occur," says Robert K. Lindsey. Lindsey retired a captain from the Jefferson Parish, Louisiana, sheriff's department. Now he's a police training consultant. "The other situations are when the shotgun malfunctions, when you're reloading, and when you're in a 'don't shoot' situation."

Lindsey has made a study of shotgun retention. He's studied everything he can learn about officer survival. And with good reason. Do you remember the infamous sniper incident on the roof of the Howard Johnson Hotel in New Orleans a few years ago? You will recall that three officers were killed. Those were Bob's men. He vowed that it would never happen again.

"The usual self-defense techniques, by themselves, are not the answer to retaining the long gun," Lindsey said. Using his knowledge of defensive tactics and the martial arts, Lindsey developed four simple procedures that virtually ensure your retaining the shotgun, whether an assailant tries to grab it (1) from the front or off side, (2) from the strong side, (3) from the front with the gun at port arms, or (4) from the rear. I'll give you the gist of his shoulder-weapon retention system, but like all defensive tactics, it should be learned and practiced under the guidance of a qualified instructor.

Grab from Front or Off Side   You're at a corner in the hallway. The subject steps out, grabs your shotgun, and tries to pull it away from you.

Use the force of his pull to your own advantage. React immediately, by stepping forward with your off foot. Thrust the barrel toward the attacker. Then quickly step forward with your strong foot, forcing the butt of the gun downward. Next, step past the attacker with your off foot while thrusting the barrel toward the outside of the attacker's body, and reach. The final move is to create distance. Get out of his reach so he can't grab the gun again.

Grab from the Strong Side   As you approach the open door on your strong side, the perpetrator reaches out and grabs your shotgun. Immediately step forward with your off foot, thrusting the barrel forward. Shove the butt downward and toward the outside as you step forward with the strong foot. Then, pivot yourself and the shotgun toward the outside of the attacker's body. Finally, create distance.

Grab from the Front, Gun in Port Arms   Immediately step forward with your off foot, thrusting the barrel upward. Then step forward with your strong foot, while quickly shoving the butt forward and toward the outside. Step forward again with your off foot and push the barrel toward the outside of the attacker's body. Then, create distance.

Grab from the Rear   This is a backward application of what's gone on before. Immediately step backward with your strong foot, thrusting the butt downward and toward the outside. Pivot toward the attacker, while shoving the barrel toward the outside of the attacker's body. Then, step back and to the side with your strong foot, pulling the gun in close to yourself. And create distance.

Grab When Gun Malfunctions   The crook sees that your gun is jammed and takes advantage of your predicament. Quickly rack the action back, wipe the shell away, and close the action. By that time, your gun is in the port arms position, and the aggressor has hands on it. Just follow the sequence above for the port arms release.

"With a shotgun, you must be continually aware of your surroundings. Weapon retention is enhanced by being alert and ready to react instantly and instinctively." Lindsey said. "Never allow an attacker to get a death grip on your gun."

30

The Gun

Anyone who wears a gun is affected by that gun. When you strap on a sidearm, you assume a responsibility you never had before. As with any other power tool, it's up to you to avoid accidents, to prevent its falling into the wrong hands, to know how to use it, and to know when to use it—or not. Call it philosophy or psychology, but the presence of a gun has an influence on the one wearing it. Having its powerful capability readily available influences how you act. The habits you develop in training with it carry over when you use it for real.

30.1 Concealing a Gun

The attitude required to properly conceal a gun is something a police officer develops over time. It's different at first. You're not accustomed to wearing one every day. It could make you so self-conscious you tip your hand.

John O'Reilly, a retired vice officer now in executive security for Holmes Detective Bureau in New York City, is trained to spot an armed person. "People carrying guns pat them constantly," he explains. "If you're wearing a shoulder holster, your arm hangs away from your body on that side." Another dead giveaway, according to O'Reilly: clothes don't hang right on someone concealing a gun. One side of the shirt collar droops lower than the other, and the buttons don't quite match up.

An ex-patrol officer friend of mine who now works in executive security must dress like a businessman. He spent four months retraining himself to wear his high-capacity auto in a front crossdraw rather than a right hip holster, but that wasn't enough. When he buys a suit of clothes, the tailor fits him with his gear on—all of it. It takes some accommodation to properly conceal a gun.

The gun must be hidden to keep that element of surprise. Yet it must be readily accessible when needed. It must be secure even when you run. Yet it must be quick to draw in an emergency.

The undercover gun isn't just a gun. It's a gun, holster, and belt. It's a system—elements that work together to accomplish their collective purpose. And if one element doesn't do its part, the system fails.

My typical rig in plain clothes is a high ride hugger, badge, and spare speedloader— normally covered by a jacket.

The choice of holster depends on where you will wear the gun. You can find holsters that hold the gun under your armpit, on your right hip, in front of your left hip, in the small of your back, in your back pocket, on your chest under your shirt, on your ankle, and almost anywhere else you can think of. Because I wear a right-hip duty holster, I insist on wearing an undercover gun on my right hip. That's where my reflexes are conditioned to reach.

If the holster is worn on a belt, what size belt? I sometimes wear a revolver belt strap that snugs the gun in close. The slots are 2¼ inches and the gun rides comfortably on a 2¼-inch lined gun belt. But put it on a decorative waist strap and the gun grip gives me a succession of kidney punches as I walk.

Snub-barrel revolvers minimize grip size for the sake of compactness. I've paid attention to grips ever since I saw a student grab for a snubby and send it sailing across the range. The small grip simply rolled out of his grasp before his fingers closed. Colt responds to this concern by equipping its snubbies with rubber combat grips. There are aftermarket accessories available for virtually any small handgun, and they're worth it.

When you grab for your gun, you want to be sure you find it quickly, draw it fast, and that it's in your hand when you try to pull the trigger.

30.2 Range Habits Are Deadly

Whatever you learn and practice on the range, that's how you'll react when facing a shootout.

In 1970, four young California highway patrolmen died in front of a diner in Newhall in a gun battle that has become known as the infamous Newhall Incident. One officer fumbled to get a sixth cartridge into his revolver as the gunman leaned over the hood of the car to put a bullet into the cop's brain. It never occurred to him that he could close the partially filled cylinder and shoot the five he had. He had been trained to load *six*. Another dead officer had an empty gun and six spent cases neatly tucked away. He had pocketed his brass *before* reloading his revolver. That's the way he did it on the range.

Those gallant men did not die in vain. The Newhall Incident changed police firearms training forever. It was a lesson bitterly learned. But much of the firearms training on the range today is still competition format, with rules and procedures and carefully marked scoring rings on targets. On the street, the targets shoot back. And they don't wait for a "Commence Firing" command.

Don't get me wrong. There is definitely a place for these competitions. Hostage situations, good-guy and bad-guy targets, situations that make you think—they're all good. They're fun. They're a challenge. In the broad sense, they help. But as long as they are practiced competitions, the danger remains that you will instinctively use competition habits in a street situation. And that can get you killed.

Just be aware of the competition shooting habits you are developing. Break the routine of competitive practice. Shoot some situations where you can attack targets just as you would on the street—from behind the mailbox, across the hood of a car, lying awkwardly behind a curbstone, one disabling shot into each of multiple targets before you put the second shot into them, double tapping a single target. Have someone else set up a situation so it's unfamiliar to you. Then think cover and tactics before exposing yourself to danger.

30.3 Revolver versus Auto

Police work today is quite different from what it was just a few years ago. The challenges we face are different. Who'd have thought there'd be situations like the Olympics in Munich? Or the armored-car robbery in Nanuet, New York, by a band of terrorists armed with high-capacity auto pistols and submachine guns? And there are too many other examples.

The traditional revolver has been a safe and reliable defensive tool for police since the turn of the century. But its capacity is limited—its potential for sustained fire before reloading is low.

The auto pistol is also a safe and reliable defensive tool. On the plus side, it offers greater firepower potential. On the negative side, it requires more training.

Departments are making the big switch from revolver to semiautomatic pistol. Some have kept the revolver and shotgun for the patrol division but armed specially trained tactical response units with high-capacity autos, scope-sighted rifles, and other special weapons. This shift to the self-loader is perhaps the biggest change in policing in decades.

Why have they switched? There are increasing incidents of attacks on officers, increasing use of sophisticated weaponry by the other side. We used to face lone criminals. Now we may well face a highly trained and well-armed terrorist attack squad. On the other hand, officers who patrol remote Western wilderness may come upon a renegade grizzly. That officer's requirements for a handgun are entirely different.

The best gun to carry depends on the potential challenges you face. And past history alone won't give you the right answer. We've all heard that the statistically average firefight is reported to be 2.3 shots fired in 2.7 seconds at an adver-

---

HOT TIPS FROM OLD HANDS

Breaking in new leather. New duty leather gear can be stretched into working shape with a light coat of mink oil. Safety straps on holsters and belt keepers, usually very tight when shipped, are especially good candidates for this treatment. Spray the strap lightly, then secure the gun in the holster with the strap snapped. It will stretch so that it can be easily secured, without getting too loose.

Officer Tim Dees
Reno, Nevada, police
department

sary less than 10 yards away. But those statistics are based on police armed with six-shot revolvers. They don't identify the situations where more shots would have been used if more than six had been available. And they are past history, not indicative of future potential. They don't reflect the trend to attack by organized groups rather than individual criminals.

The purpose of your training is to instill habits. Using your sidearm should happen without conscious thought. If you have been wearing a revolver for a dozen years, switching to an auto is much more than simply changing a pistol.

Shooting Habits Differ

A bad cartridge in a revolver just doesn't go off; pull the trigger again and the next round fires. But a bad cartridge in an auto pistol leaves it uncocked, dead in the water. A second pull on a double-action trigger *may* fire the same cartridge, but it may not. You need the instinct to jack the slide. The pistol is subject to "stovepipe" jams that can be quickly cleared with a wipe of the off hand—if you are trained to quickly identify and react properly to eliminate the problem.

The steps in reloading are similar but the procedures are not. At one department that had switched to the auto three years before, would you believe many of the men on the firing line reloaded the same way they would have with a revolver? Because their revolver habits were so deeply ingrained, when the slide locked back after the last round, those officers shifted the gun to their weak hand after dropping the magazine so their strong hand could reach for a new clip to stuff into the pistol.

With the auto pistol, it's obviously faster to reach for a full magazine on the weak side with the weak hand while the strong-hand thumb drops the empty magazine. And the spare magazine should be inserted into its pouch with the front forward. This way, you don't have to turn it. Pointing the weak-hand pointer finger up the front of the magazine lets you insert it into the pistol without looking. Then the weak-hand thumb (on some gun models) depresses the slide release and you're right back in battery with a two-hand grip ready to go.

That's just one habit that's different.

Drawing and firing the pistol is much the same as drawing and firing the revolver. But the two guns don't look at the same place. When a revolver shooter points a pistol, you can bet the muzzle is angled down. An "instinctive" reaction shot with an unfamiliar auto would likely hit the dirt in front of the target. The grip angle is different. You need to become comfortable with the different feel of the pistol.

Policemen have been armed with revolvers because it's easier to train raw recruits to handle them and because revolvers offer the utmost in safety and *ready availability*. Cops had become accustomed to a double-action trigger pull. Their guns were carried with a loaded cylinder, one chamber of which was always under the hammer. So revolver designers developed a hammer block that prevents an uncocked hammer from reaching the cartridge's primer unless the trigger is pulled.

The problem is that as new safety designs were added, not all of the old ones were replaced. Remember, the advantage of the double-action (DA) revolver is ready availability with safety. That advantage is the same with the DA auto but only if the thumb safety is left off. In autos with a firing-pin lock and the uncocked hammer blocked, there is all the safety of a DA revolver. So why complicate things with a thumb safety?

The answer is simple: you shouldn't. Gunmakers whose pistols have these internal safety mechanisms are beginning to refer to the thumb safety as a decocking lever. It still functions as a safety, in most guns, but if you *think* of it as a safety, it could be a death trap.

What about the man trained only with a revolver? He never learned to use a safety. Suddenly he's faced with remembering to release a safety latch when he draws his gun—unless he is trained to consider the thumb safety *only as a decocking lever.*

Servicing the Semi-Automatic Pistol   I would have said that auto pistols require more maintenance than revolvers. But the experience of the Connecticut state police proves my impression may be less than accurate. In the ten years prior to their switch, repairs to their older revolvers were made at an annual average of 5.6 guns for gas-check repair, 6.5 for trigger-stop repair, 10.5 for cylinder end shake, and 24.6 for timing. In the three years they'd had new auto pistols, repairs were zero.

Of course, we don't have data on what service problems might be when those pistols get more age and use on them. But this seems to say that maintenance is no more a problem with pistols than with revolvers.

When a revolver jams, that's when you wish you had a backup gun. You're not likely to clear it until it's too late. With auto pistol habits made second nature, you can have that gun firing again in less than a second—with a slam, rack, slap. Slam the bottom of the magazine, rack the slide, and slap it forward.

Too many revolver shooters relax their grip and get away with it. But an auto pistol functions against the resistance of your hand; it needs a firm grasp. Too often a malfunction can be traced to a limp grip. To get a proper grip, squeeze until your hand begins to shake, then back off a bit until it stops. Same for the weak hand. This way, the two-hand grip completely encases the grip of the gun with equal pressure all around.

With the weak-hand pointer finger wrapped around the hooked trigger guard to help control muzzle flip, a well-trained auto-pistol shooter can double tap a target so fast it almost sounds like one shot. With the isometric push-pull, the gun hardly seems to recoil. During my department's auto-pistol testing, every officer I observed used a revolver-style grip because that's the way they'd been trained. And you should have seen the muzzles flip.

No, I haven't answered the question, "Which is better, revolver or auto?" Because there is no one answer. Aside from the fact that you are probably not party to that decision, it depends on what you need the gun to do. Either can be the right choice. But I hope you understand that they are two different animals, each requiring different habits. And whatever you wear on duty, the one you wear off duty should be the same type and brand, even if it is a more compact model.

30.4 Ammunition

There are many different kinds of ammunition on the market for the gun you carry. I won't go into a technical dissertation because department policy will specify which load you carry. But what happens to that ammunition after you get it *does* depend on you.

A motorcycle officer in Arizona had completed his evening tour of duty and parked his bike behind his house. Walking along the dark path, he heard the sobering sound of a rattlesnake. He froze. With flashlight and handgun, he drew a bead on the head of the poised snake and stroked the trigger. "Click." He pulled the trigger five more times and each "shot" was another "click." He retreated to safer ground, found a rock, and killed the snake with it.

HOT TIPS FROM OLD HANDS

Check your ammo. Once I inspected duty ammo. One officer's ammo was so covered with crud, it couldn't be forced into the cylinder. Another was found carrying 200-grain "manstopper" rounds—which we quit using twenty years before.

If you're armed with a revolver, before you put ammo in your speedloaders or belt pouch, load them into the cylinder, pull back the hammer slightly, and rotate the cylinder at least one full turn. Repeat that little exercise with every cartridge. Only in this way can you be sure that each cartridge fits into the chambers and that none has a high primer to bind up the cylinder. If you use an autoloader, cycle each cartridge through the magazine, feeding it into the chamber before ejecting.

Then you can *know* the ammo you depend on to save your life will work when you need it.

Officer Ron Hackney
Detroit, Michigan,
Metro Police Academy

The next day, his department's lab technician disassembled the misfires and found both primer and powder soaked with chemicals. The officer admitted cleaning his revolver with an aerosol penetrant. And he habitually gave it another shot after loading the cylinder. That department has now issued a warning: "Do not apply lubricants or solvents directly to ammunition or a loaded firearm. Do not leave excessive oil or solvent on the weapon after cleaning it."

It's so easy to ignore something that hangs on your duty belt year after year. It's a policy in my department that qualification is followed by a Magnum course in which you must use the ammo in your duty belt. Then new duty ammunition is issued. The whole purpose is to make you spend the rounds you've exposed to the elements for several months.

If you're armed with a revolver, before you put ammo in your speedloaders or belt pouch, pull back the hammer slightly, and rotate the cylinder at least one full turn. Repeat that little exercise with every cartridge that may have to save your life. Only in this way can you be sure that each cartridge fits into the chambers and that none has a high primer to bind up the cylinder. If you use an autoloader, cycle each cartridge through the magazine, feeding into the chamber before ejecting. Then you can *know* they will feed properly.

It's a rare case to find loading abnormalities in factory ammunition. But anything's possible. I've seen culls from a production line with inverted or crushed primers, no powder, even inverted bullets. And of course a lot can happen to ammunition after it reaches you. You're out in the rain, snow, and sleet. You go from a warm stationhouse into freezing air outside. Or from summer heat into air conditioning. Such fluctuations in temperature can help penetrant sprays work their way inside a cartridge case. And haven't you read that ammunition, like so many other things, should be stored in a cool dry place?

It pays to look at duty-belt ammo every once in a while. If you find surface crud, wipe it off with a dry cloth. If you find corrosion, turn in the affected rounds and get new ones. If you use a spray to clean cartridges, dry them off thoroughly before putting them back on your belt.

The ammunition on your belt should be no older than your last qualification. Leather may retain residues of tanning chemicals that are corrosive to lead and brass. Corrosion eats into the metal and weakens the cartridge case. Leather can hold moisture; after a while, you find cartridges in belt loops with a band of green mold. Can you be sure those cartridges will chamber in your gun?

Just as complacency is the bane of officer survival, neglect is the enemy of your equipment.

30.5 Old Guns

There's always a chance you will have to render a strange gun harmless. A senile subject thinks the Indians are attacking his cabin and he grabs granddad's old heirloom out of the attic to fend off all comers. Once such a situation is cooled, someone has to make sure the old fowling piece isn't going to hurt anyone.

These old guns can hurt—and sometimes do. People don't stop to think that those old guns were usually kept loaded. It took a while to load them, so they were hung ready for instant use should they be needed.

You can encounter flintlock or percussion-lock guns even today. Antiques are still popular for decorative purposes. Replicas are being manufactured for the sports of muzzleloader target shooting and hunting.

To fully unload a muzzleloader without firing it literally requires a special tool to auger into the ball and pull it out. Since you don't have such a tool handy, here's how you can make old guns safe.

For the flintlock, or any old gun with a pan, open the pan and make sure it is empty. To render the percussion gun safe, cock the hammer and remove the copper-colored percussion cap from the nipple. Plural if it's a double barrel or revolver. Then let the hammer down, easy.

Old guns present a plethora of problems. The percussion shotgun (bottom) needs to have the caps removed from each barrel before it is safe. The Remington Cap and Ball revolver (right) has a percussion cap at each of six cylinder holes. Then how do you open the German Lugar (center)? Its bolt is held by toggle arms. The flint is missing on the flintlock pistol (left) but just opening the "frizzen" and blowing the pan clear will prevent it from firing.

31

Making the Deadly Decision

Headline in the news: "Supreme Court Limits Police Use of Deadly Force in Apprehending Suspects." What had happened?

Memphis police officers responded to a burglary-in-progress call. One took the front and another went around back. In the dark, the officer spotted a figure leaving the scene, about to scale a wall. He knew that his older and heavier torso would never keep up with the fleet figure. So he shot to prevent the escape of a fleeing felon, as Tennessee law provided—at the time.

Testimony indicated there was no apparent threat to the officer. The youth, who died from the gunshot wound, did not appear to have been armed. He was found to have property taken from the scene in his possession. The decedent's father brought suit against the city, its police department, and various individuals, alleging that the constitutional rights of his son were violated when the officer shot him to prevent his escape.

The U.S. District Court for the western district of Tennessee dismissed the complaint, ruling that the officer's actions conformed to state law. The U.S. Court of Appeals reversed the decision, holding that the statute authorizing the officer's actions violated the Fourth Amendment. The U.S. Supreme Court affirmed the Appeals Court decision.

The court could not have reached any other conclusion in *Tennessee* v. *Garner*, 471 U.S. 1 (1985). The decision, in effect, struck down the "fleeing-felon" laws of twenty-one states. But the court didn't do a thing that many jurisdictions hadn't already done by departmental policies.

31.1 Police Always in Jeopardy

It appears, however, that the Supreme Court decision was based on faulty information. Justice Byron R. White is quoted as saying that serious crimes against property, such as burglary, rarely involve violence and ordinarily would not be sufficiently dangerous to justify the use of deadly force.

A U.S. Justice Department study, on the other hand, says that a substantial proportion of violent crimes occurring in the nation's homes take place during a burglary. The Bureau of Justice Statistics reported in 1985 that 2.8 million of the roughly 73 million burglaries committed from 1973 through 1982 involved violent crimes. Three-fifths of all rapes, three-fifths of all robberies, and about a third of all aggravated assaults are committed by burglars. It also said that in 30 percent of the incidents where a burglar was confronted by a household member, a violent crime was committed. In short, burglary is potentially a far more serious crime than its classification as a property offense indicates.

The reason so much time is spent in training on proper techniques for stopping motorists is that cops are killed in just such situations. In a town near where I live, a motorist committed a minor traffic violation. The officer pulled him over, called in the stop, and got out of his car to walk up to the stopped car. The motorist, who happened to be the brother of a man who had been arrested and convicted and sentenced to jail, had been drinking. As the unsuspecting officer walked toward the stopped car, the driver leaned out of his window with a pistol and fired. The officer died.

There are any number of such examples. You never know what you're walking into whenever you respond to a call or stop to investigate something that caught your attention.

From a police point of view, the flaw in the *Garner* decision is that it can put the police officer in jeopardy. It makes officers hesitate—and that can be fatal.

Police Chief Leroy Bangham of Farmington, Connecticut, speaking for the Connecticut Police Chiefs Association (CPCA), appeared on a radio talk show the day after the decision was announced. "It [the decision] shouldn't affect any of our state's departments," Chief Bangham said. "Our CPCA model deadly force policy already provides much the same guidelines as the Supreme Court decision."

But then he explained the precarious position we put our police officers in. "Psychological screening is part of hiring. We train officers as best we can, give them a gun, and tell them to go out and protect us. But officers are human. If they make an honest mistake in a difficult situation now, they can go to prison. If a surgeon makes an honest mistake in the operating room, do we send him or her to prison?"

31.2 Training Is Critical

While twenty-one states still had unrestricted fleeing-felon laws, departments in those states had adopted more restrictive policies. Retaining those statutes protected the police officer who might make a poor judgment call in an awkward situation. But no longer.

Police training programs formerly taught deadly force only as a response to a threat of death or grave bodily injury to the officer or a third party. Now, greater emphasis is required. The consequences of poor judgment can go far beyond departmental discipline.

The challenge now is to train, train, train. You need to know instinctively how the *Garner* decision applies so you don't hesitate in the face of a deadly threat, or fail to shoot when you should, suffering grave consequences while pondering the legal situation.

But who makes that decision? The term *deadly-force decision* is a misnomer. You don't decide to shoot. You don't decide what level of force to use. Your use of force is a response to the situation presented to you by the subject.

Part of threat-response training is to learn that the subject determines the type and level of force appropriate to resolve a situation. And that's how you need to explain your actions in court. The police officer is never the aggressor in a confrontation.

31.3 Posttraumatic Stress

Even when police officers win deadly-force situations, the aftermath still leaves them devastated. There's the well-known California case where an officer responded to a neighbor's complaint, entered a vacant apartment, and untied and opened the door to the bedroom. Suddenly he was confronted in the half light by a dim figure pointing a gun at him. He fired. It turned out to be a five-year-old boy with a toy gun. The emotional impact was so great that the officer had not returned to work as this was written, and likely never will.

There are other cases where training, treatment, and support by other officers helped the officers involved to overcome their grief and become productive again. Posttraumatic stress is properly a part of training to prepare you for the time you have to take a life, then have to live with it.

But there is a new concern that we are putting so much emphasis on training officers to cope with posttraumatic stress that perhaps we are programming them to suffer it. A balanced perspective is needed. Training must teach us to recognize—and deal with—the symptoms: nightmares, sleep disorders, guilt feelings, alcohol and drug abuse, and family problems. But training must also include the mental conditioning we need for combat survival.

Not everyone suffers the same classic symptoms, nor at the same interval. It could come on after a considerable delay. And it's not always after a shooting incident. It could be the result of a particularly gruesome accident, or, as one friend told me, after he found a child who had been trapped inside a discarded refrigerator.

There's no predicting what the mental consequences will be when you take a life. In about a third of the cases, the officers suffer little or no adverse reaction; in another third, a moderate reaction; and a severe reaction in the final third. It could take you a month to get over it, or it could take a day. And if you suffer none of the consequences, it could mean just that you were mentally prepared and acted properly. You must react to a situation as you perceive it at the time. If your reaction is proper, you had no choice but to do what you did.

32

Battle over Body Armor

Everyone agrees that soft body armor saves lives, and that every police officer in harm's way should wear it. But that seems to be the only areas of agreement in a multifaceted controversy. There are divergent opinions on the new National Institute of Justice (NIJ) standard, the requirement for waterproofing, the concern over blunt trauma, the proper time to replace vests, and the best way to promote the use of soft body armor.

An International Association of Chiefs of Police (IACP) survey showed that 55 to 65 percent of patrol officers have vests—and that only 15 percent wear them regularly. FBI statistics indicate that only 20 percent of officers killed were wearing vests when they were killed. The idea that only one officer in five wears the soft body armor most of them have seems to be confirmed by a variety of sources. The reason this figure is so low has also been common knowledge for a long time. Cops don't wear vests because they are *hot* and *uncomfortable*.

32.1 The Original Concept

Richard Davis conceived the idea of soft, concealable body armor. He founded Second Chance Body Armor in 1971 and began making vests using ballistic nylon. When Du Pont commercially introduced Kevlar in 1972, Davis saw that the new fiber was two and a half times stronger than earlier ballistic nylon, and he became the first manufacturer to use Kevlar in soft body armor. He has produced a protection that officers would *use*. He blames a burgeoning bureaucracy with introducing so many additional concerns that vests meeting federal standards simply won't be worn.

32.2 The Question of Waterproofing

I repeat, the reason cops don't wear vests is that they're hot and uncomfortable. One thing that makes them hot and uncomfortable is waterproofing. Waterproofing adds heat retention and stiffness. How important is waterproofing if it causes cops to leave their armor in their lockers so it doesn't protect them in the first place?

The U.S. Army's Natick, Massachusetts, laboratory conducted tests using four Level I vests, two waterproofed and two untreated. One of each kind was worn by two officers who were put through perspiration-producing exercises on a hot, humid day. The other two were worn by security officers using a car without air conditioning and doing their normal duties. The amount of perspiration absorbed by the vest worn in the exertion exercises was enough to degrade ballistic resistance; penetration occurred. The other pair, worn during normal activity, passed the ballistic tests.

Lester Shubin, NIJ program manager for standards, says, in view of the perspiration-induced penetration, "The NIJ position is that safety should not be compromised in the name of comfort." But Richard Davis has a different opinion. "If meeting the standards for this extra margin of safety causes officers to leave their vests at home, they have no safety at all."

32.3 The Question of Blunt Trauma

When a bullet stops, its kinetic energy is transferred to whatever stopped it. In the early days, soft body armor was said to be useless because the force of the impact would knock you down, leaving you defenseless against the assailant, who could then walk up and administer the coup de grace.

Hollywood notwithstanding, physics tells us that no 125-grain pellet, even with perhaps 900 foot-pounds of residual energy, is going to knock a 185-pound man off his feet. But it took a dramatic demonstration to debunk the idea. That's what led Richard Davis to shoot himself in the chest while wearing a Second Chance vest in 1972. He fired a .38 Special, 125-grain JHP bullet to the left center of his chest at point-blank range and immediately turned to shoot three bowling pins off a table. He wasn't knocked off his feet. He continued to be functional, able to defend himself.

Blunt trauma is a reasonable concern however. In testing, it is measured by the backface signature, the depression made by the bullet in the clay backing the vest.

32.4 The Question of Replacement

NIJ conducted tests of older vests at the H.P. White Laboratory in Maryland. They were able to collect twenty-four vests issued by the Law Enforcement Assistance Administration (LEAA) back in 1975; eight had never been worn, four showed light wear, four showed moderate wear, and eight heavy wear. Front and back panels were tested individually, for a total of forty-eight test panels. All were Threat Level I types designed to protect against .38 caliber handguns.

In this test, ten-year-old armor showed no significant deterioration. All the used armor shot with .38 caliber bullets tested better than the average unused vest. When shot with a .22, light- and moderate-wear armor also tested better than the unused.

In 1980, some soft body armor was approaching seven years of age, and Du Pont was receiving questions about replacement, but they had no answer. In its "Selection and Application Guide to Police Body Armor," September 1981, NIJ had suggested a prudent five-year service life for soft body armor.

But Du Pont continued to be pressed for data. So the company gave one of Kevlar's developers, Louis H. Miner, the task. Lou tested a small number of used

Downrange, technician Larry Ragan sets up a body armor panel for testing. The chronograph screens measure the actual velocity of the bullet to make sure it's within tolerances. Nearest the camera is a bolt action receiver on a test barrel that is fired remotely for safety. **DU PONT.**

vests as a service to a large Midwestern department in April 1983. The vests met then-existing threat-level criteria, but more sophisticated tests, designed to measure ballistic performance, found decreases in bullet resistance of up to 8 percent.

Although Du Pont researchers considered the test results "satisfactory," the officer who had requested the evaluation concluded those seven-year-old vests needed replacing. This led Du Pont to begin comprehensive testing. In the first phase, 187 tests were conducted on 96 vests from 15 police departments. Of the ninety-six vests tested, three failed in dry tests, eight failed wet tests, and ten failed blunt trauma deformation; an additional forty-five showed 8 percent or greater decrease in ballistic performance. The rest tested within acceptable limits.

The second phase of testing began in October 1985 and continues at this writing. At the time I checked, it included seventy-nine vests. Three five-year-old vests failed, but nineteen vests, from three to ten years old, showed no decrease in ballistic performance.

Du Pont concludes that decreased ballistic performance varies greatly, depending upon the intensity of use, environmental factors, and the care the garment receives. It happens gradually. Extracted yarn tenacity tests indicate that fiber-strength loss from use is a principal cause of decreased ballistic performance.

Since ballistic effectiveness cannot be determined by visual inspection, Du Pont felt obligated to inform the law enforcement community of its findings. Copies of Lou's April 1987 report are available on request to T. E. Bachner, E. I. du Pont de Nemours & Co., Fibers Marketing Center, Wilmington, Delaware 19898.

32.5 The Question of Standards

Clint Davis of Second Chance resigned as chairman of the Personal Protective Armor Association (PPAA) standards committee to protest NIJ's refusal to consider a standard that would make waterproofing optional.

In May 1986, PPAA presented a proposal for a new federal standard. Its purpose, according to Du Pont's Bachner, was to promote "wearable" armor, simplify test methods, and to set reasonable protection levels. It proposed three protection levels for concealable body armor intended for continual wear. They are essentially defined as protecting against .38 Special + P, medium-velocity 9mm. and .357 Magnum, and high-velocity .357 and .44 Magnums. Another three protection levels were proposed for special-purpose armor meant to protect the SWAT team against submachine gun and rifle fire.

PPAA proposed simplified test procedures requiring a three-shot sequence for concealable armor, with only one shot fired at a 30-degree angle and optional wet testing.

The new NIJ Standard 0101.03 requires the same six-shot test sequence as the previous standard, with shots 4 and 5 fired at a 30-degree angle from each side. This causes a deformation of the clay backing material so the middle of the panel sits over a hollow, rather than flat against the chest. Shot 6 must hit between 4 and 5, right over this hollow.

For testing a IIA panel, 9mm velocities must be between 1090 and 1140 fps. That averages out to 1115 fps, plus or minus 25 fps, or 2.3 percent. The Sporting Arms and Ammunition Manufacturers Institute standard for factory ammunition is a designated velocity, plus or minus 90 fps.

The new standard does not change the requirements for wet and blunt trauma testing.

PPAA has since published its own standard.

32.6 IACP/Du Pont Kevlar Survivors' Club

The International Association of Chiefs of Police (IACP) and Du Pont cosponsor the IACP/Du Pont Kevlar Survivors' Club to recognize deserving individuals, promote the wearing of body armor, and collect statistical data. A study funded by Du Pont and supported by IACP found that most officers are aware of the dangers they face and the benefits of wearing soft body armor. But it also found a number of negatives, many predicated on erroneous information.

An officer who survives a potentially life-threatening incident is eligible, whether it's an assault with gun, knife, or other weapon, an accident, or an explosion—any time personal body armor was instrumental in saving life or preventing serious injury, on or off duty.

Candidates are nominated by the chief or supervisor, then verified by the club administrator. The club provides an attractive plaque, lapel pin, tie tack, and locket or charm for the department to present to the officer in appropriate ceremony.

So far, 210 awards have been sent to departments coast to coast. Of those, 125

Soft body armor could save you from more than bullets. Deputy Sheriff Carla Harmon of El Paso County, Colorado, was wearing her seat belt and body armor when her patrol car was hit head-on by a drunk driver during an ice storm. The seat belt saved her from going through the windshield and the body armor protected her from the crushing impact of the steering column. Accident experts agreed her chances for survival would have been nil without her personal body armor and seat belt. **DU PONT KEVLAR SURVIVOR'S CLUB.**

were saves in assaults; 85 were saves in accidents. The total number of awards for 1986 was 34. In 1987, the number jumped to 69. It will increase even faster as officers become more aware of the program.

It seems that the message to wear your armor is being heard. While felonious assaults have been declining since 1972, the number of accidental deaths is inching up. That adds up to a continuing level of threat to police officers. In this same time period, the total number of saves by the use of personal protective armor is on an upward trend. Personal body armor prevented at least seventy-eight deaths or serious injury to police officers in 1987, according to the club. "Encouraging increased use of personal body armor is the aim of the club," says Helen A. Slavin, club administrator. And that's a worthwhile goal.

"It's getting more dangerous out there," adds Charles E. Higginbotham, IACP's director of information services. "The importance of wearing personal body armor is growing. FBI statistics show that assaults on police officers have risen 15 percent in the last five years, and assaults with firearms have risen 8 percent. Accidental deaths, during the same period, rose 17 percent. More than one in ten law officers were assaulted in 1986."

"These data also show that a significant number of the officers killed each year might have been saved by lightweight, personal body armor," says Ed Bachner, Du Pont's ballistic account manager. "The vast majority of saves recorded were circumstances when officers didn't have time to go get their armor and put it on. You have to wear it all the time."

In addition to lives saved, a real benefit of the club is a better understanding gained as the data base grows. For information contact IACP/Du Pont Kevlar Survivors' Club, Room X-50680, Wilmington, Delaware 19898; phone 800-441-2746.

32.7 Invincibility

Have you seen cops act as if their badges stop bullets? Giving them a "bulletproof" vest reinforces that feeling of invincibility. Don't you believe it.

Protective soft body armor is "bullet resistant." And what if the bullet misses the armor panel? With all the publicity in general media, criminals are now aiming for the head. Officers are still shot in unprotected areas.

Body armor may save your life, but it does not replace the need for cover, concealment, and caution.

33

Who Cares?

While there are problems in every segment of the criminal justice system in America, it is my belief that real improvement must begin with the first phase, the foundation on which the whole system is built—the police. It's no easy job to be all-knowing, never forgetful, always complete in every detail, omnipotent, to do everything right and then stay alive long enough to retire.

Cops are human and no human is perfect, but people expect "their" police to be perfect. Efficient and effective law enforcement is a goal of everyone who puts on a badge. It's also a dream.

In 1977, the Vera Institute of Justice analyzed the disposition of felony arrests in New York and published its findings in a report titled "Felony Arrests: Their Prosecution and Disposition in New York City's Courts." A later analysis of the same data was published by Hans Zeisel in 1982, *The Limits of Law Enforcement* (University of Chicago Press).

Zeisel tells us that of 1,000 felonies committed, only 540 are reported to the police. Of those 540, only 65 result in arrests. Then they go to court. Of the 65 arrested, only 36 are convicted, 17 are sentenced to custody, and only 3 go to prison for more than one year. Zeisel says these figures exaggerate the apparent ineffectiveness of law enforcement. The first figures refer to events, the others to people. If one person were scored as having committed multiple events, the tally of events for which a conviction and sentence resulted would be higher.

There will always be a percentage of those arrested lost through dismissal or acquittal. But Zeisel tells us something else.

A breakdown of police arrests shows that only 18 percent were made solely on proactive (observed by police) actions. But 82 percent were based on calls to the police. Some 56 percent of the arrests were made quickly at the scene or soon thereafter. A full 80 percent resulted from observations or proactive police work, arrests at the scene or nearby, or identification of the suspect by a victim who knew the perpetrator. In his book, *The American System of Criminal Justice*, Geoffrey Alpert says this means only 20 percent of felony arrests result from other detective work or investigation. However, this is not to criticize these specialists. They usually get only the more difficult cases to work on.

In a study covering 1984, the Bureau of Justice Statistics found that 84 percent of those arrested on felony charges in 11 states were prosecuted, 62 percent were convicted, but only 36 percent ended up serving time in jail. According to the report, the highest rates of prosecutions, 90 percent, were in weapons offenses, vice cases, and parole violations. The lowest rate, 78 percent, was in drug cases. The study considered 532,000 felony cases in Alaska, California, Delaware, Georgia, Minnesota, Missouri, Nebraska, New York, Ohio, Pennsylvania, and Virginia.

In its *Sourcebook of Criminal Justice Statistics*, the Bureau of Justice Statistics publishes a wealth of information, some things you wouldn't expect. For example, what do people think of policemen?

According to a Gallop poll, public opinion of the honesty and ethical standards of policemen ranked seventh on a list of twenty-five professions. Only clergy, druggists, doctors, dentists, college teachers, and engineers rated higher. Policemen beat out bankers, lawyers, reporters, and politicians. By comparing data of prior years it's apparent that the esteem of police officers increases slightly each year. It surprised me to learn that among people under thirty years of age, 48 percent rated the honesty and ethics of policemen above average. By region, people in the East (51 percent), edged out the West (49 percent) and the South (47 percent); the Midwest scored 43 percent.

In a Roper poll, the question was asked, "Are there any situations you can imagine in which you would approve of a policeman striking an adult male citizen?" On average, 72 percent said yes in 1986, up from 69 percent in 1984 but down from 78 percent in 1983. Interestingly, the percentage of "yes" answers increases as the level of income increases.

People seem to recognize that you are justified in striking under certain circumstances but not in others. The percentage of those approving was nearly 100 when a person was attacking a police officer with his fists. It ranged around 80 percent if the person was attempting to escape from custody. But it was less than 20 percent if the person was simply saying vulgar and obscene things to the policeman. It was less than 10 percent if the person was being questioned in a murder case.

While we're on this subject, there's also data in the *Sourcebook* measuring people's opinions of courts in their own area. In 1986, 85 percent said their courts are not harsh enough on criminals. Only 3 percent said "too harsh," 8 percent "about right." This figure seems to remain fairly constant over the years but it's generally a few points higher than in the 1970s.

Considering it is the police function that feeds this entire system of justice, you can see why it is important to our profession—and our society—to attract good recruits, motivate young officers to reach beyond minimum standards, and to jog the memories of veterans so that all will learn, enhance their skills, and increase their efforts to achieve the purposes for which society created them.

Because people care.

Appendix A
Federal Agencies

There are something like 168 law enforcement and investigative units within the federal government. The number surprised me. And some are in departments you don't think of as law enforcement agencies. I won't even try to identify and describe each one of them, but here's a sampling, in alphabetical order, to give you an idea of the employment opportunities that may be found just within the federal government. For information, contact the agency whose badge you want to carry or the Federal Job Placement Center in your area.

Most federal agencies have similar employment requirements. You must be at least twenty-one but not more than thirty-five years old, possess a driver's license, a bachelor's degree or three years of responsible experience, pass a civil service exam, be in excellent physical condition, and survive a background investigation. Then you complete a period of training at the Federal Law Enforcement Training Center in Glynco, Georgia.

Investigators begin at grade GS-5, with promotions to 5, 7, and 11 following at one year intervals. Then promotions are earned through the federal merit promotion system.

A.1 Agriculture

The U.S. Department of Agriculture has special agents in the office of the inspector general who plan and conduct investigations into alleged violations of federal laws pertaining to programs and operations of the department. This involves gathering physical and documentary evidence, interviewing witnesses, examining files and records, and performing undercover and surveillance work that is often dangerous. Investigators' reports are used to assist in prosecution, and special agents testify at trials.

Special agents, as designated federal law enforcement officers, carry firearms, make arrests, and conduct searches.

A.2 Air Force

The U.S. Air Force has its military law enforcement function like the other services, but we include it here because, within the Office of Special Investigations (OSI), about 200 of the 1,800 special agents are civilians. Though few in number, the civilian agent force consists of individuals with unique talents for protecting Air Force and government resources worldwide.

Brig. Gen. Richard S. Beyea, Jr., commander of AFOSI, points out that his people have a higher degree of job satisfaction than those in most other career fields in the Air Force.

"We get involved in all sorts of complex criminal and fraud investigations. We help protect Air Force resources from hostile intelligence services. And we help protect Air Force people with antiterrorism and protective service operations," Gen. Beyea said.

"It's an exciting and challenging career, like trying to piece together a jigsaw puzzle but the pieces may not all be part of the puzzle. It takes ingenuity, creativity, and perseverance to solve some of our cases, but we must provide commanders with accurate information."

AFOSI special agents work closely with the Secret Service, State Department, CIA, the FBI, foreign law enforcement agencies, and local police. AFOSI uses agents with a knowledge of electronics, mechanics, languages, procurement and contracting, accounting and finance, administration, law, computers, and a range of other areas. Special agents work independently of base authorities but not without the knowledge of the requesting commander.

About 43 percent of AFOSI investigative efforts involve criminal cases, ranging from housebreaking to drug abuse to homicide. Because of the potential for computer-related crime, a new Computer Crime Investigative Assistance Program is being developed and expanding the methods for using computers as investigative tools.

About 25 percent of AFOSI resources are devoted to fraud investigations. Its counterintelligence mission is to identify and assess the threat by hostile intelligence services and terrorist groups and to protect senior officers and other U.S. officials.

A.3 Border Patrol

Within the Immigration and Naturalization Service, the U.S. Border Patrol is a specialized and highly trained officer corps with a mission to detect and prevent smuggling and illegal entry of persons into the United States. While it is part of INS, I list it separately because of its esteem as a law enforcement agency.

The new agent is likely to see service first in the southern border states of California, Arizona, New Mexico, and Texas. He uses pursuit vehicles, four-wheel drives, fixed-wing aircraft and helicopters, complex communications, and electronic sensing devices.

One of the most famous Border Patrol agents is Bill Jordan, famous because he was an NRA lifetime master with every gun he carried and was involved in so many gun fights he became a recognized authority on gun handling. He authored *No Second Place Winner* in 1965; it's still worth your reading.

It was Bill Jordan who, at the National Matches at Camp Perry, Ohio, in 1954, described the ideal law enforcement sidearm for then Smith & Wesson president Carl Hellstrom. Jordan wanted the power of the .357 Magnum cartridge in a medium-size .38 Special frame revolver. Training then used mid-range target loads. Jordan is the "father" of the S&W Combat Magnum, Model 19.

A.4 Bureau of Alcohol, Tobacco, and Firearms

The Bureau of Alcohol, Tobacco, and Firearms (BATF) is under the U.S. Treasury Department. It is responsible for the administration of some of the newest federal laws, but its history dates back to the earliest days of the United States.

Special agents of BATF investigate violations of federal laws relating to explosives, arson, firearms, illicit liquor, and tobacco. Investigations may involve surveillance, participation in raids, interviewing suspects and witnesses, making arrests, obtaining warrants, and searching for physical evidence. They work closely with other law enforcement officers, prepare case reports, and assist in the prosecution of violators.

Special agents are eligible for retirement at age fifty with twenty years federal service, may earn premium pay, and join group health and life insurance plans with the government sharing the cost.

Sales of new guns are reported to BATF, and these records have aided criminal investigations, some of them quite spectacular.

On March 30, 1981, President Ronald Reagan was shot while leaving a Washington hotel. The assailant was arrested on the spot by Secret Service agents, and the gun was recovered. Within minutes, BATF's National Firearms Tracing Center ran a trace on a Roehm model RG14, serial number L731332. A phone call to the manufacturer in Florida found the gun was shipped to a North Carolina wholesaler in 1980. The wholesaler's records led investigators to Rocky's Pawn Shop in Dallas. Rocky's records revealed the gun had been sold on October 13, 1980, to a twenty-five-year-old identifying himself as John Hinkley Jr. It took just fourteen minutes to add this important piece of corroborative evidence.

Tracing has become increasingly successful in investigating narcotics traffickers. In the first eighteen months of the President's Organized Crime Drug Enforcement Task Forces, BATF developed 146 criminal cases involving 210 defendants and the seizure of 1,171 firearms, including submachine guns and silencers.

A.5 Drug Enforcement Administration

The Drug Enforcement Administration (DEA) is responsible for the detection and apprehension of drug traffickers. In 1985, DEA's 3,000 agents stationed through the country and in forty-four other countries arrested more than 20,000 suspected dealers and confiscated controlled substances with a street value of about $500 million.

DEA's head, John C. Lawn, has updated the administration's training program and made it perhaps the toughest law enforcement academy in the world. New recruits spend thirteen weeks at Quantico, Virginia, in a program that aims to combat "a growing sophistication" among drug dealers and a "marked increase" in violence directed against agents during arrests and investigations, to use Lawn's words.

Lawn says his reasons are compelling. Five agents were killed in the line of duty between 1983 and 1988; dozens of others have been wounded or beaten. There are two shootings a week on average, involving agents and suspected dealers. On average, agents seize an automatic weapon each day of the year, including M-16s, AK-47s, MAC-10 and 11 machine pistols, and Uzi submachine guns. More than a third of the inmates in federal prisons were arrested in cases that DEA agents helped to investigate.

Recruits are required to have a bachelor's degree; about a quarter have master's or other advanced degree. Nearly a third speak a second language. Only one of every 100 applicants is accepted. The starting salary is about $23,000 a year.

There are typically four academy classes a year with about forty-two students each. Typically, about half have law enforcement experience. About 10 percent are women. "We are very serious about what we do here," says training director Robert A. Bryden. "People can lose their lives in this profession, and shame on us if we're not prepared for it."

A.6 Environmental Protection Agency

The Inspector General Act of 1978 created the Office of Inspector General (OIG) in the Environmental Protection Agency (EPA). It reviews EPA's financial trans-actions, program, and administrative activities and investigates allegations or evidence of possible criminal and civil violations. Within the OIG is the Office of Investigations, apart from audit and technical assessment.

During fiscal year 1986, EPA investigative efforts resulted in eighty indictments and convictions, and $2.8 million in fines and recoveries from persons or firms who defrauded the agency. Most recoveries involved bid rigging and other fraud on competitively awarded contracts. As examples of other cases, two project officials were investigated, indicted, and convicted of embezzling nearly $65,000 in grant funds. Another former employee was investigated jointly by OIG and the Secret Service for theft of checks and forging endorsements. A contractor was convicted on a forty-seven-count indictment of defrauding the government on a sewer project.

A.7 Federal Bureau of Investigation

In 1908, Attorney General Charles Bonaparte directed that Department of Justice investigations be handled by a small group of special investigators in the Bureau of Investigation. In 1935, Congress designated it the Federal Bureau of Investigation.

The FBI investigates violations of certain federal statutes and collects evidence in cases in which the United States is or may be an interested party. It investigates incidents that occur on federal jurisdictions, involve a federally chartered or insured financial institution, or where the crime is such that precedent presumes interstate travel. In kidnapping, for example, the law provides that unless the victim is located or released within twenty-four hours, it is presumed that he or she has been transported across state lines. Most federal statutes concerning organized crime are aimed at interstate gambling, loan sharking, infiltration of legitimate business, and interstate travel in aid of racketeering. The FBI investigates foreign-inspired terrorism because of its interstate nature.

There's a lot more to the FBI than just investigations. By the end of 1986, more than 178 million fingerprint cards representing some 60 million persons were in the FBI files. The FBI's Disaster Squad can help identify victims of catastrophies.

The FBI National Academy trains some 5,000 local, county, and state police officers each year. It runs the National Crime Information Center (NCIC), a computerized information system detailing missing persons, serialized stolen property, wanted persons, and criminal histories on individuals arrested for serious offenses.

Through NCIC, local police can access the Criminalistics Laboratory Information System (CLIS), which includes a general rifling characteristic file used to identify the manufacturer and type of weapon used to fire an evidence bullet. The FBI laboratory spends about a third of its time processing evidence for outside agencies. The FBI compiles crime reports into four quarterly reports and a comprehensive annual report called "Crime in the United States."

To become a part of the FBI, you must be a citizen of the United States, at least twenty-three but not more than thirty-five, and be available for assignment anywhere within FBI jurisdiction, plus the general requirements mentioned above.

The FBI employs more than 12,000 support personnel in nonagent positions: computer programming, chemical analysis, clerical, cryptanalysis, electronics and radio, engineering, explosives, firearms and ballistics, foreign languages, metallurgy, photography, spectroscopy, stenography, system analysis, and typing.

A.8 Immigration and Naturalization Service

The Immigration and Naturalization Service (INS) administers and enforces immigration and nationality laws, and they have to find out facts to do it. That's the job of the INS criminal investigator. He may plan and conduct investigations, surveillance, and undercover assignments. He also cooperates with other federal and local agencies.

The immigration inspector is stationed at points of entry into the United States. His job is to prevent illegal entry. The deportation officer provides control and removal of persons who have been ordered deported. He works with foreign consulates to facilitate the issuance of passports and travel documents required for deportation.

A.9 Internal Revenue Service

Criminal investigation as part of the Internal Revenue Service (IRS) began soon after the first tax law, the Revenue Act, was passed in 1913. When you think about it, you realize that infamous underworld figures often go to prison on income tax charges, rather than for other crimes.

About 2,800 special agents, most of them accountants or attorneys, or both, have the backup of some 30,000 trained personnel as part of this "operations team." These include revenue agents and tax auditors.

IRS Criminal Investigation makes cases in tax evasion, fraud, money laundering, and banking violations. Such cases usually involve criminal acts committed over a period of years, complicated by the number and variety of business transactions and varied methods of evasion employed. IRS special agents are recognized as the financial experts in the multi-agency Organized Crime Drug Enforcement Task Forces.

A.10 Marshals Service

George Washington appointed the first thirteen U.S. marshals. The service now has ninety-four marshals supported by more than 2,500 employees.

For eighty-one years before the creation of the Department of Justice, U.S. marshals were "federal law enforcement." Today, the Marshals Service reports to the Attorney General. Each U.S. marshal heads a district office throughout the United States, Puerto Rico, Virgin Islands, Guam, and the Northern Mariana Islands.

The backbone of the Marshals Service is the deputy U.S. marshal, famous as subjects of movies and popular television shows. Today, deputy marshals pursue and arrest fugitives, parole violators, and those who fail to appear. They secure the federal court and provide personal protection for judges. They transport prisoners by land and air, serve processes and warrants, and ensure the safety of endangered witnesses. They deprive the criminal of ill-gotten gains by seizing and managing assets acquired from criminal activity.

There's also a Special Operations Group (SOG), an elite and highly trained unit of volunteers who provide a swift law enforcement response to significant national emergencies requiring federal intervention. The SOG is on call twenty-four hours a day and can put an operational force anywhere in the country within six hours.

A.11 Office of Federal Investigations

The assassination of President Garfield by a frustrated job-seeker spurred Congress to pass the Pendleton Act in 1883. Conducting investigations was one of the original functions of the old Civil Service Commission, renamed the Office of Personnel Management (OPM) in 1978.

With the creation of the Office of Federal Investigations (OFI), additional responsibilities were added for conducting security investigations of sensitive positions in the federal government. For example, OFI checks out contractors for the Department of Energy, Nuclear Regulatory Commission, and other federal agencies.

Today, OFI is under OPM's associate director for training and investigations. There are about 700 investigators assigned to more than 135 duty stations throughout the country. It has two main purposes for investigations: (1) to determine whether a person should be granted a security clearance and (2) to determine a person's suitability for federal employment.

An OFI investigator could well develop information of past undetected crimes, ongoing criminal activity, or planned criminal activity. Then OFI cooperates with appropriate agencies to assist in the resolution of such cases.

A.12 Postal Service

The right of the people to be secure in their papers against unreasonable searches and seizures is guaranteed by the Fourth Amendment of the U.S. Constitution. When those papers are entrusted to the U.S. Postal Service, this right is embodied in the concept of the "sanctity of the seal." Since colonial times, protecting this right has been the responsibility of the Postal Inspection Service.

There are some 1,880 postal inspectors and 1,800 postal police officers who investigate criminal offenses; provide security for the mail, personnel, and property; and conduct the internal audit of the Postal Service.

Offenses could include robbery of mail, burglary of a postal facility, assaults on postal employees, theft of mail, letter bombs, mail fraud, extortion, obscenity, counterfeiting, accidents—virtually any crime involving postal interests.

A.13 Secret Service

The U.S. Secret Service claims to be the first general law enforcement agency of the federal government. At the close of the Civil War, as much as half of all paper currency in circulation was counterfeit. To combat the threat, the Secret Service was created on July 5, 1865, as a division of the U.S. Department of the Treasury. Within a decade, counterfeiting was sharply reduced.

In its early years, the Secret Service was called upon to investigate such diverse cases as the Teapot Dome oil scandals, the Ku Klux Klan, government land frauds in the west, and counterespionage activity during the Spanish-American War and World War I. As other federal law enforcement agencies were created, the service's jurisdiction became limited to Treasury-related crimes.

Today the service investigates counterfeiting of currency and securities, and fraud and forgery of U.S. checks, bonds, and other obligations. In 1984, Congress expanded the mission to include fraud related to false identification documents, credit and debit cards, and computer fraud, including the electronic transfer of U.S. Treasury funds.

When President William McKinley was assassinated in 1901, Congress directed the service to protect the new president, Theodore Roosevelt. It wasn't until 1906, however, that legislation was passed making presidential protection a permanent Secret Service responsibility.

Since then, Secret Service protective duties have increased dramatically. Included are the President and Vice President and their families; former Presidents, their spouses, widows, and minor children; major candidates for President and Vice President and their spouses; visiting heads of foreign states; and others at the direction of the President.

The Secret Service today has some 4,300 employees, including two uniformed forces: the U.S. Secret Service uniformed division and the Treasury police force. More than 1,900 special agents are rotated throughout their careers between investigative and protective assignments. A number of specialists serve, including security specialists, electronics engineers, communications technicians, research psychologists, armorers, computer experts, forensic experts, and other professionals.

The uniformed division was formed to protect the White House during the Civil War. In 1922, President Warren G. Harding created the White House police and President Herbert Hoover made it part of the Secret Service in 1930. In 1970, responsibilities were expanded to include foreign diplomatic missions in the Washington, D.C. area, and the force was renamed the Executive Protection Service. It took on its present name in 1977.

The Treasury police was established in 1789, making it one of the oldest in America. It became part of the Secret Service in 1937. In the early years, officers accompanied money shipments, guarded currency in the Treasury vault, and ensured security in the Treasury's cash room. Today, these officers maintain security over Treasury facilities, guard the Secretary, and assist in investigations of crimes committed within Treasury buildings.

A.14 State Department

The Department of State's Bureau of Diplomatic Security (DS) was created in November 1985 to provide a secure environment for the conduct of American diplomacy and the promotion of American interests worldwide, and to increase security awareness among all Americans living, working and visiting abroad. The security of every U.S. embassy, mission, and consulate abroad is the responsibility of this agency.

The Diplomatic Security Service is the operational arm of the bureau. Only 7 percent of those who apply are selected for special agent training. These professionals work with foreign and other federal and local law enforcement agencies to protect American facilities and personnel here and abroad.

DS manages a security-awareness program for U.S. government employees and their dependents. Security training teams visit high-threat missions to instruct employees in such protection tactics as self-defense, hostage survival, and defensive driving.

The first line of defense at U.S. facilities abroad are 13,000 foreign contract guards who stand watch under the supervision of DS agents. Inside are the 1,400 Marine security guards. DS has developed standards to upgrade physical security and has designed and installed sophisticated alarm systems, bomb detection devices, and architectural barriers. Crisis-management teams assist in testing emergency action plans and train personnel in crisis-management techniques.

DS security engineers monitor and negate the electronic threat facing embassies, and DS intelligence experts brief personnel on counterintelligence. Information on terrorist activities is gathered and analyzed. Alleged espionage incidents are investigated. Confirmed acts of espionage are assessed.

DS has security professionals in 116 embassies and consulates throughout the world and at field offices in 9 U.S. cities.

A.15 Interpol

I saved this for last because it isn't really a law enforcement agency. Contrary to what you've seen in the movies, Interpol doesn't send agents around the world to investigate crime.

The International Criminal Police Organization (INTERPOL) was created in 1923 by a small number of European nations to promote mutual assistance and cooperation among various law enforcement entities to suppress international crime. It was so successful that, despite a period of disruption during World War II, some 142 nations are members today.

Interpol is a unique organization in which each nation maintains its own sovereignty. It supports a worldwide telecommunications network and addresses criminal activities that have been spawned by modern technology. Current major programs include international terrorism, illicit drugs, economic and financial fraud, capture of international fugitives, and the tracing and recovery of stolen works of art.

Each participating country operates a National Central Bureau (NCB) as that nation's point of contact with the international law enforcement community. In most countries, this is an office in the national police. In the United States, it is under the Departments of Justice and Treasury, staffed by personnel from those and other federal law enforcement agencies, with regional offices around the country.

State and local law enforcement agencies can contact the NCB through the National Law Enforcement Telecommunications System (NLETS) to request investigative assistance in any of the Interpol member countries.

Because acts of terrorism are often politically motivated, it was thought they were covered under the prohibition against Interpol intervening in matters of a racial, military, political, or religious nature. At the General Assembly meeting in Luxembourg in 1984, delegates reasoned that whatever the motive, the act itself should not be interpreted as political if the target is not directly connected with the aims or objectives of the offenders. Thus, acts of terrorism became crimes against society.

The 1985 General Assembly meeting in Washington D.C. approved further response to terrorism. Interpol's International Terrorism Group came into being in January 1986. It's a focal point for all information concerning terrorist activity, compiling and analyzing data as it comes available. As one of its first tasks, the group developed a manual outlining what can be done using existing organizational methods such as publication of international lookouts, wanted notices, information of property, and other identifying information.

Appendix B
Helpful Agencies

Many agencies and organizations aid law enforcement. This is by no means a complete list, nor are descriptions all inclusive. Individuals are identified, if known.

B.1 NIJ/TAPIC: Information for Law Enforcement

Look at any catalog of police equipment to see the diversity of technologies available for your purchase. There's a wide choice of brands and flavors, and a lot of it is beyond the capacity of a small police department to properly evaluate. Picking and choosing isn't as easy as it once was. But whether you're buying handcuffs for a dozen-man department or a fleet of cars for a 1,000-man state patrol, you need to make the right decision, which means you need good, complete information.

Say you are selecting a sidearm. Your firearms instructor will want to take the candidates out to the range. Given the dedication, time, and enough ammunition, he can give you a fairly definitive evaluation. But does he have a chronograph? A pressure tester? A Ransom rest? He isn't really equipped to give you a comprehensive laboratory analysis.

More than a decade ago, the National Institute of Justice began a program of establishing performance standards, testing products for conformance to those standards, then publishing consumer products lists and test reports. It was formerly administered by the International Association of Chiefs of Police (IACP). This information now comes from the Technical Assessment Program Information Center (TAPIC).

TAPIC publishes a periodic newsletter, *TAPIC Alert,* to keep criminal justice officials informed. Consumer reports (CRs) tabulate test results of products in a particular category. CRs do not recommend product brands but do discuss trade-offs to consider before making a purchase. Products that are found to conform to standards are listed in consumer product lists (CPL). Updated CPLs are issued as additional products are tested.

Patrol car testing is conducted annually by the Michigan State Police. Fourteen different cars were tested for braking, acceleration, top speed, vehicle dynamics, ergonomics, and communication capabilities. Tests in 1986 were on the Dodge Diplomat 183-4bbl, Ford Crown Victoria 351-vv, Plymouth Gran Fury 318-4bbl, and Chevrolet Caprice 350-4bbl. The report on radio batteries was originally issued in 1984. Later tests examined sixty-four different nickel-cadmium battery models against the TAP standard. The report summarizes test results and discusses such other considerations as size and weight.

Sharing information with private industry enables manufacturers to design or redesign equipment so that it more closely meets the needs of criminal justice agencies. When a report on handcuffs was issued, for example, two manufacturers introduced entirely new and improved handcuff designs that complied with the standards.

Through TAPIC, the Law Enforcement Standards Laboratory produces guides on how to purchase and use equipment; they do not include test results but show you how to select equipment. Guides are available on communications systems, procedures for collecting and preserving physical evidence, and selecting body armor.

There's a special report that's neither a CR nor a guide. The Relative Incapacitation Index is a research report that ranks common ammunition according to its ability to incapacitate violators while providing a margin of safety for bystanders.

Most publications of The Technical Assessment Program are available through the National Criminal Justice Reference Service, Law Enforcement Standards Laboratory (LESL), or TAPIC. For information call 1-800-24-TAPIC, or write TAPIC, Box 6000, Rockville, MD 20850.

B.2 National Auto Theft Bureau

NATB is a crime-prevention organization supported by more than 600 property and casualty insurance companies. It provides assistance to law enforcement, insurance companies, and the public.

NATB develops and implements policies for the prevention of vehicle theft, vehicle arson, and vehicle fraud. It aids in the prosecution of persons engaged in these activities and in locating and identifying stolen vehicles. It promotes vehicle theft-prevention programs and conducts training for law enforcement officers. Through its *NATB Journal*, it shares information about successful cases breaking up vehicle theft rings.

The executive office of NATB is at 10330 South Roberts Road, #3A, Palos Hills, IL 60465; phone 312-430-2430.

B.3 Aviation Crime Prevention
Institute

ACPI is a nonprofit organization funded by the aviation insurance industry and others to combat aviation-related crime and to provide education in aviation crime prevention. The *Alert Bulletin Quarterly* lists stolen and unrecovered aircraft and avionics that are reported to ACPI on its toll-free number: 800-234-5444. As of January 1, 1988, there were 260 aircraft on the stolen list.

ACPI just published an *Aviation Identification Manual for Police Officers*, single copies free on request. It illustrates various general aviation aircraft, explaining registration numbers and showing vehicle identification number (VIN) locations.

ACPI picks up where the National Crime Information Center (NCIC) leaves off. NCIC aircraft records remain in the data base for four years plus the year of entry. ACPI lists stolen equipment indefinitely, and aircraft when identified as a bona fide theft. ACPI records date back to 1973, when the original International Aviation Theft Bureau was formed.

ACPI headquarters address is P.O. Box 3443, Frederick, MD 21701; phone 301-694-5444; Robert J. Collins, president.

B.4 Insurance Crime Prevention Institute

In its role to investigate suspicious claims and secure the arrest and prosecution of insurance criminals, ICPI functions as a highly productive channel for communications and cooperation between the insurance industry and the criminal justice system.

Typically, ICPI will conduct an investigation sufficient to determine whether a crime has been committed. At the appropriate time, evidence will be presented to a public law enforcement agency for further investigation or indictment, arrest, and prosecution.

ICPI also initiates investigations on the basis of requests for cooperation from law enforcement agencies engaged in insurance-related investigations, and will provide public law enforcement with training resources on a variety of fraud schemes. ICPI is not involved in adjusting claims or providing information to insurance carriers for adjusting or underwriting purposes.

National headquarters of ICPI is at 15 Franklin Street, Westport, CT 06880; phone 203-226-6347; Wendall C. Harness, director. There are regional offices in Illinois and California.

B.5 National Crime Prevention Council

"We're not just stopping something, we're starting something." That's the title of the brochure explaining the NCPC. Since 1982, NCPC has worked with an alliance of national, state, and local organizations, businesses, and government agencies, to generate crime-prevention awareness and action at every level of society.

You've seen and heard "Take a Bite out of Crime" advertisements. This campaign has generated more than $200 million in donated space and air time.

"Crime has two victims," says Executive Director John A. Calhoun, "the individual and society." Education is one of our most powerful weapons against crime. NCPC is the focal point of a network of information services. It publishes, receives, and exchanges a variety of public education materials. It maintains a computerized data base of crime-prevention activities with information on thousands of programs to assist law enforcement agencies and others.

A staff of twenty-five is headquartered at 733 15th Street N.W., #540, Washington, DC 20005; phone 202-393-7141.

B.6 Search Group

Search Group, Inc., the National Consortium for Justice Information and Statistics, is a nonprofit organization of states dedicated to improving the criminal justice system through technology. Since 1969, it has provided leadership in information systems, responsible law and policy, and national statistical research. It is funded by state membership dues, grants, contracts, and donations.

I learned about Search through the National Clearinghouse for Criminal Justice Information Systems. They create software packages and put them in public domain. Most recent are a jail-management system for small and medium-sized jails called LOCKUP; a prosecutor's management support system called DA's ASSISTANT; and MICRONYM Plus, a system for state identification bureaus. They maintain a data base of all public-domain police computer programs they know about, more than 1,500 systems so far.

With the Criminal Justice Statistics Association, Search developed the National Criminal Justice Computer Laboratory and Training Center in Washington D.C., an expansion of its model center in Sacramento, California.

Search Group Inc., is headquartered at 925 Secret River Drive, #H, Sacramento, CA 95831; phone 916-392-2550.

B.7 Other Helpful Groups

There are many more agencies and organizations whose purpose is to aid law enforcement and criminal justice agencies. Here is an alphabetical listing of those identified at this writing, with contacts included where known.

Association of American Railroads
Police and Security Section
1920 I Street NW
Washington, DC 20036
202-639-2100

Conducts the National Railroad Police Academy in conjunction with the State Law Enforcement Officer's Training Academy in Jackson, Mississippi.

Commission on Accreditation of Law Enforcement Agencies
4242-B Chain Bridge Road
Fairfax, VA 22030
703-352-4225

A nonprofit corporation founded in 1979, the commission works to promote excellence, efficiency, and professionalism in law enforcement agencies nationwide. Accreditation is a process of improvement and change. Agencies must meet some 900 standards that require sound, effective policies and procedures in management, operations, and support services. The commission's book of standards has eleven chapters dealing with personnel issues and six addressing traffic operation. There are chapters on public information, community relations, internal affairs, and crime prevention. The chapter titled "Law Enforcement Role and Authority" speaks to the limits of authority and the use of force.

National Alliance for Safe Schools
501 North Interregional
Austin, TX 78666
512-396-8686

Created in 1977, this is a research, training, and technical assistance center funded by the National Institute of Justice. Robert J. Rubel.

National Center for Computer Crime Data
2700 North Cahuenga Boulevard, #2113
Los Angeles, CA 90068
213-874-8233

NCCCD is principally a research institute and publisher of the *Computer Crime Law Reporter* and a source book called *Introduction to Computer Crime*. In 1986, it published results of a study on computer crime, computer security, and computer ethics. NCCCD serves as a clearinghouse for information about computer crime. Presently in the works is "Computer Crime Fighting, Career of the Future." Case summaries are covered in the Computer Crime Chronicles series. "The Defense of a Computer Crime" is a 197-page analysis covering the current law, recently litigated cases, and the implications of the laws and cases for trial strategy. J. J. BloomBecker, director.

National Criminal Justice Reference Service
U.S. Department of Justice
Box 6000
Rockville, MD 20850
800-851-3420 outside the Washington metropolitan area
Maryland and Alaska: 301-251-5500

Periodically publishes lists and reports of studies, publications, and other materials of interest to the law enforcement community.

National Institute of Corrections
320 First Street NW
Washington DC 20534
202-724-7995

NIC is a small federal agency that provides a range of assistance services to improve policy and practice in the field of corrections. The full program is described in NIC's Annual Program Plan available by calling NIC at 202-724-8449.

NIC Information Center
1790 30th Street #130
Boulder, CO 80301
303-444-1101

Information center that distributes all NIC documents.

Personal Protective Armor Association
28 Belcaro Circle
Nashville, TN 37215
615-665-1000

PPAA was formed in 1977 by those involved in the manufacture, sale, supply, or distribution of soft body armor, to promote its use by the law enforcement community. Larry Gates.

Police Executive Research Forum
2300 M Street NW
Washington, DC 20037
202-466-7820

As its name implies, PERF aims to improve police services and crime control through research and policy development, debate of criminal Justice issues, and providing management, technical support, and leadership services to law enforcement agencies. General membership is made up of executive heads of public law enforcement agencies with 100 or more employees or serving a population of 50,000 or more people. The Forum's professional staff provides research, technical assistance, and management service. It has been involved in the development of police problem-solving models, new approaches to coping with repeat offenders, criminal investigation models, differential police response strategies, and police executive selection criteria.

Appendix C
Police Organizations

There are many associations aimed at aiding various law enforcement specialties in the exchange of information, improving professional skills, or refining new techniques. This section refers not to official procedures for sharing criminal intelligence, such as the National Crime Information Center (NCIC), or regional cooperation in a computerized fingerprint system or training academy, but rather, membership organizations that respond to the special needs of their members. Membership organizations usually publish a magazine or newsletter, hold an annual convention, and provide other training and assistance to its members.

This is an alphabetical list of those I found. Comments are included where organizations responded with information. I won't repeat the usual member services or detail the programs of each organization. If known, the name and title of the contact person are included. While I made every effort to make this list as complete and accurate as possible, new groups form and addresses change. You should write to the association of interest to you for the latest information.

C.1 Membership Associations

Airborne Law Enforcement Association
1450-A North Airport Road
Naples, FL 33942
916-923-1446

> ALEA is dedicated to enhancing the airborne presence in law enforcement through the exchange of information and providing training in both fixed- and rotary-wing aircraft. Carl Meadows, executive director.

American Probation and Parole Association
c/o Council of State Governments
P.O. Box 11910
Lexington, KY 40578
606-252-2291

Conducts training programs, seminars and disseminates information to members through its quarterly publication *Perspectives.* Membership represents adult and juvenile probation, parole, and community agencies throughout the United States and Canada. Ben Jones, staff director.

American Society for Training and Development
1630 Duke Street, Box 1443
Alexandria, VA 22313
703-683-8100

While not strictly a police group, ASTD is the world's largest association in the field of employer-based training. It represents some 50,000 professionals.

American Society of Law Enforcement Trainers
P.O. Box 1003
Twin Lakes, WI 53181-1003
414-279-5700

ASLET is a group of law enforcement trainers, educators, and administrators in all fields. Its purpose is to advance progressive and innovative law enforcement training. Edward Nowicki, executive director.

American Society for Industrial Security
1655 North Fort Myer Drive #1200
Arlington, VA 22209
703-522-5800

ASIS was founded in 1955 to foster professionalism in the field of security. It sponsors the Certified Protection Professional (CPP) program for those meeting education and experience requirements and pass a written test. Sue Melnicove.

Associated Public-Safety Communications Officers, Inc.
P.O. Box 669
New Smyrna Beach, FL 32069
904-427-3461

APCO works for the improvement of all forms of public safety communications. Founded in 1935, it is open to those employed by a public safety agency or company that provides products or service to the field. Bob Buttgen, executive director.

Association of Firearms and Toolmark Examiners
80 Mountain View Avenue
Rensselaer, NY 12144
518-286-3912

AFTE was formed in 1969 to advance and improve the knowledge and techniques of examining firearms and toolmarks. Some 500 members worldwide include laboratory examiners, firearms and ammunition industry personnel, and consultants in firearms identification and related fields. AFTE is pledged to establish and maintain standards, to sponsor and support research, and to collect and disseminate information relevant to firearm and toolmark examination. Andy B. Hart, membership secretary.

Criminal Justice Statistics Association
444 North Capitol Street #606
Washington, DC 20002
202-347-4608

CJSA assists those involved in statistical analysis of criminal justice information for policy and management.

Eastern Armed Robbery Conference, Ltd.
P.O. Box 607
Wilmington, DE 19899

Dedicated to the exchange of intelligence among police agencies, EARC was founded in 1971 by Simon G. Edwards, Bureau of Police, Wilmington, Delaware, as a nonprofit, tax-exempt organization. Attendance at its bimonthly conferences is high, and information exchanged has resulted in clearing many felony cases. Membership is largely from the eastern United States and Canada. Representatives of individual agencies are encouraged to present discussions of such serious crimes as homicide, robbery, and hijacking, with special emphasis on those committed by transient criminals. Photos and information sheets are distributed.

International Association of Auto Theft Investigators
255 South Vernon
Dearborn, MI 48124-1340
313-561-8583

IAATI has more than 1,600 members from the United States, Canada, United Kingdom, Puerto Rico, Sweden, Australia, and Portugal. Active members represent all levels of law enforcement. Affiliate members represent insurers, manufacturers, and car rental firms. Goals are to encourage high professional standards of conduct among auto-theft investigators; disseminates technical information and conducts seminars.

International Association of Arson Investigators
25 Newton Street, P.O. Box 600
Marlboro, MA 01752

IAAI, founded in 1951, is dedicated to the control of arson and related crimes. Membership is open to those engaged in arson investigation, detection, and prosecution in the public or private sector. Dan Lemieux.

International Association of Campus Law Enforcement Administrators
638 Prospect Avenue
Hartford, CT 06105
203-233-4531

IACLEA is dedicated to promoting professional ideals and standards of campus security and law enforcement. Membership is composed of colleges and universities throughout the United States, Canada, and Mexico, individual campus law enforcement directors and staff, as well as criminal justice faculty and municipal police chiefs.

International Association of Credit Card Investigators
1620 Grant Avenue
Novato, CA 94947
415-897-8800

IACCI was formed in 1968 by a group of credit card investigators and law enforcement professionals to aid in the establishment of effective card and check safety programs, to suppress fraudulent use of cards and traveler's checks, and to detect and aid in the apprehension of violators. Membership classification is determined by the relationship of the applicant to the investigative function. D. D. Drummond, executive director.

International Association of Chiefs of Police
13 Firstfield Road, P.O. Box 6010
Gaithersburg, MD 20878
301-948-0922

IACP was founded in 1893, which makes it the oldest on this list. Membership is open to chiefs and superintendents of police, command and administrative level officers. It offers many assistance programs and subsidiary groups. Carol Bennette, membership director.

International Association for Identification
P.O. Box 2423
Alameda, CA 94501-2423

IAI was established in 1915 to bring together people internationally who are actively engaged in the profession of scientific identification and investigation of crime. The goals are to foster ethical standards, promote cooperation, stimulate improvements in forensic sciences through research, and to disseminate such advancements. An annual international educational conference is supplemented by state and regional conferences. The *Journal of Forensic Identification* is published bimonthly. Ashley R. Crooker, Jr., secretary.

International Association of Airport & Seaport Police
580-2755 Lougheed Highway
Port Coquiltlam, BC
Canada V3B 5Y9
604-942-2132

The International Association of Port Police was founded in March 1970 in Boston to improve the security of the world's maritime facilities. In 1974, it reorganized to include aviation and became the IAASP. Through international communication, cooperation, and consultation, IAASP works to improve operational effectiveness of airport and seaport law enforcement officers. Its objectives are to prevent and detect crime, study and recommend uniform practices for safeguarding international cargo, exchange information among law enforcement agencies, and encourage cooperation for improved security in the international trade community.

IAASP has 205 members in 40 countries and now maintains a full time secretariat. T. Ciunyk, executive director.

International Association of Law Enforcement Firearms Instructors
R.F.D. 3, Box 57N
Laconia, NH 03246
603-279-8869

IALEFI was formed in October 1981 by firearms instructors to promote more relevant firearms training programs and enhance instructor skills. It publishes a quarterly newsletter and sets criteria for training programs and instructor certification. Bob Bussey, executive director.

International Association of Law Enforcement Intelligence Analysts
P.O. Box 876
Washington, DC 20044

Formed in December 1980, IALEIA aims to establish qualification standards and enhance understanding of intelligence analysts in law enforcement. It isn't a lobbying or collective bargaining organization and does not exchange substantive intelligence. The association keeps its members abreast of new analytical techniques, training courses, career advancement opportunities, and other developments of interest to the profession. Jack Morris, president.

International Association of Women Police
P.O. Box 15207, Wedgewood Station
Seattle, WA 98115
206-625-4465

IAWP is the second oldest police association I found; it was formed in 1915. It develops standards for the service of women police, encourages proper training and increased use of women in law enforcement. Beryl Thompson, executive director.

International Conference of Police Chaplains
Rt. 5, Box 310
Livingston, TX 77351
409-327-2332

ICPC supports volunteer and paid chaplains and helps law enforcement agencies develop chaplaincy programs. It provides its members with educational opportunities and a network for sharing information. It was founded in 1973 and has members in all fifty states, seven provinces of Canada, and six other countries. Chaplain David W. De Revere, executive secretary.

International Juvenile Officers Association, Inc.
P.O. Box 2224
Florissant, MI 63032
314-298-7788

IJOA was founded in 1957 and is dedicated to improving organization techniques and education, promoting research and establishing juvenile control councils, institutes for learning, and more effective programs for working with youths. Provides technical assistance and training. Charles J. Fumagalli, executive director.

International Narcotic Enforcement Officers Association, Inc.
112 State Street, #1310
Albany, NY 12207
518-463-6232

INEOA membership is open to those involved in narcotic law enforcement. It was founded in 1960. Joe J. Bellizzi, executive director.

National Association of Chiefs of Police
1000 Connecticut Avenue NW, #9
Washington, DC 20036
202-293-9088

NACP was founded in 1976. Membership is open to those holding a command rank in law enforcement and private security managers involved in national defense. Chief Edward Turner.

National Association of Federal Investigators
1612 K Street NW, #202
Washington, DC 20006
202-466-7288

AFI is the only professional association dedicated to the enhancement and protection of the federal investigator. It publishes a monthly newsletter and an annual *Investigator's Journal* and offers insurance benefits, professional development, and an awards program. A. Leigh Stewart, executive director.

National Disabled Law Officers Association
75 New Street
Nutley, NJ 07110

NDLOA was founded in 1972 by Peter Frazza. As a police officer in 1963, Frazza was pursuing a criminal in a car chase when his cruiser was struck by another vehicle. He was severely injured in his chest, head, and neck. Physically devastated, he was forced to retire at the height of his career.

Peter Frazza has built an organization of some 5,000 disabled police officers around the country. Joining is easy. All you have to do is ask. There are no dues.

Police officers, like sports heros, are respected. But strip them of badge, power, and uniform, and they lose confidence and may become confused, angry, hurt. They become candidates for emotional disaster. NDLOA provides emotional support. Frazza is an understanding sympathizer, a counselor. He provides the kind of therapy not available through conventional counseling. He fights forced retirement, saying there are many police jobs a disabled officer can do.

National Organization for Victim Assistance
717 D Street NW
Washington, DC 20004

NOVA is a private, nonprofit organization of victim and witness assistance practitioners, criminal justice professionals, researchers, former victims, and others committed to the recognition of victim rights. Its purposes are to help pass federal and state legislation and to help change local policy that affects the rights of victims, to help victims, to work with local programs in victim counseling and reparations, and support its membership and provide an information exchange.

National Sheriffs' Association
1450 Duke Street
Alexandria, VA 22314
703-836-7827

NSA was established in 1940 to represent sheriffs throughout the country. It has more than 30,000 members, including sheriffs, deputy sheriffs, police executives and officers, corrections personnel, and other criminal justice professionals. NSA is the force behind such programs as Neighborhood Watch, Jail Training, and Victim Assistance.

National Tactical Officers Association, Inc.
P.O. Box 1412
La Mirada, CA 90637
213-943-4223

NTOA, founded in 1983, includes active or retired officers involved in SWAT or tactical units. Its purpose is to provide an information exchange and operational evaluation service. John Kolman, director.

Tactical Response Association
P.O. Box 17354
Salt Lake City, UT 84117
801-277-1513

TRA is an organization of professionals dedicated to combatting international terrorism. It is composed of law enforcement officers, hostage negotiators, SWAT team members, intelligence officers, and selected private security personnel. Its purpose is to exchange intelligence and information to combat terrorism. To be an active member, you must work with tactical response problems on a daily basis. Associate and team memberships are available. Kim T. Adamson, secretary-treasurer.

United States Police K-9 Association, Inc.
P.O. Box 26086
Shoreview, MN 55126
612-450-6432

This group was founded to establish minimum standards for police K-9 dogs. Membership is open to K-9 officers, handlers, trainers, and administrators. Donald Slavik, national secretary.

Glossary

For your ready reference, here are some practical explanations of various terms used by law enforcement officers. However, the only accepted source for legal definitions is *Black's Law Dictionary*. Another helpful source is the *Dictionary of Criminal Justice Data Terminology*, published by the U.S. Department of Justice, National Criminal Justice Information Service.

ABSCOND.   To depart from a geographical area prescribed by conditions of probation or parole without authorization, or to intentionally absent or conceal oneself unlawfully to avoid a legal process.

ACQUITTAL.   A judgment by a court finding a defendant not guilty of the offenses with which he was charged.

ADJUDICATED.   Having been the subject of completed criminal or juvenile proceedings, and convicted or determined to be a delinquent, status offender, or dependent.

ALIAS.   Any assumed or additional name used for an official purpose that is different from a person's legal name.

ALS.   Advanced Life Support is the highest level of medical response unit providing the skills of paramedics.

APPEAL.   A request by either prosecution or defense that a completed case be referred to a higher court for review.

ARRAIGNMENT.   A hearing in the court of original jurisdiction at which an accused is informed of the charges against him or her.

BLS.   Basic Life Support is the level of skill that must be provided by any ambulance crew, in most states, regardless of their sponsor.

BOOKING.   Administrative procedure of recording an arrest and identifying the person, place, time, arresting authority, and reason for the arrest.

CERTIORARI.   When the U.S. Supreme Court agrees to hear a case, it issues a writ of certiorari to call up the records of an inferior court.

CHARGE.   A formal allegation that a specified person committed a specific offense.

CITATION.   A written order issued by a law enforcement officer directing an alleged offender to appear in a specific court at a specified time to answer a criminal charge.

COMPLAINT.   A formal written accusation filed in court, alleging that a specified person committed a specific offense.

CONVICT.   An adult who has been found guilty of a felony and confined in a confinement facility.

CORRECTIONS.   A generic term including all government agencies, facilities, programs, procedure, personnel, and techniques concerned with the investigation, intake, custody, confinement, supervision, or treatment of alleged or adjudicated adult offenders, delinquents, or status offenders.

COUNT.   Each separate offense listed in a complaint, information, or indictment.

CRIME.   A violation of law for which a possible jail or prison term may be imposed.

DELINQUENT.   A juvenile who has been adjudicated by a juvenile court as having committed a delinquent act, an act for which an adult could be prosecuted in a criminal court.

DE NOVO.   Anew, afresh, as if there were no earlier decision.

DEPENDENT.   A juvenile offender over whom a juvenile court has assumed jurisdiction because the court has found his care by parent, guardian, or custodian to fall short of a legal standard of proper care.

DETENTION.   The legally authorized holding in confinement of a person subject to criminal or juvenile court proceedings until he is confined or released.

EMT.   Emergency Medical Technician is a more advanced rating than MRT, requiring more than 100 hours of training plus regular refresher courses.

EXPUNGE.   The sealing or purging of arrest, criminal, or juvenile record information.

FELONY.   A crime punishable by a term of at least a year and a day.

FUGITIVE.   One who has hidden or fled from a jurisdiction to avoid prosecution or confinement.

INDICTMENT.   A formal written accusation made by a grand jury and filed in a court, alleging that a specified person committed a specific offense.

INFORMATION.   A document prepared by the prosecutor formally charging an alleged offender with a crime.

INFRACTION. An offense punishable by fine or other penalty but not incarceration.

INTENT. A design or determination to cause recognized consequences as a result of a particular act.

JAIL. A place for incarceration of prisoners with terms of up to one year.

JUDGMENT. Statement of the decision of the court that the defendant is convicted or acquitted of the offense charged.

MISDEMEANOR. A crime punishable by a term of not more than one year.

MRT. Medical Response Technician, roughly equivalent to Red Cross Advanced First Aid, is the minimum rating, requiring about forty hours' training. The MRT can assess the situation, control bleeding, aid breathing, and perform some stabilization.

NEGLIGENCE. Omission of doing something a reasonable man should, or doing what a reasonable man should not do. The actor fails to perceive the risk that a reasonable man should perceive.

NIBRS. The National Incident-Based Reporting System, a more comprehensive statistical analysis to replace the old UCR.

NOLO CONTENDERE. A defendant's answer in court that he does not contest the charges. While not an admission of guilt, this plea subjects the defendant to the same consequences as a plea of guilty.

PARAMEDIC. Requires some 500 hours of training beyond the basic EMT level. Maintains full advanced life support, including administering drugs, heart defibrillation and monitoring, and inserting endotracheal and esophageal tubes for breathing. Paramedics work under orders from emergency room doctors.

PARDON. An act of executive clemency that absolves an individual in part or in full from the legal consequences of a crime or conviction. A full pardon erases both guilt and punishment and restores civil rights. A pardon may be conditional, usually leaving the guilt and conviction intact.

PAROLE. The status of a prisoner conditionally released from confinement before completion of his sentence, and put under the supervision of a parole agency.

PLEA. An accused's formal answer in court to the charges brought against him.

PLEA BARGAIN. A means of avoiding trial by an agreement to plead guilty to a lesser offense, or a recommendation by a prosecutor for a reduced sentence in exchange for a plea of guilty.

PRISON. A place for incarceration of prisoners with terms of more than one year.

PROBABLE CAUSE. Facts and circumstances that would lead a reasonably intelligent and prudent person to believe that a crime had been committed and that the accused person committed it.

PROBATION. Conditional freedom granted to an accused person by the court as long as he meets certain conditions of behavior. Probation may be in lieu of confinement but may include a suspended sentence that could be imposed if the probationer fails to meet the conditions of his probation. One requirement is to report at specified intervals to a probation officer for supervision.

REASONABLE AND PRUDENT MAN.   An interesting term that isn't defined anywhere.

RECIDIVISM.   Repetition of criminal behavior after having served a prior sentence.

RECKLESS.   Careless, indifferent: aware of but conscientiously disregarding possible consequences. An actor shows substantial disregard of human life by action that could cause loss of life. He perceives the risk but acts anyway, although he didn't specifically intend to cause injury.

RESPONSE TIME.   The length of time it takes an emergency vehicle to reach the scene after being called.

REVOCATION.   The administrative act by a parole or probation authority, or an order by a court removing a person from parole or probation in response to a violation by a parolee or probationer.

SENTENCE.   The penalty imposed by a court on a convicted person.

STATUS OFFENSE.   An act or conduct declared by statute to be an offense but only when committed or engaged in by a juvenile. It can be adjudicated only by a juvenile court.

SUBPOENA.   A written order issued by a judicial officer requiring a specified person to appear in a designated place at a specified time to give testimony or to bring specified material to the court.

SUMMONS.   A written order requiring an accused person to appear in a designated court at a specified time to answer charges. As an alternative to an arrest warrant, it is used in cases where complaints are filed with a magistrate or prosecutor's office.

SUSPENDED SENTENCE.   A threat to take more drastic action if the offender commits another crime during a specified period of time. May be conditional, limiting the defendant's mobility, associates, activities, or making restitution, or participating in a rehabilitation program.

UCR.   The Uniform Crime Report form used by the FBI in developing crime statistics.

VENUE.   Geographical area of a court.

VERDICT.   The decision by a jury or judicial officer that a defendant is either guilty or not guilty of the offenses for which he was tried.

VOIR DIRE.   In a criminal trial, the jury selection process.

WARRANT, ARREST.   A document issued by a judicial officer directing a law enforcement officer to arrest a person accused of an offense.

WARRANT, BENCH.   A document issued by a judicial officer directing that a person who has failed to obey an order or notice to appear to be brought before the court.

WARRANT, SEARCH.   A document issued by a judicial officer directing a law enforcement officer to conduct a search for specified persons or property at a designated location, to seize the property or persons, if found, and to account for the results of the search to the issuing authority.

WITNESS.   A person who has personally seen an event or thing, or who has expert knowledge relevant to the case.

YOUTHFUL OFFENDER.   A person, adjudicated in criminal court, who may be above the statutory age limit for juveniles but is below a specified upper age limit, for whom special correctional commitments and special record-sealing procedures are made available by statute.

Bibliography

There are many good books and training manuals that go into greater detail on subjects that were just touched on here. You will find them helpful in broadening your knowledge and advancing your career. If you know of other good books I didn't find, please let me know; send recommendations for additions to me, in care of the publisher.

Allen, Bud, and Diana Bosta. *Games Criminals Play.* Sacramento, Calif.: Rae John Publishers, 1981.

Allen, Harry E., and Clifford E. Simonsen. *Corrections in America: An Introduction.* 4th ed. New York: Macmillan Publishing Co., 1986.

Alpert, Geoffrey P. *The American System of Criminal Justice.* Beverly Hills, Calif.: Sage Publications, 1985.

Aubry, Arthur S., Jr., and Rudolph R. Caputo. *Criminal Interrogation.* Springfield, Ill.: Charles C. Thomas, 1980.

Ayoob, Massad. *Fundamentals of Modern Police Impact Weapons.* Concord, N.H.: Police Bookshelf, 1984.

————. *In the Gravest Extreme.* Concord, N.H.: Police Bookshelf, 1980.

————. *Stressfire.* Concord, N.H.: Police Bookshelf, 1984.

Bureau of Justice Statistics. *Sourcebook of Criminal Justice Statistics.* Washington, D.C.: Government Printing Office, 1987.

Clede, Bill. *Police Handgun Manual: How to Get Street Smart Survival Habits.* Harrisburg, Pa.: Stackpole Books, 1985.

————. *Police Nonlethal Force Manual: Your Choices This Side of Deadly.* Harrisburg, Pa.: Stackpole Books, 1987.

————. *Police Shotgun Manual: How to Survive Against All Odds.* Harrisburg, Pa.: Stackpole Books, 1986.

Duncan, Thomas Stanley. *Domestic Crisis Intervention.* Lawrenceville, Va.: Brunswick Publishing Co., 1985.

Eden, R. S. *Dog Training for Law Enforcement.* Calgary, Alberta, Canada: Detselig Enterprises, 1985.

Ellison, Katherine W., and John L. Genz. *Stress and the Police Officer.* Springfield, Ill.: Charles C. Thomas, 1983.

Ezell, Edward Clinton. *Small Arms Today: Latest Reports on the World's Weapons and Ammunition.* Harrisburg, Pa.: Stackpole Books, 1984.

Hall, Robert F., and Steven R. Schutt. *The Gentle Art of Interviewing and Interrogation.* Englewood Cliffs, N.J.: Prentice-Hall, Inc., 1976.

Hess, Karen M., and Henry M. Wroblewski. *For the Record: Report Writing in Law Enforcement.* 2nd ed. Eureka, Calif.: Innovative Publications, 1987.

Holcomb, Richard L. *Police Patrol.* Springfield, Ill.: Charles C. Thomas, 1971.

Inbau, Fred E., and John E. Reid. *Criminal Interrogations and Confessions.* Baltimore: Williams and Wilkins Co., 1967.

Jacoby, Joan E., *The American Prosecutor: A Search for Identity.* Lexington, Mass.: Lexington Books, 1980.

James, Pat, and Martha Nelson. *Police Wife: How to Live with the Law and Like It.* Springfield, Ill.: Charles C. Thomas, 1975.

Jordan, Bill. *No Second Place Winner.* Des Moines, Iowa: Shooting Times Books, 1965.

Lindell, James. *Handgun Retention.* Kansas City, Mo.: Odin Press, 1981.

Murphy, Gerald R. *Improving Police Response to the Mentally Disabled.* Washington, D.C.: Police Executive Research Forum, 1986.

Niederhoffer, Arthur, and Elaine Niederhoffer. *The Police Family.* Lexington, Mass.: Lexington Books, 1978.

Parsons, Kevin. *Techniques of Vigilance.* Rutland, Vt.: Charles E. Tuttle Publishing Co., 1980.

Peters, John G., Jr. *Defensive Tactics with Flashlights.* Albuquerque, N.M.: Reliapon Police Products, 1982.

Remsberg, Charles. *The Tactical Edge: Surviving High-Risk Patrol.* Northbrook, Ill.: Calibre Press, 1986.

Remsberg, Charles, Ronald J. Adams, and Thomas M. McTernan. *Street Survival.* Northbrook, Ill.: Calibre Press, 1980.

Russell, Harold E., and Allan Beigel. *Understanding Human Behavior for Effective Police Work.* New York: Basic Books, 1976.

Schultz, David O. *Police Pursuit Driving Handbook.* Houston: Gulf Publishing Co., 1979.

Swendsen, David H. *Badge in the Wilderness: My 30 Dangerous Years Combating Wildlife Violators.* Harrisburg, Pa.: Stackpole Books, 1985.

Tegner, Bruce. *Defensive Tactics for Law Enforcement.* Ventura, Calif.: Thor Publishing Co., 1978.

Thompson, George J. *Verbal Judo.* Springfield, Ill.: Charles C. Thomas, 1983.

Weston, Paul B. *The Police Traffic Control Function.* Springfield, Ill.: Charles C. Thomas, 1968.

Wood, J. B. *Beretta Automatic Pistols: The Collector's and Shooter's Comprehensive Guide.* Harrisburg, Pa.: Stackpole Books, 1985.

Zelman, Aaron S., and Lt. Michael L. Neuens. *Consumer's Guide to Handguns.* Harrisburg, Pa.: Stackpole Books, 1986.

Index

Case Index